Alien Rule

This book argues that alien rule can become legitimate to the extent that it provides governance that is both effective and fair. Governance is effective to the degree that citizens have access to an expanding economy and an ample supply of culturally appropriate collective goods. Governance is fair to the degree that rulers act according to the strictures of procedural justice. These twin conditions help account for the legitimation of alien rulers in organizations of markedly different scales. The book applies these principles to the legitimation of alien rulers in states (the Republic of Genoa, nineteenth- and twentieth-century China, and modern Iraq), colonies (Taiwan and Korea under Japanese rule), and occupation regimes, as well as in less encompassing organizations such as universities (academic receivership), corporations (mergers and acquisitions), and stepfamilies. Finally, it speculates about the possibility of an international market in governance services.

Michael Hechter is Foundation Professor of Political Science at Arizona State University and Emeritus Professor of Sociology at the University of Washington. Author of *Internal Colonialism: The Celtic Fringe in British National Development*, *Principles of Group Solidarity*, and *Containing Nationalism*, he has edited five books and written numerous articles in academic journals. A Fellow of the American Academy of Arts and Sciences, his works have been translated into Chinese, Japanese, French, Italian, Polish, Spanish, Arabic, Romanian, Hungarian, and Georgian.

Cambridge Studies in Comparative Politics

General Editor

Margaret Levi   University of Washington, Seattle

Assistant General Editors

Kathleen Thelen   Massachusetts Institute of Technology
Erik Wibbels   Duke University

Associate Editors

Robert H. Bates   Harvard University
Gary Cox   Stanford University
Stephen Hanson   The College of William and Mary
Torben Iversen   Harvard University
Stathis Kalyvas   Yale University
Peter Lange   Duke University
Helen Milner   Princeton University
Frances Rosenbluth   Yale University
Susan Stokes   Yale University
Sidney Tarrow   Cornell University

Other Books in the Series

(continued after the index)

Alien Rule

MICHAEL HECHTER

Arizona State University

CAMBRIDGE
UNIVERSITY PRESS

CAMBRIDGE
UNIVERSITY PRESS

32 Avenue of the Americas, New York, NY 10013-2473, USA

Cambridge University Press is part of the University of Cambridge.

It furthers the University's mission by disseminating knowledge in the pursuit of
education, learning, and research at the highest international levels of excellence.

www.cambridge.org
Information on this title: www.cambridge.org/9781107617148

© Michael Hechter 2013

First published 2013

Printed in the United States of America

A catalog record for this publication is available from the British Library.

Library of Congress Cataloging in Publication data
Hechter, Michael.
Alien rule / Michael Hechter.
    pages cm.   (Cambridge studies in comparative politics)
Includes bibliographical references and index.
ISBN 978-1-107-04254-4 (hardback) – ISBN 978-1-107-61714-8 (paperback)
 1. Legitimacy of governments – Case studies.   2. Sovereignty – Case studies.
 3. Military occupation – Case studies.   4. Imperialism – Case studies.   I. Title.
JC497.H43   2013
325′.3–dc23   2013014271

ISBN 978-1-107-04254-4 Hardback
ISBN 978-1-107-61714-8 Paperback

For Oscar, Caroline, and Katharine

Melians: *And how could it be just as good for us to be the slaves as for you to be the masters?*

Athenians: *You, by giving in, would save yourselves from disaster; we, by not destroying you, would be able to profit from you.*

– Thuycidides

Contents

Figures and Photographs

Figures

Photographs

Preface

The idea for this book dates from a conference that I organized at the University of Washington on June 3 and 4, 2005, on Alien Rule and Its Discontents, supported by the Earl and Edna Stice Endowment. Alien rule occurs whenever the members of a given collectivity, such as a state or a less-encompassing organization, are ruled by nonmembers of that collectivity. As such, the concept applies to a broad range of situations taking place at different levels of social organization, including multinational societies, colonial societies, occupation regimes, research universities, corporations, and even stepfamilies.

Although many distinguished scholars participated in the conference, most of their papers touched only glancingly on the general phenomenon. As the conference proceeded, it dawned on me that despite the evident importance and relevance of the subject – if nothing else, the United States had recently instigated a military occupation in Iraq – very little research explicitly focusing on the general phenomenon of alien rule was currently being done, as opposed to detailed case studies of colonialism or military occupation. As someone with a penchant for studying relatively uncharted territory it seemed worthwhile to begin thinking about exploring this one, if only because alien rule is likely to have greater relevance in an increasingly interdependent world. After all, a host of problems that have arisen on a global scale – from climate change, to epidemic disease, failed states, human rights violations, terrorism, and piracy – can only be addressed by international authorities who, by definition, will be alien to the inhabitants of any state. *Alien Rule* is the result. The reader should regard it as a preliminary foray rather than anything like a definitive statement.

This is the fourth of my books examining collective action, and its nationalist strain in particular.

In my first book, *Internal Colonialism*, I asked why Welsh, Irish, and Scottish identity and subsequent nationalist mobilization have persisted to the present day, despite all expectations that it should have vanished long ago. I argued there that the members of low-ranking ethnic groups in a cultural division of labor are likely to develop a collective identity that predisposes them to nationalist politics. Although this explanation has gained some support in subsequent empirical research, it is clearly incomplete. Because not all groups having a strong collective identity mobilize, something important must be missing from any purely social-structural explanation of collective action. In *Principles of Group Solidarity*, I attempted to fill that gap. *Principles* explored the microsociological mechanisms of dependence and control that lead to the formation and maintenance of group solidarity. Whereas group solidarity is a prerequisite for much collective action, it is neither a necessary nor sufficient condition. In some circumstances, the members of a highly solidary group might elect to pursue their common interests by means other than engaging in collective action. In *Containing Nationalism*, I argued that the state's form of governance also matters. Indirect rule can provide the members of aggrieved national groups with enough decision-making capacity to slake their demand for self-determination, thereby limiting the prospects for nationalist mobilization. Now, *Alien Rule* contends that there are a small number of general conditions under which the members of aggrieved solidary groups not only fail to engage in collective action, but also come to accept foreign domination as legitimate. This is the antithesis of everything that nationalist ideology has always proclaimed.

In the years since the conference was held in Seattle, I have profited a great deal from comments made by many colleagues, including Yoram Barzel, Michael Banton, Ronald Breiger, John Breuilly, Daniel Chirot, Bruce Cumings, Debra Friedman, Ellis Goldberg, John Ross Hall, Eliana Hechter, Stathis Kalyvas, Resat Kasaba, Edgar Kiser, William Kornblum, C. J. Lammers, Doug McAdam, Steven Pfaff, Dan Posner, Nicholas Sambanis, Andrew Walder, and Steven Wilkinson, as well as Allison Demeritt and Tuna Kuyucu. I am very thankful to all of them.

Portions of the contents were presented at seminars held at Stanford University (Sociology); the University of Haifa (Sociology); the Hebrew University of Jerusalem (Sociology); Institut Barcelona d' Estudis Internacionals; Singapore Management University (School of Social Sciences); University of Hawaii-Manoa (Sociology); City University of New York Graduate Center (Sociology); the U.S. State Department Foreign Service Institute in Yokohama, Japan; University of California at Los Angeles (Global Studies); Emory University (Sociology); Duke University (Political Science); Arizona State University (Political Science); University of Arizona (Sociology); London School of Economics (Government); George Mason University (Economics); University of Edinburgh (Sociology); University of Gothenberg (Political Science); University of Stockholm (Sociology); Koç University in Istanbul (Department of International Relations); the European Academy of Sociology; Nuffield College, Oxford; and Queen Elizabeth House, University of Oxford; (Centre for Research on Inequality, Human Security, and Ethnicity).

Parts of the book were also presented at conferences organized at Columbia University (the School of International and Public Affairs); University of California, San Diego; Yale University; the Fourth Beijing Forum; the Central European University; the Swiss Federal Institute of Technology (ETH); and the Laboratory in Comparative Ethnic Processes meeting in Kampala, Uganda.

This volume was written during my fellowship at the Center for Advanced Study in the Behavioral Sciences at Stanford University in 2011–2012. If there is a better place in the world to write a book in the social sciences, I am not aware of it. I am proud to be a recidivist Fellow of this fine institution. Among my colleagues at the Center, Arlene Saxonhouse and Barbie Zelizer were particularly helpful. In addition, Johan Elverskog, Pam Hieronymi, Nancy Kollman, Michael Macy, John Mollenkopf, Dina Okamoto, Emily Ozer, Rachel Prentice, William Roy, Zach Shore, and Marla Stone provided me with an optimal mix of encouragement and criticism. I am indebted to Yoav Peled for information about Israeli collaborators in the Palestinian West Bank. Two anonymous reviewers for Cambridge University Press raised issues that I have attempted to address. Naturally, I take full responsibility for all of the book's shortcomings.

Ravi Shivanna of the Center designed the figures. And Lynne Withey offered me sage advice about publication. I am also grateful for the research assistance of Chris Hale, Nika Kabiri, Devin Kelley, Stefan Kubicki, Emy Matesan, and Oriol Vidal-Aparicio.

Some of the material in this volume was previously published in a variety of outlets.

- Chapter 2 is a revised version of Michael Hechter, "Alien Rule and Its Discontents." *American Behavioral Scientist*, 53, 3 (2009): 289–310. Reprinted with permission from SAGE Publications.
- Chapter 3 is a revised version of Michael Hechter and Nika Kabiri, "Attaining Social Order in Iraq," in *Order, Conflict and Violence*, edited by Stathis N. Kalyvas, Ian Shapiro, and Tarek Masoud. Copyright © 2008 Cambridge University Press. Reprinted with permission.
- Chapter 4 is a revised version of Michael Hechter, Ioana Emy Matesan, and Chris Hale, "Resistance to Alien Rule in Taiwan and Korea." *Nations and Nationalism* 15, 1 (2009): 36–59. Reprinted with permission from John Wiley and Sons.
- Parts of Chapter 5 were borrowed from Michael Hechter and Oriol Vidal-Aparicio, "Dynamics of Military Occupation," in *The Handbook of the Political Economy of War*, edited by Christopher J. Coyne, 432–452. Cheltenham, UK: Edward Elgar, 2011. Reprinted with permission.

The photographs in this volume are reprinted with the permission of the United States Holocaust Memorial Museum. Finally, Chapter 6 is written by Gail Dubrow and Debra Friedman; the first draft of their chapter was originally presented at the Washington conference.

Phoenix, 2012

I

Introduction

> *The difference between inbred oppression and that which is from without is essential, inasmuch as the former does not exclude from the minds of the people a feeling of being self-governed; does not imply (as the latter does, when patiently submitted to) an abandonment of the first duty imposed by the faculty of reason.*
>
> *– William Wordsworth*

In July 1808, a new constitution was presented to the Spanish people by King Joseph. For the first time in the country's history, Spain was offered an independent judiciary, freedom of the press, and the abolition of aristocratic and ecclesiastical feudal privileges. At this time, 3,148 towns and villages were owned by clerical overlords who ruled over some of Europe's most impoverished tenants. However, as Goya's iconic paintings of the turmoil in Madrid in May of that year reveal, far from welcoming greater political liberty and freedom from feudal rule, Spain's peasants instead followed their priests and rose up against the constitution and the king who proposed it. Why did they spurn the freedoms they had been offered? Why did they reject a regime that promised them greater opportunities and superior material conditions? They did so because Joseph, the brother of Napoleon Bonaparte, had been installed on the Spanish throne by French troops in the previous month (Luttwak 2005). In the end, the peasants preferred poor rule by Spaniards to the promise of better rule by Frenchmen.

In this respect, not much has changed. Alien rule continues to be widely disparaged in the world today. It has no defenders because it is blamed for fostering underdevelopment, ethnic divisions, racism, genocide, and a host of other malign outcomes.[1] Indeed, some political theorists hold that alien rule

---

[1] This is particularly evident in the American literature on colonial history, which is frequently viewed exclusively through nationalist lenses (Wilder 2005: 127). According to Owen (2000:

is incompatible with human freedom (Abizadeh 2012: 867). What is an alien ruler? Because rulers promulgate and enforce rules, the answer largely hinges on the definition of aliens. Legally speaking, an alien is someone who has neither the privileges nor the obligations of citizenship in a state (Bosniak 2006). On this view, an alien ruler is an individual who is not a citizen of the state he or she is ruling. Colonial rulers and military occupiers are among the most common examples of such alien rulers. However, this definition is overly restrictive: alien rule can exist in organizations far less large and encompassing than the state. For the purposes of this book, alien rulers are authorities in a given collectivity, who are themselves not members of that collectivity.

Unlike rule, the meaning of which is relatively straightforward, alienness is a more slippery concept: it is defined by the ruled, and their perception of it can change over time.[2] One means alien rulers often have used to diminish their alienness in the eyes of the ruled is the adoption of some of the cultural forms and institutions of the recently subdued native society. Alexander the Great's temples along the Nile incorporated many elements of Ancient Egyptian culture – from temple architecture, to the use of hieroglyphics, to the recognition of Egyptian gods – as a means of making himself appear to be less alien. The Manchu conquerors of Ming China adopted Ming institutions wholesale in their long-lived dynasty. Following the expulsion of the Moors from Cordoba, Spanish Catholics built their cathedral over a preexisting mosque. Likewise, after conquering Tenochtitlán, the conquistadores constructed their cathedral on Aztec ruins, incorporating many Aztec elements in the church. These examples reveal alien rulers' attempts to reduce their alienness in the eyes of the ruled by acknowledging native culture, rather than wholly disparaging it.

The present volume makes the case that assertions regarding the pervasive antipathy to alien rule are overdrawn and potentially at odds with the pursuit of better governance in the modern world. It considers the possibility that good alien governance may be better than bad native governance. To do so it argues that popular resistance to alien rule emanates from two different sources. One source comes from a general, and possibly ancient, fear of aliens. The other comes from a core principle of liberal political philosophy – the right of individual self-determination – that takes issue with the idea of rulership pure and simple. Neither of these bases of opposition to alien rule is set in stone, however. The aliens in one era often become the natives in another. And even in

---

20), for example, the colonial state led "to the familiar dialectic by which imperial rule cannot help but generate the nationalist forces that will eventually drive it out." Lawrence (2013) offers an insightful critique of this literature.

[2] Membership can be determined either legally, as in the case of citizenship, or informally, as in social groups. The criteria involved in determining which individuals qualify as citizens of a given state or members of a social group are often contested and may change over time, but an analysis of the complex issue of boundary formation lies beyond the scope of this analysis (for one such attempt, see Shelef 2010).

the most liberal societies, individuals voluntarily surrender control over some domain of their activities to others whom they trust. They also surrender some of their control to political representatives and the state. Individuals comply with costly state policies such as conscription and taxation either out of coercion or because they grant the state legitimacy to demand these kinds of sacrifices of them. For their part, states attain compliance and social order more effectively from legitimation than from coercion. But can alien rulers manage to attain legitimacy? This chapter introduces the view that all rulers – whether domestic or foreign – ultimately rely on the same means of legitimation. They can do so to the degree that rulers effectively produce the right kinds of collective goods,[3] and allocate these goods fairly to the ruled.

It is hardly a secret that we live in an era of global communications and trade. World cities like New York, London, and Paris are well-known multicultural hotspots: the range of languages spoken on their streets and cuisines represented in their restaurants is nothing short of stunning. One often hears comments that New York is not really American, that London is not really English, and – albeit less frequently – that Paris is not really French. However, cultural diversity also figures prominently in many smaller urban areas in both developed and less-developed societies. For instance, Des Moines, Iowa, is the home of a thriving community of Nuers, who – as Evans-Pritchard (1944) would have been gratified to learn – are largely employed in the meatpacking industry. Increasingly, the composition of professional sports teams, corporate offices, and university departments is diverse, polyglot, and cosmopolitan.

One of the few exceptions to this growing approbation of cultural diversity is in the realm of government. There seems to be near-universal consensus that it is unacceptable for a country to be ruled by someone other than a native-born citizen. This consensus derives from a pervasive norm of national self-determination.[4] This norm is avowed in the United Nations' Charter, which states that the organization's goal is "to develop friendly relations among nations based on respect for the principle of equal rights and self-determination of peoples" (Ch. 1, Article 1). This commitment is reinforced in Article 15 of the United Nations' Universal Declaration on Human Rights, which states that "everyone has the right to a nationality, and no one shall be arbitrarily deprived

---

[3] Throughout this book, I have generally chosen to substitute the term *collective goods* for what is usually termed *public goods* in the literatures of economics and political science (see Olson 1965). Unlike public goods, which are not excludable, collective goods, in principle, can be excluded from individuals who are not members of specific groups. For example, a range of welfare benefits can be excluded from individuals who are not citizens of a given state. The argument in this book hinges in part on consequences of the differential allocation of collective goods across groups.

[4] Political theorists, however, disagree about the reasons that ostensibly justify this norm (Buchanan 2004; Moore 1998). For a recent argument about the structural conditions that promoted the development of the norm of national self-determination, see Wimmer (2013).

of his nationality nor denied the right to change his nationality." Article Two of the U.S. Constitution famously contains the requirement that the president must be a natural-born citizen of the United States. On this account, advocates of the birther movement sought to delegitimate Barack Obama's presidency by claiming that he fails to meet this criterion.[5] Likewise, following her party's victory over the National Democratic Alliance in India in 2004, Sonia Gandhi, a natural-born Italian, was dissuaded from becoming prime minister of India on account of her foreign origin. In what is perhaps the most revealing sign of the disreputability of alien rule, even the World Trade Organization, that militant advocate of free trade, goes out of its way to deny that it supports an international market in governance services. Opposing alien rule is as natural as upholding mom and apple pie.

By the same token, alien rulers have often encountered stiff resistance. The historical record is rife with examples of such defiance. The earliest historians of ancient Greece wrote about the resistance of Greek city-states, united in the Delian League, to defend themselves against the threatened incursion by the Persian Empire (a brief description is found in Bridges, Hall, and Rhodes 2007: 7–10). Following this, Athens built an empire and subjected other city-states to its will. The Peloponnesian War was made "inevitable [by] the growth of Athenian power and the fear which this caused in Sparta" (Thucydides 1954: I: 23). Judea erupted several times against Roman rule, most notably at Masada. Alexander Nevsky mobilized the Rus against Swedish and Teutonic invaders (Martin 2007). In the Indian subcontinent, Hindus battled against Muslim invaders from the thirteenth through the sixteenth centuries. Joan of Arc asserted that God had instructed her to recover her homeland from English domination late in the Hundred Years' War. The Mongols fought against the expansion of China during the Qing Dynasty (Perdue 2005). Similar resistance movements emerged in late-medieval Europe (Gorski 2000).

Yet we cannot read *popular* opposition to alien rulers from the mere existence of these premodern resistance movements. Nor is there much reason to believe that their opposition was motivated by a norm of national self-determination, for no such norm could be said to exist prior to the eighteenth century. If this is so, however, then what can account for this resistance to alien rule? Most premodern societies were largely rural. As such, they tended to be made up of a large majority of serfs, peasants, or tenant farmers who were lorded over by

---

[5] As this statement from a conservative political scientist suggests, hostility to Obama is not just a matter of his ostensibly foreign birth, but his ostensibly foreign values: "I finally realized that the Obama administration and its congressional collaborators almost resemble a foreign occupying force, a coterie of politically and culturally non-indigenous leaders whose rule contravenes local values rooted in our national tradition. It is as if the United States has been occupied by a foreign power, and this transcends policy objections. It is not about Obama's birthplace. It is not about race, either; millions of white Americans have had black mayors and black governors, and this unease about out-of-synch values never surfaced. The term I settled on is 'alien rule' – based on outsider values, regardless of policy benefits – that generates agitation" (Weissberg 2010).

a small minority of large landowners.[6] When aliens conquered these territories, they could either rule indirectly by delegating authority to the traditional rural elites, or they could attempt to strip power from these elites and replace them with alien retainers. The bulk of the rural population remained dependent on the landowners for their very survival, however. Thus it was the disposition of the *landowners*, a small elite, rather than the peasantry, the bulk of the population, that was responsible for resistance against alien rulers. To the degree that alien rulers threatened the power and privileges of the native elites, these elites had an incentive to mobilize their dependent peasants against them (Hechter 2000: 60).[7]

Genuinely popular resistance to alien rule – that which constitutes the phenomenon of nationalism, in short – is often thought to have emerged following the American and French revolutions (Kedourie 1960) and the European revolutions of 1848 (Dowe, Haupt, Langewiesche, and Sperber (2001). These dramatic events provided seeds for the development of a norm of national self-determination. Ernest Gellner (1983: 1) enunciates the content of the norm squarely:

If the rulers of the political unit belong to a nation other than that of the majority of the ruled, this, for nationalists, constitutes a quite outstandingly intolerable breach of political propriety.

To take just one example, the American South reacted violently to Northern overlordship during the era of Reconstruction, as graphically depicted in D. W. Griffith's landmark film, *The Birth of a Nation*.[8] The norm of national self-determination gained further strength at Versailles, which claimed it as a universal ideal. In the years following World War II, a virtual cascade of anticolonial liberation movements swept across the globe (Strang 1990; Wallerstein 1961). In the wake of this massive decolonization, detailing the many warts of alien rule turned into a booming academic industry.[9] This critique of colonialism

---

[6] The situation was rather different in the ancient Greek city-states. Each city-state tended to be divided into two class-based parties: the oligarchs, favored by the Spartan empire, and the democrats, favored by Athens (Thucydides 1954: cf. the discussion of the civil war in Corcyra). Resistance against the threat of Athenian domination, then, was determined not by the sentiments of the citizenry writ large but by the relative power of the two local parties.

[7] See also Chapter 5.

[8] Viewers of *The Birth of a Nation* may wonder which nation Griffith was referring to: the United States, which had successfully prevented the division of its territory, or white Southern society, which bred the Ku Klux Klan. Evidently, Griffith did not believe that the Confederate States of America was a nation, despite its secession from the United States in 1860. For a discussion of the era of Reconstruction as an early exercise in nation building, see Suri (2011); for a historical account of the rise of the Klan, see Foner (1988: 424–444). Interestingly, Nevsky and Joan of Arc – each also the subject of feature films – were both granted sainthood by their respective state churches.

[9] The postcolonial branch of this industry has been justly criticized for its ahistoricity: "Postcolonial studies has brought before a large and transcontinental public the place of colonialism in world history, yet it has tended to obscure the very history whose importance it has highlighted.

profited from a great deal of empirical support.[10] Similar conclusions were reached about the German occupation of Europe (Mazower 2008) and the Japanese occupation of East Asia (Duus et al. 1996) during World War II. Even Italy's high rate of tax evasion – a hindrance to its current struggle to reduce its public debt – has been ascribed to a cultural legacy emanating from opposition to pervasive alien rule.[11]

Why has alien rule in the modern era generated such popular resistance? One reason is because often it has been imposed by conquerors rather than chosen by the ruled themselves.[12] This makes it easy to perceive alien rulers as predatory rather than beneficent. And in many cases this perception was entirely accurate. More fundamentally, however, rule by imposition is totally at odds with liberal and democratic norms. As far back as the seventeenth century, John Locke could write that "a Man can never be oblig'd in Conscience to submit to any Power, unless he can be satisfied who is the Person, who has a Right to Exercise that Power over him" (Locke 1988: Section 81.25, p. 203).

There is something fundamentally misleading about this story, however. Resistance to alien rule is hardly universal. Alien rule has long been accepted in human history. Prior to the eighteenth century it was a commonplace; there was no attempt to engender cultural homogeneity within polities. Indeed quite the contrary: rulers preferred to govern culturally *heterogeneous* territories, the better to divide their subjects (Gellner 1983: 10–13). In the absolutist monarchies of premodern Europe, for instance, the national identity of the rulers was politically insignificant.[13] Royal weddings were quintessentially instrumental affairs designed to cement advantageous geopolitical alliances. Likewise, the Manchus, an alien people from the north of the heartland, ruled China for almost four centuries (Perdue 2005).

> A generic colonialism – located somewhere between 1492 and the 1970s – has been given the decisive role in shaping a postcolonial moment, in which intellectuals can condemn the continuation of invidious distinctions and exploitation and celebrate the proliferation of cultural hybridities and the fracturing of cultural boundaries. ... [More weight should be placed on] the specificity of colonial situations and the importance of struggles in colonies, in metropoles, and between the two" (Cooper 2005: 400). For an analysis of the variable effects of colonialism on present-day civil violence, see Lange and Dawson (2009).

[10] Indeed, my own first book (Hechter 1975) was a part of this anticolonial literature.

[11] In the United States, the first forms of taxation were in the far west for the defense of the community, and tax evaders were expelled from the community. By contrast, in Italy, the first forms of taxation were largely imposed by foreign princes to pay for their own battles, and Italians did everything they could to avoid paying taxes because they saw nothing in return (Donadio and Povoledo 2011).

[12] See, however, the discussion of the Genoese *podesteria* in Chapter 2.

[13] In this context, it is notable that the account of Spanish resistance to Napoleonic rule with which this chapter begins has been called into question. "Indeed, as one perceptive British officer noted of the Spanish peasantry, 'had they been permitted to live in peace, it would have been a matter of the greatest indifference to them whether their king was Joseph [French], Ferdinand [Spanish] or the ghost of Don Quijote'" (Esdaile 2001: 94).

Support for alien rule can also be found in the modern era. Progressive social theorists and colonial authorities alike justified the imposition of alien rule by claiming that it brought progress and civilization to the benighted peoples of Africa and Asia (Muthu 2003). At least some of the native collaborators who profited from colonialism no doubt agreed. More recently, UN peacekeepers became alien rulers (Doyle and Sambanis 2006; Fortna 2008), and nongovernmental organizations have assumed control over many different substantive domains in the international economy (Koppell 2010).[14] Finally, at the time of this writing, the European Union is engaged in a prolonged struggle to protect its currency, the euro, by increasing its financial oversight at the expense of the fiscal sovereignty of its members.

This book is about the conditions that have made, and that might continue to make, alien rule legitimate in the eyes of the ruled. This issue matters for several reasons. First, the massive gap between the haves and have-nots in the world increases the prospect of international intervention to prop up failed or failing states. Second, vital social problems concerning climate change, the spread of infectious disease, financial stability, and terrorism are global rather than national in scale. Solutions to these problems therefore will have to be global and will increasingly challenge Westphalian notions of state sovereignty. As a result, it appears that more of the state's prerogatives will come to be assumed by alien institutions and actors in the future.

Yet the prevalence of the norm of national self-determination ensures that state sovereignty will not go gently into that good night. There are two distinct sources of discontent with alien rule. The first involves the term "alien," whereas the second involves the term "rule."

Roots of the Antipathy toward Foreigners

Consider the roots of xenophobia, defined by the Oxford English Dictionary as "a deep antipathy to foreigners." On one view, these roots derive from our ancestral past. Evolutionary accounts of xenophobia in humans suggest that conflicts over territory, reproduction, and status led to the development of xenophobia (Thorpe 2003).[15] An early statement holds that natural selection was responsible for xenophobia:

Our brains do appear to be programmed to the following extent: we are inclined to partition other people into friends and aliens, in the same sense that birds are inclined to

---

[14] The Peace of Westphalia (1648) is conventionally thought to have established the norm of national sovereignty in the international system, but in reality it did no such thing. For a comprehensive historical survey of the multifarious violations of so-called Westphalian sovereignty since the seventeenth century, see Krasner (2001).

[15] Something akin to xenophobia – which evolutionary biologists generally explain by low genetic relatedness (Hamilton 1964) – exists in many other organisms, from social insects to mammals. Many primates, such as chimpanzees, exhibit intense hostility toward the members of alien

learn territorial songs and to navigate by the polar constellations. We tend to fear deeply the actions of strangers and to solve conflicts by aggression. These learning rules are most likely to have evolved during the past hundreds or thousands of years of human evolution. (Wilson 1978: 119)

This view, however, ignores the possibility that it is also adaptive to cooperate with neighboring groups, and all the more so when our ancestors sometimes were prey rather than predators. After all, one may be more skeptical of strangers than locals, but it is wise to keep one's options open (Cashdan 2001: 760). Where might the suspicion of strangers come from? From an evolutionary point of view, contemporary xenophobia may be derived from adaptations selected to manage the threats posed to ancestral humans by their social environments. Individuals banded together in small groups to acquire and protect critical resources and to ensure against threats (Hechter 1987), but this openness to others could not have been universal. After all, some kinds of interactions – those that expose one to the risk of physical harm, contagious disease, and free riders – are costly. To overcome the potential costs of involvement in group life, mechanisms would have evolved to enable individuals to characterize others as potential threats and to lead them to either avoid or eliminate these threats. "Just as eyelids, blink reflexes, eyelashes, and tear ducts evolved to protect the eye and its important functions, prejudice and discrimination processes may have evolved to protect ultrasociality and its important functions" (Neuberg and Cottrell 2006).

Beliefs about alien groups are likely to be unfavorable because aliens, who are necessarily strangers about whom relatively little can be known, lack a reputation for cooperative behavior. Any person who acts in a manner inconsistent with normative standards may be implicitly viewed by others as a threat to the integrity of the group (Neuberg, Smith, and Asher 2000). Unlike the members of in-groups, aliens have not participated in the repeated reciprocal exchanges of effort and goods that contribute to a favorable reputation. This suggests that aliens should be perceived as untrustworthy and potentially dangerous until their behavior suggests otherwise. Alien individuals – those who do not share some of the in-group's norms – are likely to be regarded as such a threat and thereby to inspire antipathy.

That there may be an evolutionary basis for categorizing individuals into members of in-groups and out-groups is of course plausible, but xenophobia is far from a universal outcome of intergroup contact. The concept of alien is evidently a social construction that is not set in stone. For example, following

groups. More surprising, perhaps, something akin to xenophobia is found in extremely small organisms such as microbes. The recognition of relatives is important in microbes because they engage in many behaviors that entail costs to the individual while benefiting neighbors. Microbes cooperate for nourishment, movement, virulence, iron acquisition, protection, quorum sensing, and production of multicellular biofilms or fruiting bodies. Likewise, cells benefit their own kind by poisoning alien cells (Strassmann, Gilbert, and Queller 2011).

the French Revolution, many inhabitants of the Celtic-dominated region of Brittany regarded the French as culturally alien, and the French felt likewise about the Bretons, but today the inhabitants of both territories reserve that label for the Mahgrebis, among others. One source of differential antipathy to aliens is the variable level of threat they pose. In this view, one is more likely to fear manifestly warlike neighbors than manifestly cooperative ones. So even if there is an evolved tendency to be suspicious of strangers, this belief can be modified in the face of contradictory evidence. This conclusion points to the importance of contextual and historical contingencies.

Hostility to aliens could also arise from competition over resources such as land and food. Yet there is little evidence of an association between land shortage and intergroup conflict (Thorpe 2003: 148–159). In contrast to this expectation, the archaeological record does not reveal a significant increase in conflict following the adoption of agriculture. The social psychological version of this materialist theory – realistic group conflict theory – is also undermined by much empirical research (Hewstone, Rubin, and Willis 2002). Doubtless, competition for material and human resources sometimes spurs intergroup hostility, but this is neither a necessary nor a sufficient explanation of xenophobia. After all, intergroup contact may also yield both reproductive and political benefits to individuals and groups (Gluckman 1955; Lévi-Strauss 1969).

Another root of the antipathy to alien rule concerns the term "rule" rather than "alien." Criticism of rule goes hand in hand with the growing acceptance of the right of individual self-determination.

Roots of the Antipathy to Rule

The concept of individual self-determination – which asserts one's right to control one's own actions – emerged in the seventeenth century out of the notion that individuals have certain natural, inalienable rights. Key among these is freedom from depending on the will of others (Macpherson 1962: 263).[16] In previous eras – and in other parts of the contemporaneous world – no such right was presumed. In premodern societies, individuals, far from being wholly

---

[16] This formulation assumes that individuals have free will and the goals they decide to pursue are their own rather than those imposed on them by a predatory or manipulative ruler bent on pacifying and exploiting them, as in *Brave New World* (Huxley 1946). As Rawls (2005: 137) puts it, "our exercise of political power is fully proper only when it is exercised in accordance with a constitution the essentials of which all citizens as free and equal may reasonably be expected to endorse in the light of principles and ideals acceptable to their common human reason." The view that legitimacy rests on a commitment to equally respect all persons is widely held by normative political theorists (Grafstein 1981; Lukes 1974; Rehfeld 2005). Much of the corpus of sociological theory discounts the realism of this view of free will; by contrast, sociologists regard social institutions as key determinants of individual preferences and values. If internal states such as preferences and values are in large part determined by such institutions, then it is naïve to assume that they are entirely sovereign.

independent agents, were largely understood as members of communities (*Gemeinschaften*) and were defined, and defined themselves, by their status within these communities (Macpherson 1962; Maine 1986; Tönnies 1988).[17] If groups are conceived as essential to human welfare and survival, then the idea that membership in them imposes obligations that limit individual sovereignty is easy to accept.

The emergence of liberalism as a political philosophy brought concern for the individual to the forefront.[18] If previous social thought conceived of the premodern community as a harmonious collective, much like the colonies of ants or bees (Hollingsworth 2001), liberalism highlighted the existence of conflict between individuals and the groups to which they belonged. The rise of liberalism invariably raised questions about governance and rule. As Hobbes (1996) had argued, some sort of governance was required to mitigate interpersonal conflict and foster civilization and social order. Such collective goods could only be provided if individuals surrendered some part of their liberty to the ruler. But by what criteria should the performance of these rulers be assessed? Their commitment to individual self-determination led liberals to argue that governments should be assessed by the degree to which they satisfied the demands of the ruled.

Not that individualists agreed on the trade-off between individual liberty and state prerogatives. Elevated to the level of a political philosophy, the untrammeled right of individual self-determination lies at the core of anarchism, which denies that the state is a prerequisite for the attainment of social order. Not only is the state unnecessary; anarchists also believe that it is malign. Consider Pierre-Joseph Proudhon's indictment of the nineteenth-century state:

To be GOVERNED is to be watched, inspected, spied upon, directed, law-driven, numbered, regulated, enrolled, indoctrinated, preached at, controlled, checked, estimated, valued, censured, commanded, by creatures who have neither the right nor the wisdom nor the virtue to do so. To be GOVERNED is to be at every operation, at every transaction noted, registered, counted, taxed, stamped, measured, numbered, assessed, licensed, authorized, admonished, prevented, forbidden, reformed, corrected, punished. It is, under pretext of public utility, and in the name of the general interest, to be place[d] under contribution, drilled, fleeced, exploited, monopolized, extorted from, squeezed, hoaxed, robbed; then, at the slightest resistance, the first word of complaint, to be repressed, fined, vilified, harassed, hunted down, abused, clubbed, disarmed, bound, choked, imprisoned, judged, condemned, shot, deported, sacrificed, sold, betrayed; and

---

[17] Indeed, classical sociology was erected on the basis of this distinction between premodern and modern societies. Marx's feudal and capitalist social formations (Marx, Engels, and Hobsbawm 1998), Durkheim's mechanical and organic solidarity (Durkheim and Simpson 1933), Weber's (1978) patrimonial and rational-legal forms of legitimation, and Simmel's (1955) concentric and juxtaposed forms of group affiliation all attest to the centrality, if not the details, of the distinction.

[18] This is not to deny that various communitarian and other nonindividualist philosophies also continue to attract adherents today.

to crown all, mocked, ridiculed, derided, outraged, dishonored. That is government; that is its justice; that is its morality. (Proudhon 1923: 293–294)[19]

The powers of the state have been on steroids since Proudhon's time. Lest one think that no one believes in anarchism anymore, notable modern champions include Robert Nozick (1974), whose views have been buttressed by game-theoretic analyses of the evolution of cooperation (Axelrod 1984). And *Atlas Shrugged* (Rand 1957) – a fictional paean to anarcho-capitalism – remains a best seller to this day.

If anarchists want to do away with the state in the name of individual freedom, liberals hold that individual freedom must be sacrificed, albeit to a limited extent, by the state.[20] This is because they regard the state as necessary to produce collective goods – such as the enforcement of property rights and contracts – that individuals cannot provide for themselves (Hayek 1973). Liberalism also allows decision-making authority to be stripped from individuals because they are deemed to be incompetent (Buchanan and Brock 1989) or self-destructive. Thus in liberal societies there are limits on individual self-determination for children, the mentally ill, illegal drug users, and motorcyclists who do not use helmets, among others (Sartorius 1983).

Fair enough, but sometimes the individuals in liberal regimes voluntarily surrender their liberty by vesting control of (at least some) of their actions to others. Patients surrender their control to doctors, passengers to airline pilots, novitiates to a religious order, members of intentional communities to their gurus, workers to their unions, and quite often, citizens to their states. This surrender can be limited to specific contexts and domains in life, or it can be more general. The reasons for this vesting of control seem to be counterintuitive, however. If the right of individual self-determination lies at the very heart of liberalism, how can this voluntary surrender of this (so-called natural) right ever be justified on individualistic grounds? At the simplest level, there are two reasons why individuals accept the rule of others and voluntarily surrender control over some set of their actions (Coleman 1990). First, individuals may surrender control because they believe that they will be better off following another's leadership. In this case they give up control unilaterally, without any expectation of extrinsic compensation.[21] Second, they can transfer

---

[19] The desire for self-determination is hardly confined to anarchists. The protection of autonomy, or turf, is one of the principal goals of bureaucrats everywhere (Wilson 1989: ch. 10).

[20] Thus, John Stuart Mill's *On Liberty* sought to defend "one very simple principle, as entitled to govern absolutely the dealings of society with the individual in the way of compulsion and control..... That principle is, that the sole end for which mankind are warranted, individually or collectively, in interfering with the liberty of action of any one of their number, is self-protection. That the only purpose from which power can be rightfully exercised over any member of a civilized community, against his will, is to prevent harm to others. His own good, either physical or moral, is not a sufficient warrant" (Mill 1956: 13). See also Manin (1987: 338–339).

[21] This belief is likely to hinge on one's knowledge of the other person's incentives to fulfill the trust placed in him (Hardin 1993: 509).

rights of control without holding this belief, but in return for some extrinsic compensation.[22]

Because the reasons for the second kind of surrender of control seem straightforward, why would anyone ever select the first kind? One reason is that, on account of personal knowledge or reputational information garnered from individuals whom they already trust, they believe that the other party has qualities that make it possible for the other party to provide them with more satisfactory outcomes than they could provide for themselves (Coleman 1990). After all, this kind of exchange of control is the principal theme of Victorian novels by Austin, the Brontë sisters, and George Eliot, whose female protagonists seek to secure an appropriate social station for themselves by dint of marriage. Another reason is that even without such knowledge those who surrender self-control believe the other party has sufficient incentives to fulfill the trust that has been placed in him (Hardin 1993: 509).

A striking, if highly controversial, example of this surrender of control may be found in Rousseau's discussion of marital relations. According to Rousseau,

in the romantic dyad there is a physical exchange whose "sweetness" derives precisely from the confusion of coercion and consent: desire intensifies in the ambiguous interplay of force and will. For this reason a woman's sexual submission, like a citizen's obedience to the general will, is consistent with consent because her desire, like his interest, materializes only through relations with another whom she has "let" be stronger. (Wingrove 2000: 3–4)[23]

The relation of dominance and submission that Rousseau advocates in marriage has been described as *consensual nonconsensuality*, meaning "the conditions in which one wills the circumstances of one's domination" (Wingrove 2000: 5). The key term in this construction is *consent*, for consent is what makes a relationship of ruler and ruled legitimate (Weiss and Harper 2002). "Rousseau's fundamental teaching about sexuality ... involves a political relationship of command and obedience.... Sexual relationships are political because they normally entail the interchange of ruling and being ruled between the two partners" (Schwartz 1984: 99). Whereas relations of dominance and submission between genders are hardly surprising in highly patriarchal societies, there is evidence that such relationships are also relatively common in Western, liberal societies as well.[24] This willingness to allow others to control

[22] One relevant instance is the practice of logrolling in legislatures (Coleman 1986).

[23] For an opposing, equalitarian view of the link between intimate relationships and political life, see Giddens (2000: ch. 3).

[24] This is attested to, among other things, by the popularity of bondage-discipline-sadomasochistic (BDSM) communities in many U.S. and foreign cities (see for instance the Web site of the Till Eulenspiegel Society [TES] in New York). There is also a movement among evangelical Christians to foster domestic discipline: http://site.themarriagebed.com/domestic-discipline and http://www.takeninhand.com/an.overview.of.taken.in.hand. Note that the practitioners of master/slave relationships also have their own communities in the developed world. Khan (1979: 197–210) offers a psychoanalytic interpretation of these relationships. Finally, at the time of this

some domain of one's life is often, but not exclusively, selective rather than promiscuous.[25]

A more sweeping example is offered by Fromm (1941) who argued that modernity freed individuals from the bonds of pre-individualistic society, which provided them with security and limited their life prospects. Whereas freedom expands individual horizons, it also leads to feelings of isolation and anxiety and the sense of powerlessness. As a result, people are tempted to escape from the burden of this freedom into new dependencies and submission. Echoing themes previously developed by Durkheim (1951) and Simmel (1955), Fromm's diagnosis refers to the widespread popular submission to authoritarian regimes that occurred in Nazi Germany and Fascist Italy. A similar logic, however, can explain the appeal of fundamentalist religions, intentional communities, and urban gangs. In all of these kinds of groups, members willingly surrender much of their individual sovereignty – and sometimes their material resources – to God, Jesus, Allah, or particular charismatic leaders.[26] More prosaically, people who use popular Web sites such as Google and Facebook are surrendering their individual privacy, which can lead to a host of consequential outcomes.[27]

writing one of the top-rated pop songs in this country is Katy Perry's *ET* (extraterrestrial), which glamorizes this kind of dyadic relationship in the context of alien rule: "/Infect me with your love and/Fill me with your poison/Take me, take me/Wanna be a victim/Ready for abduction/." The *Fifty Shades of Grey* trilogy, strongly featuring a dominant/submissive relationship, was a publishing sensation in 2012. For a discussion of the recent impact of these themes in contemporary American culture and organizations, see Chancer (1992).

[25] Likewise, it has been argued that early modern rulers were impelled to cede some of their political control to representative assemblies to gain the funding necessary to conduct war against their external enemies (Acemoglu, Johnson, and Robinson 2005; North and Weingast 1989; North and Thomas 1973). For a qualifying view, see Stasavage (2011).

[26] Indeed, Judaism and Christianity place great stress on the believers' obligations to obey to God's will in return for worldly or otherworldly benefits (this is often referred to as a covenant). And the term *islām* actually means the manifesting of humility or submission and outward conformity with the law of God. Thus, the Quran [33:36]: "It is not fitting for the believing man nor for the believing woman, that whenever Allah and His Messenger have decided any matter, that they should have any other opinion." An individual's willingness to submit to a leader's will is a defining characteristic of charisma. For Weber (1978: 1111–1112), "the 'natural' leaders in moments of distress – whether psychic, physical, economic, ethical, religious, or political – ... [were] the bearers of specific gifts of body and mind that were considered 'supernatural' (in the sense that not everybody could have access to them)."

[27] "Whether you can obtain a job, credit, or insurance can be based on your digital doppelgänger – and you may never know why you have been turned down. Material mined online has been used against people battling for child custody or defending themselves in criminal cases. LexisNexis has a product called Accurint for Law Enforcement, which gives government agents information about what people do on social networks. The Internal Revenue Service searches Facebook and MySpace for evidence of tax evaders' income and whereabouts, and United States Citizenship and Immigration Services has been known to scrutinize photos and posts to confirm family relationships or weed out sham marriages. Employers sometimes decide whether to hire people based on their online profiles, with one study indicating that 70 percent of recruiters and human resource professionals in the United States have rejected candidates based on data found online. A company called Spokeo gathers online data for employers, the public, and anyone else who

Trust is required for the voluntary surrender of control. The person who willingly surrenders control to another will only tend to do so if he or she trusts that the other person will provide the desired benefit (leadership, expertise, security, sexual gratification, and so forth). In a sense, the placement of trust may be conceived as a wager. If so, trust will be placed only when the expected net benefit is positive (Coleman 1990: 99).[28] The decision to place trust is therefore affected by three variables: the probability of gain if the trustee is trustworthy, the potential loss if the trustee is untrustworthy, and the potential gain if the trustee is trustworthy.

Often information about these three variables is hard to come by. Perhaps the least well-known variable is the probability that the trustee will be trustworthy. This analysis is directly applicable to the realm of politics. When the individual vests some of his control to a ruler – or government – he is obligated to comply with its laws and regulations. He knows full well what each candidate promises to deliver, for that is enunciated in their campaigns. But he cannot be sure whether the candidates would honor their campaign promises were they elected. The degree to which he believes campaign promises is limited, at least in part, by the trust he has in the candidate.[29]

Legitimacy

If trust is required for individuals to voluntarily surrender control (at least in particular domains of activity), under what conditions do citizens surrender their sovereignty, liberty, and self-determination to a political regime rather than to another individual? The trust that people place in their rulers cannot rest on the kind of knowledge they require for the vesting of interpersonal trust, for their personal knowledge of rulers is vanishingly small. They may well have beliefs about the nature of rulers' incentives to take their political interests into account, however.[30] These beliefs about rulers' incentives are likely to affect their perception of the regime as more or less legitimate.[31]

Concern about legitimacy has flourished in the news recently. The so-called surge in Iraq was motivated by a changed occupation strategy, built on counterinsurgency theory, that was designed to increase the legitimacy of the U.S.

---

wants it. The company even posts ads urging 'HR Recruiters – Click Here Now!' and asking women to submit their boyfriends' e-mail addresses for an analysis of their online photos and activities to learn 'Is He Cheating on You?'" (Andrews 2012: 7).

[28] A more specific list of the attributes that warrant the placement of trust is offered by Bachrach and Gambetta (2001: 153–154).

[29] "When one trusts, one *forgoes* the opportunity to influence decision-making, on the assumption that there are shared or convergent interests between truster and trustee" (Warren 1999: 4).

[30] These incentives are supposedly maximized in democratic polities (Dahl 1963), but as is discussed later there are differences in this respect between direct and representative democracy.

[31] "Clearly citizens' ability to trust in government is an integral element of political legitimacy" (Williams 1998: 31).

military presence there. In 2009 prolonged demonstrations erupted in Iran in protest of a rigged election. Shortly thereafter Xinjiang erupted in violence against what many Uighurs considered the colonization of their homeland by Han Chinese. The Arab Spring of 2011 consisted of movements protesting the illegitimacy of regimes in Egypt, Tunisia, Bahrain, Syria, and Libya. Suffice it to say that at this moment questions of political legitimacy have assumed great salience in the world at large.

In his sweeping survey of the history of government, S. E. Finer (1997: 28–29) observes that

> rulers cannot maintain their authority unless they are legitimated, and … they are legitimated by belief systems. It would be completely useless for a British monarch today to claim absolute powers on the grounds that these had been conferred on him by God, but this was taken as read in Archaic Egypt and Mesopotamia. Where the claim of the ruler to authority is out of kilter with the prevalent belief system of the society, he must either "change his plea," that is, make himself acceptable in terms of that belief system, or else delegitimize himself and fall. The belief systems are stronger than the ruling authorities because it is by their virtue that rulers rule.

The concept of legitimacy was invented to help account for social order in large societies. As such, the concept, if not the term, has an ancient lineage (Zelditch 2001). Because it is too costly to attain order in the long run on the basis of sanctions or naked coercion, it stands to reason that political stability must also rest, in part, on some normative basis. Rousseau understood that "the stronger is never strong enough to be forever master unless he transforms his force into right and obedience into duty" (Rousseau and Gourevitch 1997: Book i, ch. 3, p. 43). Legitimacy refers to this basis of the social order (Hurd 2007). The existence of a large public relations industry and of other agencies that spin reality to suit their clients' interests provides compelling indirect evidence of the importance of legitimacy in modern society. In fact, one of the principal weapons the U.S. government has employed in its campaign against terrorism is delegitimation.[32]

More precisely, legitimacy is the perception that the actions of some entity are desirable, proper, or appropriate according to a socially constructed system of norms, values, and beliefs (Suchman 1995: 574).[33] This definition leaves

---

[32] If illegitimacy fosters protest, then it follows that delegitimation would be a strategy employed in counterinsurgency. Although many terrorists claim moral or theological legitimacy for their actions, one aim of the U.S. counterinsurgency strategy is to raise questions about the moral legitimacy of using weapons of mass destruction. "Many terrorists value the perception of popular or theological legitimacy for their actions," said Stephen J. Hadley, Mr. Bush's national security adviser. "By encouraging debate about the moral legitimacy of using weapons of mass destruction, we can try to affect the strategic calculus of the terrorists" (Schmitt and Shanker 2008).

[33] Compare this definition with that of Stinchcombe (1968: 160–163), who argues that in circumstances where such a perception is not commonly held, a ruler who has the ability to call on other powerful actors in society to uphold his claim to authority can also be regarded as legitimate.

the nature of causality open, however, and about this there is considerable disagreement.

Normative legitimacy is widely discussed by political theorists and some sociologists. For Meyer and Rowan (1977) and others (Berger et al. 1998; Dimaggio and Powell 1983; Zucker 1977), legitimation is a process that begins at the macro level – in the cloud, as it were, which contains a mythlike cultural (or institutional) framework that explains and supports the existence of social entities at lower levels of analysis. This cultural framework, entailing institutionalized practices and procedures, leads to a "taken-for-grantedness" of the social entity (Baum and Powell 1995). On this view, a state attains legitimacy by conforming to global norms about what proper states should – and do – look like. Hence approval of the government is a necessary but insufficient cause of legitimacy. In ancient China, the emperor's authority derives from the Mandate of Heaven (Zhao 2009); in medieval Islam, the caliphate's authority derives from the Sharia (Binder 1955: 236); in Christendom these norms entailed the divine right of rule, as justified in Romans XIII. In an era in which democratic norms seemingly have won the day, a nondemocratic regime cannot be deemed to be normatively legitimate even if its citizens consent to its rule (Grafstein 1981: 456; see also Manin 1987; Rehfeld 2005).[34]

Because the norm of national self-determination is so pervasive in the modern world, no type of alien rule can possibly qualify as normatively legitimate. For this reason, this book adopts an *instrumental* conception of legitimacy that proceeds from the micro to the macro. On this view, the legitimacy of a state is conferred not by disembodied ideas floating somewhere in the ether, but by its all-too-human individual subjects (Lipset 1960; Weber 1978).[35] In general, a government is legitimate to the extent that its rules are considered rightful by both dominant and subordinate members of society. In this circumstance, compliance with governmental rules demonstrates consent with the regime. Note that this is an exceedingly demanding condition to meet. Among other things, it implies that the government's rules and obligations will be honored even when it is powerless to enforce them. When an individual or group obeys these rules because they anticipate that failure to do so will be met with sanctions, compliance owes more to the government's power than its legitimacy.[36]

---

[34] Even a critic of the consent theory of legitimation concedes that "any plausible account of legitimacy and obligation must center on whether the state is for the most part responsive to the people" (Herzog 1989: 205). Despite its vagueness, Herzog's position can easily be interpreted as offering support for an instrumental view of legitimation.

[35] The normative view has been criticized – rightly in my view – for holding that "collective representations manufacture themselves by opaque processes, are implemented by diffusion, are exterior and constraining without exterior people doing the creation or the containing" (Stinchcombe 1997: 2).

[36] As Kuran (1995) points out, the publically expressed consent with a given regime may conceal strong private reservations about the regime's legitimacy.

These two views of legitimacy have quite different empirical implications. On the normative view, a contemporary state such as the Peoples' Republic of China is deemed to be illegitimate – whatever its citizens may think of it – because it fails to adopt global norms that mandate democratic practices and procedures. On the instrumental view, Chinese citizens are the arbiters of the regime's legitimacy whether or not the regime conforms to global norms about democracy. If collective action to resist the regime is an indicator of illegitimacy, then according to the normative view of legitimation, the Chinese regime should be facing more or less constant resistance on account of its continuing nondemocratic nature. In contrast, the instrumental view implies that resistance to the regime should erupt only when the government performs poorly – by failing to deliver sufficiently rapid economic growth and other collective goods (La Porta et al. 1999) or by failing to apply state policy and distribute its largesse fairly, according to the norm of impartiality. This norm dictates that the exercise of state power should accord with existing laws and apply equally to all citizens and subjects (Rothstein 2011: 20).[37]

Instrumental legitimacy is indicated by compliance with authority in the absence of coercion. For instrumentalists, the legitimacy of rulers depends on the degree to which they satisfy the demands of the ruled – providing them with the collective goods they desire at the least possible cost and allocating these goods fairly. What kinds of political institutions are most likely to generate this outcome? A number of plausible political mechanisms may produce it. The hallmark of collective self-determination in liberal societies is *direct democracy* (Mansbridge 1983). This is because direct democracy under a unanimity rule best preserves individual self-determination (Manin 1987: 363). For this very reason it is impractical, however, because it gives everyone veto power (Buchanan and Tullock 1965).[38] Ironically, the powers that direct democracy affords individuals – thereby maximizing their self-determination – preclude its utility in collective decision making for large groups.

Representative democracy – which is how most people define democracy these days – is the default response to the impracticality of direct democracy. In representative democracy, the individual voter surrenders control

[37] If this is so, then what are we to make of the divine right of kings? According to this doctrine, rulers are legitimate regardless of the quality of their performance – that is, the effectiveness and fairness of their governance. Although the divine right of kings was a (disjoint) norm that rulers and their ecclesiastical allies attempted to impose on their subjects, its imposition was far from universal even in absolutist Europe. The hollowness of the norm was revealed whenever peasants mobilized in food riots and other rebellions against their rulers (Tilly 1975). Ecclesiastical authorities increasingly lost power to kings as state formation proceeded in modern European history (the English Reformation is a particularly clear example of this). As such, the legitimation of rulers in Europe shifted gradually from religious to nationalist bases.

[38] Note that many important powers of government in classical Athens, which is often taken as an exemplar of direct democracy, were not decided on by the assembly but by magistrates chosen by lot (Manin 1997). For some experimental evidence that direct elections promote legitimacy, see Baldassarri and Grossman (2011).

Key quolyude - but what desi mean (actual, hundered, prover? mind or well a physial?)

over legislative decisions to an elected representative.[39] Although this solution sounds straightforward, in fact it is not. Representation connotes a number of different things (Pitkin 1967). Political representatives are expected to act on behalf of their constituency's interests. They are chosen by a set of standard procedures and are generally held accountable by free and fair elections (Rehfeld 2006: 3).[40] Under any concept of the term, representative democracy deals with large numbers of ruled, but by doing so it deprives individuals of some quantum of self-determination.[41] It has long been recognized that the distance between representatives and their constituencies drives a wedge between these groups (Rehfeld 2005: 6).

There is substantial consensus that representative democracy is beset by what has come to be known as the agency problem (Jensen and Meckling 1976; Michels 1999; Przeworski, Stokes, and Manin 1999).[42] "Elected representatives are not bound by promises made to voters. If people vote for a candidate because they favor the policy he proposes, their will is no more than a wish. In this respect, the election of modern representatives is not a far cry from the election of deputies to the Estates General under the *Ancien Régime*" (Manin 1997: 237).

The representatives decide what citizens must and cannot do, and they coerce citizens to comply with their decisions. They decide how long children must go to school, how much individuals should pay in taxes, with which countries men must go to war, what

---

[39] Once constitutional matters have been settled in favor of representative democracy, this surrender of political control is not, however, voluntary. That is, the prospective voters only have the liberty of choosing between prospective representatives. They cannot choose between direct and representative democracy.

[40] Under this standard definition, many national representatives of global institutions, such as the UN, fail to attain legitimacy. The same is true of ambassadors, who – at least in the United States – are nonelected appointees who nonetheless are taken to represent their states.

[41] "What today we call representative democracy has its origins in a system of institutions (established in the wake of the English, American, and French revolutions) that was in no way initially perceived as a form of democracy or of government by the people" (Manin 1997: 1). According to Madison, the effect of representation is "to refine and enlarge the public views by passing them through the medium of a chosen body of citizens, whose wisdom may best discern the true interest of their country and whose patriotism and love of justice will be least likely to sacrifice it to temporary or partial considerations" (Hamilton et al. 1961: 82).

[42] Agency costs loom large despite Edmund Burke's Panglossian denial: "It ought to be the happiness and glory of a representative to live in the strictest union, the closest correspondence, and the most unreserved communication with his constituents. Their wishes ought to have great weight with him; their opinions high respect; their business unremitted attention. It is his duty to sacrifice his repose, his pleasure, his satisfactions, to theirs – and above all, ever, and in all cases, to prefer their interest to his own. But his unbiased opinion, his mature judgment, his enlightened conscience, he ought not to sacrifice to you, to any man, or to any set of men living. These he does not derive from your pleasure – no, nor from the law and the Constitution. They are a trust from Providence, for the abuse of which he is deeply answerable. Your representative owes you, not his industry only, but his judgment; and he betrays, instead of serving you, if he sacrifices it to your opinion" (Burke 1857: 95–96).

agreements private parties must adhere to, as well as what citizens can know about the actions of governments. And they enforce such rules, even against the wishes of the individuals concerned. In this sense, they rule. (Przeworski et al. 1999: 1–2)

Mansbridge (2009: 369) explains that

many political scientists, most economists, and almost all citizens who demand more "accountability" and "transparency" routinely rely on a ... model of principal-agent relations [in which] the interests of the principals (in politics, the constituents) are assumed to conflict with the interests of their agent (the representative). The principals must therefore monitor the agent closely, rewarding the good behavior and punishing the bad.

The point is that representative democracy erodes constituents' direct political control.[43] The motivations, views, and desires of representatives may conflict with those of at least some of their constituents. This loss of control can only be redressed by mechanisms that provide constituents with institutions that align the interests of representatives and constituents. There are at least two different kinds of mechanisms by which a constituency can advance its collective self-determination. The first relies on sanctions: if the representative fails to vote in line with the constituency's view, it may not reelect that representative (Przeworski et al. 1999). The second relies on differential selection: the constituency can deliberately choose a representative whose views are congruent with its views (Kingdon 1989; Mansbridge 2009; Miller and Stokes 1963). To the degree that these mechanisms fail to solve the agency problem, the legitimacy of the government is threatened. This reduction in legitimacy leads to a decrease in the willingness of the ruled to comply with the government's rules and regulations. The most extreme consequence is the rise of resistance against the regime.

Measuring Legitimacy

Although compliance often is observable, it is difficult to discern legitimacy in the absence of reliable subjective evidence. As Max Weber (1978) famously noted, "the merely external fact of the order being obeyed is not sufficient to signify" that it is seen as legitimate. Because reliable evidence about the internal states of collectivities was impossible to come by before the advent of the sample survey in the 1930s – and even now such evidence often is tantalizingly elusive (Hechter, Kim, and Baer 2005; Hechter et al. 1999) – the measurement of legitimacy poses a formidable challenge. On this account, many empirically oriented social scientists refrain from discussing it.

---

[43] Of course, by giving up political control to their representatives, constituents gain other goods – such as more time to attain their favorite private goods. I am indebted to Arlene Saxonhouse for this insight.

But the concept is so fundamental that it is difficult to avoid. Thus, after Samuel Huntington (1991: 46) cautions his readers that "legitimacy is a mushy concept that political analysts do well to avoid," he goes on to devote no less than thirteen pages in the same book to an insightful analysis of it. Only recently has serious attention been paid to the measurement of legitimacy. Perhaps the most sustained body of empirical literature about legitimacy is social psychological (Jost and Major 2001). Much of this work attempts to link attitudinal and other subjective variables (such as concerns about identity) with variations in legitimacy (Weatherford 1992). From a political perspective, this research is limited in that it considers these internal states to be exogenous. That is, investigators typically rely on custom-made survey data or experiments that tend not to be linked to the institutional and structural variables that would be required to analyze the effects of different forms of governance on legitimacy. Even so, there are exceptions. Among these, Tyler's (2001; 2006) research is especially notable. Tyler's basic point is that the key determinant of the legitimacy of a state is the perceived fairness of the decision-making process rather than its provision of resources, opportunities, or outcomes.[44] Findings such as these suggest that experiencing fair procedures builds social values, and these values lead people to feel a long-lasting, personal obligation to accept decisions and support rules. Therefore, when a decision is made in a manner that people regard as fair, they become committed to that decision and feel personally responsible for following it (see also Levi 1988). This commitment is indicated by their continued compliance with the decision over time, even in situations in which the incentives for compliance and the risks of sanctions for noncompliance are weak or nonexistent (Tyler 2001: 420).

Political scientists often employ macroscopic measures of legitimacy. Gilley (2006a; 2006b), for example, created a data set that purports to measure the legitimacy of regimes in seventy-two countries, enabling him to analyze its determinants cross-nationally. He considers legitimacy to be composed of three subcomponents: views of legality, views of justification, and acts of consent. He derives an index of legitimacy based on this conceptualization ranking from the highest (Denmark) to the lowest (Russia) and attempts to test the validity of the index. The attitudinal scores in the index are closely associated with behavioral ones.

Another recent cross-national study (Anderson et al. 2005) takes a different tack. It builds on the well-appreciated notion that a political system is legitimate to the degree that the people who are on the losing end of government

---

[44] The high value placed on fair allocation is not only pervasive in humans, but it is found in some of our primate ancestors as well (Brosnan and de Waal 2003). According to Trivers (2002: 16–17), a sense of fairness evolved as a means of "regulating reciprocal tendencies, a way of judging the degree to which other people were cheating you (and you them!).... [This argument] suggested that a sense of fairness was not some arbitrary cultural construct of an easily changed effect of socialization. It suggested, instead, that there were deep biological roots to our sense of fairness that to me would seem to encourage a commitment to fairness or justice."

policies and decisions nevertheless continue to support the regime. In many ways, this is a defining characteristic of legitimacy. To that end Anderson and colleagues propose the *winner–loser gap* in support for elections as a measure of legitimacy. The gap measures the difference between the answers of respondents who supported the winning party and those who supported the losing party. The larger this gap is, the less legitimate the regime.

Finally, Fry (2005) analyzes official government responses to the killing of their own subjects. She collected a large sample of cases of state violence to determine how, and if, these acts were legitimated verbally. In 56 percent of these cases, governments responded with language that was consistent with the country's values and previously stated political claims. She then sought to find out whether such verbal legitimation efforts effectively preserved these political systems from post-violence civil war, system change, and the emergence of new social movements.

In contrast, this book seeks to measure legitimacy by compliance with the laws and regulations of the regime that does not stem from coercion, repression, or other kinds of obstacles to collective action. Although this kind of compliance is somewhat observable, this is probably not true of the mechanisms responsible for it. Compliance that mainly arises from state coercion is not an indicator of legitimacy, nor is compliance that arises from an inability of the ruled to engage in collective action – because of internal class, cultural or geographical divisions, spatial deconcentration, or other factors. In the chapters that follow I attempt to distinguish between legitimate and illegitimate sources of compliance, a task that is made feasible because state repression is usually apparent in the historical record. Whereas compliance may arise from legitimation as well as coercion, incidents of noncompliance – such as collective resistance to alien rule – can only indicate the absence of rulers' legitimacy.

Legitimacy and Alien Rule

To this point I have argued that even in liberal regimes founded on the principle of individual sovereignty, people often voluntarily cede control to others at certain times and in specific domains of their lives. The principle of representative democracy is built on such a surrender of control in the realm of politics. Why should the willingness to cede control be different for natives opposed to aliens?[45] To what extent does the identity of the rulers – specifically, whether

[45] With respect to the most extreme example of alien intrusion – potential visitors from another planet – a recent article suggests that humanity has greater reason to fear such contact than to seek it out. The analysis concludes that extraterrestrials are likely much stronger than humanity because humanity is a young civilization relative to astronomical time scales. As such the extraterrestrials could intentionally attack and kill us, enslave us, or potentially even eat us. They could attack us out of selfishness or out of a more altruistic desire to protect the galaxy from us. We might be a threat to the galaxy just as we are a threat to our home planet. They could also

they are alien or native – affect the legitimacy of a regime? One popular answer derives from John Stuart Mill:

A portion of mankind may be said to constitute a Nationality, if they are united among themselves by common sympathies, which do not exist between them and any others – which make them cooperate with each other more willingly than with other people, desire to be under the same government, and desire that it should be government by themselves, or a portion of themselves, exclusively. This feeling of nationality may have been generated by various causes. Sometimes it is the effect of identity of race and descent. Community of language, community of religion, greatly contribute to it. Geographical limits are one of its causes. But the strongest of all is identity of political antecedents; the possession of national history, and consequent community of recollections; collective pride and humiliation, pleasure and regret, connected with the same incidents in the past. None of these circumstances, however, are necessarily sufficient by themselves. (Mill 1963: 546)

The idea that a representative must have the same kind of social identity as his constituency has been termed *descriptive representation* (Pitkin 1967). Descriptive representation implies that blacks should represent predominantly black constituencies, Asians should represent predominantly Asian constituencies, and women are required to adequately address issues of gender equity. The concept of descriptive representation denotes not just visible characteristics – such as skin color and gender – but also shared experiences.

This criterion of shared experience, which one might reasonably expect to promote a representative's accurate representation of and commitment to constituent interests, has a long history in folkways and even in law. Long-term residents in a town often argue for electing to office someone born in the town on the implicit grounds that lifetime experience increases the representative's common experiences with and attachment to the interests of the constituents. Similar arguments appear against "carpetbaggers" in state legislatures. The United States Constitution even requires that a president of the nation be born in the United States. "Being one of us" is assumed to promote loyalty to "our" interests. (Mansbridge 1999: 629)

Is descriptive representation – in which representatives are in some sense of typical of the larger class of persons whom they represent – required for the legitimation of rule? The question has been the subject of considerable debate.

On the one hand, descriptive representation lowers informational barriers between representatives and their constituents. Representatives whose own culture differs from that of their constituents may not be able to accurately take into account, or even comprehend, the latters' interests and demands (Scott 1998). The same is likely to be true of centrally located representatives who are at a physical remove from constituents in peripheral territories (Hayek 1973). Moreover, descriptive representation often will be preferred by the members of

---

harm us unintentionally by giving us a biological or computer disease that our defenses cannot handle, among other things (Baum, Haqq-Misra, and Domagal-Goldman 2011).

historically underrepresented groups because it gives them the impression that they have a seat at the table.[46]

On the other hand, morons probably should not represent morons.[47] And there is much empirical evidence that descriptive representatives do not necessarily represent the actual interests of constituents (Swain 1995).[48] Hence the idea of descriptive representation garners little support even among the advocates of group rights (Mansbridge 1999: 630). Proponents of descriptive representation make the questionable assumption that the members of given groups are always highly solidary and thereby share common interests that trump whatever other interests may divide them.

Although descriptive representation typically contributes to a regime's legitimacy in multicultural societies, it is neither a necessary nor a sufficient condition. This book extends arguments about political representation to natives and aliens and holds that legitimacy in the contemporary world is largely[49] a function of the effectiveness and fairness of rulers, rather than their identity.[50] As such, the determinants of legitimacy – which revolve around the concept

---

[46] "A history of dominance and subordination typically breeds inattention, even arrogance, on the part of the dominant group and distrust on the part of the subordinate group. In conditions of impaired communication, including impairment caused by inattention and distrust, the shared experience imperfectly captured by descriptive representation facilitates vertical communication between representatives and constituents. Representatives and voters who share some version of a set of common experiences and the outward signs of having lived through those experiences can often read one another' signals relatively easily and engage in relatively accurate forms of shorthand communication. Representatives and voters who share membership in a subordinate group can also forge bonds of trust based specifically on the shared experience of subordination" (Mansbridge 1999: 641). As Hardin (1993: 508) puts it, "experience molds the psychology of trust."

[47] Clearly, Senator Roman Hruska of Nebraska (R) disagreed. In response to questions about the competence of Richard Nixon's (unsuccessful) nominee to the U. S. Supreme Court in 1970, G. Harrold Carswell, Hruska said ,"Even if he were mediocre, there are a lot of mediocre judges and people and lawyers. They are entitled to a little representation, aren't they, and a little chance (Honan 1999)?"

[48] There is evidence, however, that rulers in sub-Saharan Africa do provide disproportionate resources (leading to lower rates of infant mortality and higher educational attainment) to the members of their own ethnic groups (Franck and Rainer 2012).

[49] Whereas it is often contended that legitimacy in premodern societies rests on notions such as the divine right of kings or the mere acceptance of traditional authorities, evidence about individual consent in such regimes is quite hard to come by. It is therefore possible that effective and fair rule also drive legitimacy in such societies, although I make no such claim here.

[50] Similar to all other organizations, states that work well "do so by paying people to serve values, to try to be competent, to conduct their business with integrity" (Stinchcombe 1997; 16). Likewise, Gellner (1983: 22) sees the state's production of collective goods to be key to its attainment of legitimacy in modern societies but also points out the downside of this strategy: the state's "favoured mode of social control is universal Danegeld, buying off social aggression with material enhancement; its greatest weakness is its inability to survive any temporary reduction of the social bribery fund, and to weather the loss of legitimacy which befalls it if the cornucopia becomes temporarily jammed and the flow falters."

of good governance (Rothstein 2011) – should be the same for both natives and aliens.

Plan of the Book

Because alienness is a social construction, it does not necessarily correspond to any particular type of person or group. Whereas most – but not all – of the chapters in this book define aliens as foreigners, many kinds of individuals or groups can be deemed to be alien.[51] For example, in some places and times, ethnic, racial, or religious groups are commonly considered to be alien. And if the Earth is ever visited by beings from another planet, we can be confident they will be considered to be the echt aliens among us. The present analysis applies to aliens of all stripes.

The book proceeds as follows. It is commonplace to explain nationalist movements by adverting to the demand for national self-determination. Indeed, nationalism is frequently defined in precisely these terms. Discontent with alien rule – the obverse of national self-determination – is often assumed to be pervasive, if not universal. There is no shortage of explanations of the antipathy to alien rule, and a great deal of corroborative evidence. Many believe – with the early nineteenth century Spanish peasantry – that people seem to prefer to be badly ruled by their own kind than better ruled by aliens. Yet if this is true, then identity trumps competence in the assessment of rulers, implying that we are all liable to suffer from suboptimal governance. In contrast, Chapter 2 argues that the evidence for the pervasiveness of antipathy to alien rule is overdrawn. To that end, it distinguishes between two different types of alien rule, elected and imposed; provides a brief portrait of each; and suggests that when aliens are confronted with incentives to rule fairly and efficiently, they can gain legitimacy. This demonstrates that even though one might expect imposed alien rule to be nefarious, it is the incentives for aliens to govern well that determines their legitimacy. Thus imposed alien rule can sometimes be less threatening than native rule. This conclusion has implications for the prospects of an international market in governance services.

If effective and fair governance is required to attain legitimacy – and its by-product, social order – then it should follow that unfair and ineffective governance should result in disorder and intergroup conflict. Chapter 3 demonstrates the point by analyzing the history of governance in Iraq from its status as an Ottoman principality to British overlordship and, finally, native rule under Saddam Hussein. Each of these regimes experimented with direct and indirect rule as a means of mitigating resistance to alien rule, on the one

---

[51] In this sense, the alien is an instantiation of what postmodernists regard as "the Other." Of course, the groups to which this designation is applied are likely to vary over time and across social contexts. For an interesting discussion of the changing meaning of the term alien in Imperial Russia, see Slocum (1998).

hand, and communal conflict between Sunni, Shi'i, and Kurdish groups, on the other. Indirect rule is the closest approximation to native rule in multinational states. Yet this chapter shows that indirect rule was no more effective – and perhaps less effective – than direct (alien) rule in the modern history of Iraq. Neither form of rule – indirect (native) nor direct (alien) – is by itself capable of sustaining social order. Because none of these experiments resulted in effective and fair governance, both nationalist resistance and intergroup conflict have persisted in Iraq.

Evidently, nationalist resistance to alien rule varies across time and space. Chapter 4 analyzes the mechanisms responsible for this variation in two former Japanese colonies. It explores why there was greater nationalist resistance to Japanese rule in Korea than Taiwan from the turn of the twentieth century to the end of World War II. Resistance to alien rulers requires both a supply of participants in nationalist collective action and a demand for national self-determination. The chapter assesses two principal propositions: the supply of participants increases to the degree that native elites are stripped of their traditional authority and offered few incentives to collaborate, and the demand for national self-determination decreases to the degree that alien rule is fair and effective. A comparative analysis of the effects of Japanese alien rule in Taiwan and Korea suggests that nationalist resistance is greater in the earliest phases of occupation; the greater native elites' opportunities, the weaker the resistance to alien rule; and the fairer the governance, the weaker the resistance to alien rule.

Historically, the most extreme form of alien rule is military occupation. Because occupation is often justified as serving the occupier's interests alone, and because it is defined as temporary, the occupier's incentives to employ good governance are usually much weaker than those of native rulers. As such, military occupation usually breeds nationalist resistance. Chapter 5 presents a general theory of variation in that kind of resistance and illustrates its plausibility by reference to the literature on military occupation. Following Chapter 4, it pays especial attention to the role of collaboration in legitimating occupation, drawing on recent attempts by Israeli authorities to recruit Palestinian collaborators in the West Bank.

The legitimation of alien rulers can also occur in organizations that are less encompassing than the state. The notion that a single theory can apply to states as well as to the organizations found within them is controversial. Evidently, states differ in many ways from all such organizations: among other things, they alone claim to have a monopoly of the means of violence, they alone have the right to imprison deviants, and they are far less permeable than most other kinds of organizations, thereby imposing high exit costs on their members – that is, citizens. What is often overlooked is that the very concept of *the state* is itself an abstraction concealing a multitude of institutional differences that distinguish one democracy from another, let alone from its authoritarian counterparts. Despite these differences, comparative analysts find it useful to employ the concept because all states share key attributes in common. Likewise, many of the problems of legitimation faced by alien rulers in states are also to be found in less-encompassing organizations. Chapter 6 treats the unusual case of academic receivership – a relatively rare event in which the chair of an academic department is imposed by a dean or provost when that unit is considered unable to govern itself effectively – as an example of alien rule within the university. It explores the questions of what aspects of identity make an academic leader an alien, under which conditions are outsiders chosen to lead academic departments, why the department prefers leaders of "one's own kind," and why the disciplinary affinity of a leader might matter. Additionally, it discusses why there is such a truncated market for academic leadership of departments. To inform the analysis, it draws on case studies of receivership and interviews with former receivers at a number of universities.

Chapter 7 extends the analysis of alien rule to other smaller-scale organizations: corporations, where the issue concerns mergers and acquisitions, and stepfamilies. It then considers the future of alien rule in an increasingly globalized world. Although legitimation typically is not taken to be problematic in corporate firms, scholars and practitioners have long noted that mergers and acquisitions sometimes lead to employee resistance toward the newly merged firm's integration activities. The most common explanation for this resistance is attributed to culture clash: namely, the idea that employees from different firms value their own cultures and are unwilling to adopt new practices, outlooks, and authorities as legitimate. There is evidence, however, suggesting that the potency of cultural differences in creating resistance has been overstated, and the importance of more instrumental factors entailed in effective and fair governance has been overlooked in much of the existing literature. By the same token, the rise of stepfamilies also creates problems of integration not unlike those faced by alien rulers. Cinderella's evil stepmother is a trope that is found in countless societies. Despite evidentiary limits, it appears that effectiveness and fairness go a long way to dampen children's resistance to stepparents. Finally, the possibility of the collapse of the Euro – which has raised new fears of alien rule in the southern economies of the European Union – suggests that the prospects for alien rule may be on the upswing in the years ahead. The book concludes by speculating about the prospects for the development of an international market in governance services.

2

Alien Rule and Its Discontents

Actions are held to be good or bad, not on their own merits, but according to who does them, and there is almost no kind of outrage – torture, the use of hostages, forced labour, mass deportations, imprisonment without trial, forgery, assassination, the bombing of civilians – which does not change its moral colour when it is committed by "our" side.

– George Orwell

One of the principal means of coping with cultural conflict in multicultural societies is adopting some form of indirect rule (Hechter 2000).[1] The usual explanation for the ubiquity of this institution is the claim that people prefer to be ruled by members of their own cultural group than by aliens.

At the most basic level, alien rule exists whenever one or more culturally distinct groups are governed by individuals of a different cultural group. This description encompasses the legally distinct situations of colonialism, foreign occupation, and those multinational states whose discontented nations regard their rulers as alien. It also encompasses alien rule in smaller-scale organizations such as corporations, academic departments, and the family. Even so, this definition is even less straightforward than it seems because *governance* and *cultural distinctiveness* are contested terms. In this chapter, governance refers to administration – that is, management of the affairs of an organization, institution, or government.[2]

---

[1] The notion that indirect rule is a superior means of governing in multicultural societies is an old one in social theory. Thus, in *The Prince*, Machiavelli advises that "if one wants to preserve a city that is accustomed to living in freedom, it is more easily held by the means of its own citizens than in any other way" (Hörnqvist 2004). See also Althusius (1964).

[2] "There is no distinction between 'policy' and 'administration'; almost every administrative act has policy implications and may, indeed, *be* policy whether intended or not" (Wilson 1989: 41).

For their part, cultural distinctions cannot be read out of a list of objective differentiae like language or religion but exist largely in the eyes of the beholders.[3] What is regarded as alien rule at one point in time or social setting is often reframed as native rule in another.[4] As is the case with respect to all social boundaries (Barth 1969), the distinction between alien and native is socially constructed (Hale 2004; Tilly 2004).[5] In the Middle Ages and in some less developed countries today, individuals tend to identify with relatively small units such as the village, clan, or tribe.

In developed societies, however, the state often takes pride of place. When the boundaries of the relevant community expand, then the entities described by the terms native and alien also must reflect these changes. In classical colonialism the meaning of alien is intuitive – it distinguishes conquerors hailing from the metropole from the indigenes who have been subjected by them. Likewise, in the early stages of Western European state building, centralized authorities were considered by many people in the periphery as alien rulers. Now, however, most of the residents of these territories no longer regard central authorities as foreign. Instead, they are likely to reserve that designation for immigrants from Africa and the Middle East. Such transformations have occurred throughout history; they are, in fact, a necessary step in the process of nation building (Weber 1976).[6]

The hallmark of alien rule concerns the identity of the rulers rather than the provenance of the ruling institutions.[7] The most familiar example is colonialism, but alien rule can also occur in settings of widely varying size and scope. Broadly conceived, alien rule is widely scorned in groups as small as families, and as large as international organizations. Fairy tales like Cinderella portray stepparents as alien rulers who ill-treat their stepchildren.[8] Indeed, stepchildren are subject to greater parental abuse than genetically related children (Daly and Wilson 1985; 1996). University faculty members react with dismay when

---

[3] For example, there are relatively few such objective differences between the cultures of American southerners and northerners (but see Nisbett and Cohen 1996), Americans and Anglophone Canadians, Northern and Southern Italians, East and West Germans, or Czechs and Slovaks. Despite this, individuals on both sides of these respective divides subjectively perceive that these distinctions entail substantial cultural distinctions and behave accordingly.

[4] For example, Thomas Schelling recounted (personal communication) that once Colin Powell became U.S. Secretary of State, he was regarded as an alien by the Department of Defense.

[5] The concept of alien rule must also be distinguished from that of problematic political representation. As discussed in Chapter 1, democratic elections typically yield native representatives who are different – more privileged, more educated – than the electorate. Moreover, despite their native status, these representatives may not be entirely responsive to the interests of their constituents.

[6] For a useful review of the literature on the cognitive bases of categorization with respect to group formation, see Brubaker, Loveman, and Stamatov (2004).

[7] Alien rule entails alien rulers. Thus despite the heavy American influence on the constitutions of postwar Japan and Germany, neither of these countries is today subject to alien rule. I am indebted to Ning Wang for this distinction.

[8] See the discussion of stepparenting as an instantiation of alien rule in Chapter 7.

their departments are relegated to academic receivership – a euphemism for alien rule (Chapter 6). And employees whose firms have been subject to corporate takeovers often fear their new alien rulers (Demeritt 2012).

The ubiquity of nationalism in the modern world attests to pervasive political discontent with alien rule. In country after country the strongest norms and sanctions are reserved for those individuals who support alien rulers against their native counterparts (*treason* is often punishable by death, and people who collaborate with occupying powers can meet a similar fate).

Alien rule is often shunned even when there is reason to believe that it would provide superior governance. I have already referred to the Spanish peasants' resistance against King Joseph's proposed liberal constitution; a similar fate befell another Napoleonic ruler in Naples in 1799. According to most available measures, K–12 public education in the United States lags far behind its Singaporean, Finnish, and South Korean counterparts. Yet it is hard to imagine that any American school district would ever consider hiring Singaporean, Finnish, or South Korean administrators to run their schools.[9] In a *New York Times* op-ed article, Brent Staples (2005) makes such a proposal, but he doubts that it will come to fruition because "the United States will need a radically different mind set to catch up with high-performing competitors.... We will also need to drop the arrogance and xenophobia that have blinded us to successful models developed abroad."

International organizations like the European Union, the International Monetary Fund (Vreeland 2003), the World Bank, and the World Trade Organization are frequently targets of mass protests.[10] Finally, hostility to alien rule has been held to be the principal motivation for suicide bombing (Pape 2005).

The apparently pervasive discontent with alien rule has been accounted for in many different ways. Some argue that there is a biological drive for individual self-determination that leads to resentment of rule of any kind, whether native or alien. According to Freud (1961), for example, the newborn – a quintessential egoist whose motivations are exclusively hedonic – is loath to countenance any interest lying beyond its own epidermis. By contrast, modern evolutionary theory (Hamilton 1964) contends that all who are not closely related kin are considered to be aliens and therefore not to be cooperated with or trusted. Indeed, recent research in cognitive neuroscience suggests that the sight of a stranger of another race causes a reaction in the nervous system that may have evolutionary roots (Olsson et al. 2005).

Social explanations abound, as well. For anarchists, all forms of rule essentially are alien because they violate the principle of self-determination.

---

[9] Despite this, parts of alien curricula – such as Singapore math – have been adopted in some American and Israeli elementary schools.

[10] This discontent occurs despite the World Trade Organization's explicit exemption of governance from its otherwise capacious view of free trade.

Less controversially, the antipathy to alien rule may just be an instantiation of the more general phenomenon of homophily – the process by which social similarity fosters interaction (McPherson, Smith-Lovin, and Cook 2001). Because mutual communication is essential for social interaction, it stands to reason that the more similar two individuals are, the more easily they can communicate. Much social psychological research demonstrates that self-conscious groups (and thus group boundaries) can be formed on almost any basis.[11] Moreover, the greater the cultural homogeneity of a group, the more likely it is to develop common and exclusionary political dispositions that may set the stage for antipathy to out-group members.

Hostility to alien rule may also derive from intergroup differences in values. Alien rulers are likely to devalue the hallowed cultural practices and even the lives of natives, thereby stimulating resentment.[12] The normative controls that regulate intragroup behavior are liable to be suspended when dealing with out-groups (Browning 1992; Hochschild 1998).[13] By the same token, native rulers may be more politically accountable than foreigners as a result of the high costs of exiting one's own country.[14] Corrupt or nefarious rulers are subject to criminal prosecution in all democratic regimes, but natives are more vulnerable to this sanction than aliens. Aliens may simply return to their own native countries to escape retribution – especially in the absence of extradition treaties.[15]

Despite these arguments, Orwell's observation at the beginning of this chapter is troubling because we take it for granted that in modern society government agents will be evaluated on the basis of their *competence* rather than their

---

[11] Whereas differences in resource endowments were once thought to be necessary for the formation of intergroup boundaries, Tajfel (1982) showed that experimental subjects would form self-conscious groups – exhibiting in-group bias – on the basis of a distinction between those who preferred paintings by either Klee or Kandinsky. Subsequent research in this vein demonstrated that such groups could even be formed after subjects were randomly assigned to different groups by an experimenter. One possible explanation for the prevalence of homophily is that the social identities of native and alien are uncertainty-reducing mechanisms that act as a kind of "social radar" (Hale 2004).

[12] Mazzini (1892: 59–60), the principal ideologist of Italian nationalism, focused on the alien threat to culture: "Our country is our Home, a house God has given us, placing therein a numerous family that loves us, and whom we love; a family with whom we sympathize more readily and whom we understand more quickly than we do others; and which, from its being centred round a given spot, and from the homogeneous nature of its elements, is adapted to a special branch of activity." In contrast, Fanon (1968: 311) seemed more concerned about the threat to native lives: "Leave this Europe where they are never done talking of Man, yet murder men everywhere they find them, at the corner of every one of their streets, in all the corners of the globe."

[13] Thus, at various times the British authorities resisted attempts by their colonial subjects in India and Sudan to wear Western dress (Sharkey 2003: 47–8).

[14] The lack of accountability is also an argument against the privatization of government services (Verkuil 2007).

[15] See Hechter (1987) for an analysis of the effect of high exit costs on compliance.

personal *identity*.[16] The belief that competence should trump identity when it comes to governance was enunciated strongly, if not unanimously (Muthu 2003), in the Enlightenment.[17] For this reason, writers of far different political stripes – from John Stuart Mill to Karl Marx – could be found endorsing European rule as a progressive force in the African and Asian colonies they considered to be backward. Some contemporary economic historians echo this view by claiming that European imperialism provided a number of key collective goods – from infrastructural investment to modern legal and fiscal institutions – to colonial peripheries that otherwise would have forgone these (Ferguson and Schularick 2006; Mitchener and Weidenmier 2005). A similar view was also taken by the George W. Bush White House with respect to the Middle East (Shweder 2004).

Indeed, the requirement that officials and staff be selected on the basis of their technical competence and expertise is arguably the principal distinguishing characteristic of the modern, bureaucratic state.[18] To attain their primary goal of promoting corporate efficiency, bureaucracies aim to hire the best and the brightest. The officer corps of the Habsburg Emperor Franz Joseph (1830–1916) is a case in point. The Habsburg officers acted as the glue that enabled the emperor to largely overcome the national differences that threatened to dissolve the social order (Deák 1990). In virtually every American research university the faculties – especially in technical fields – comprise a virtual United Nations. If we have the ill fortune to be faced with a risky operation, we are more likely to select surgeons on the basis of their track record in the given procedure, rather than their ethnicity, gender, nationality, or religion.[19]

[16] The locus classicus for this expectation is Weber's (1978: 223–226) analysis of monocratic bureaucratic organization.

[17] According to Lord Acton, "The coexistence of several nations under the same state is ... one of the chief instruments of civilization; and, as such, it is in the natural and providential order, and indicates a state of greater advancement than the national unity which is the ideal of modern liberalism. The combination of different nations in one state is as necessary a condition of civilized life as the combination of men in society. Inferior races are raised by living in political union with races intellectually superior. Exhausted and decaying nations are revived by the contact of a younger vitality. Nations in which the elements of organization and the capacity for government have been lost ... are restored and educated anew under the discipline of a stronger and less corrupted race" (Acton [1862] 1907: 290).

[18] Indeed, the opposite principle – that is, selection to office on the basis of identity – is characteristic of Weber's two other non-modern modes of organizational legitimacy: traditional and charismatic.

[19] Even so, there is considerable evidence that gender, race, and sexual orientation are salient characteristics in the choice of physicians for some procedures. Thus, some women so strongly prefer a female colonoscopist that they are willing to delay the procedure for a month or pay up to $200 more to have a woman perform it. In one study (Menees et al. 2005) nearly 50% of the women surveyed preferred a woman endoscopist: 75% of these cited embarrassment as the primary reason, 50% thought a woman would have more empathy, and 36% thought they were better listeners. Whether these factors are equally salient in critical procedures – like the neurosurgery mentioned – is questionable.

Yet Orwell suggests that when it comes to matters of governance, this modern idea that competence trumps identity is far from accurate. Does this ostensibly universal antipathy to alien rule mean that we are all condemned to suffer from rule that is less optimal than we might attain were there an international market in governance services?

Not necessarily. None of these explanations explain why alien rule is sometimes tolerated and accepted. In the first place, for most of history empires were run by rulers who were alien to large proportions of their subjects, but this caused no great outcry (Gellner 1983; McNeill 1986). If one of its principal sources was conquest, another was aristocratic marriages that were arranged for dynastic considerations (Coontz 2005: Ch. 6). Alien rule only becomes problematic after the emergence of the norm of national self-determination. Most analysts regard the emergence of this norm as a modern phenomenon. Some trace it back to Kant's emphasis on self-determination and its influence in the French Revolution (Kedourie 1960); others date it from the Dutch Revolt of the seventeenth century (Gorski 2000), still others (Gellner 1983) from the onset of industrialization. Whatever its provenance, that such a norm has gained strength in modern times cannot be denied (Jackson 1990: 17–18). However, the application of the norm in international politics is far from universal (Hechter and Borland 2001). Many national claimants to statehood are continually frustrated by the United Nations; Palestine and Iraqi Kurdistan are but two notable current examples.

In the second place, alien rule is not always scorned.[20] This chapter argues that the evidence for the pervasiveness of antipathy to alien rule is overdrawn. To that end, it distinguishes between two different types of alien rule – elected and imposed – provides a brief portrait of each, and suggests that when aliens are confronted with incentives to rule fairly and efficiently, they can gain legitimacy even if they have been imposed on native populations.

Alien Rule Elected

Examples of the election of alien rule are hard to come by.[21] One of the best documented instances is provided by the economist Avner Greif who analyzes the

---

[20] For example, the U.S. Declaration of Independence did not regard alien rule as the justification for the colonists' rebellion. The poor quality of British governance was what mattered: "When a long train of abuses and usurpations, pursing invariably the same Object evinces a design to reduce them [the people] under absolute Despotism, it is their right, it is their duty, to throw off such government, and to produce new Guards for their future security. – Such ... is now the necessity which constrains them to alter their formal Systems of Government." Ronald Breiger called my attention to this example. Moreover, aliens have often been implicated in the founding myths of democratic institutions, especially the law (Honig 2001).

[21] Much, of course, depends on the meaning of *election*. Sometimes one faction in a divided polity summons a partisan alien ruler to join forces in subduing a common rival. Thus English Protestants invited William of Orange (in 1688) to assume the throne, thereby forestalling a Catholic succession. Needless to say, this outcome was far more popular in England

emergence and persistence of the *podesteria* in the thirteenth-century Republic of Genoa (Greif 1998).[22] Under this institution the alien ruler (the *podestà*) was installed by the Genoese to end years of internecine rivalry between competing clanbased parties: the Menacianos and Camadimos (analogues to Guelfs and Ghibellines whose conflicts in northern and central Italy were made famous in Dante's *Inferno* and to Shakespeare's fictional Capulets and Montagues in Verona[23]).

Although the thirteenth century had little conception of a norm of *national* self-determination, something akin to *civic nationalism* was in full force in much of the Italian peninsula. Whereas the Italian city-states shared a common culture derived from the remnants of the Roman Empire, they were fiercely patriotic – thus to the Genoese, the residents of other city-states were alien. "Lineage ties, noble affinities, and family rivalries occur everywhere in Europe in these centuries but nowhere else with the intensity and passion of Italy, just as nowhere else was the attachment to one's native town, to the *patria*, so deeply felt, so committed" (Finer 1997: 961). This attachment was fueled by pervasive conflicts between rival city-states over territory and boundaries and nurtured by the promulgation of civic symbols such as the *carroccio*, a special wagon that bore the city's standard in battle, as well as communal coats of arms, state seals, and patriotic literature (Chittolini 1989; Jones 1997; Waley 1988).[24]

than in the Catholic regions of Ireland and Scotland. Jean-Baptiste Bernadotte, a French Revolutionary general, was elected Crown Prince of Sweden in 1810 and King eight years later; his is the dynastic line of the current Swedish monarchy. Bernadotte's election owed to political conflicts unleashed within Sweden during the chaotic period of the Napoleonic Wars. In contemporary times, several small islands – including Bermuda (United Kingdom), Tokelau (New Zealand; see Parker 2006) and Réunion (France) – have opted to retain colonial status rather than independence because the former comes with hefty subsidies. A 2011 opinion poll revealed that 60% of a representative sample of Jamaicans believed that their country would have been better off if it had remained a British colony (BBC News 2011). Australia never severed its ties to the British Crown; Queen Elizabeth II is titled Queen of Australia. Likewise, she is also de jure head of the Canadian state. Moreover, Westphalian sovereignty has sometimes been honored in the breach: sovereign states have often been subject to externally imposed (alien) restrictions on their treatment of minorities, for example (Krasner 1999; Sheehan 2006).

[22] Although the accuracy of Greif's archival research recently has been challenged (Boldizzoni 2011: 56–60), this criticism does not apply to his analysis of the podesteria.

[23] "Faction, born of private hatreds, remained essentially war, cut-throat *werra*, and ...war of increasing virulence and thoroughness, that turned communal annals into a lengthening and long-remembered record of devastation and slaughter, atrocity and public revulsion" (Jones 1997: 605). Unlike Genoa and many of the other Italian city-states that experienced alien rule, Venice was not crippled by interclan feuding; the doge was a native Venetian who served for life (Brown 1895).

[24] In spite of more than a century of political unification, cultural differences between Italian cities persist to the present day, maintained by low rates of geographic mobility and the exceptional resilience of the Italian family (Ginsborg 2003).

Despite this civic nationalism, alien rule appealed to the conflicting parties of the Italian city-states because owing to their position in the social structure strangers are bound to exhibit a certain kind of objectivity:

> [The stranger] is not radically committed to the unique ingredients and peculiar tendencies of the group, and therefore approaches them with the specific attitude of "objectivity." But objectivity does not simply involve passivity and detachment; it is a particular structure composed of distance and nearness, indifference and involvement. I refer to the ... dominating positions of the person who is a stranger in the group; its most typical instance was the practice of those Italian cities to call their judges from the outside, because no native was free from entanglement in family and party interests. (Simmel [1908] 1950: 402–403)

The Genoese accepted an alien ruler – a podestà – to ensure the acquisition of trading privileges in Sicily that were promised by Henry VI, the son of the Holy Roman Emperor, Frederick Barbarossa. Foregoing these privileges would have damaged Genoa's economy as well as its standing relative to Pisa, a major rival. Many other podestàs were installed by the Emperor as a means of gaining control over the notoriously independent Italian city-states. When the imperial podestà died, however, the Genoese took the unprecedented step of nominating their own without imperial approval. By so doing, they altered the nature of the institution. Why would not the most powerful clan simply attempt to subdue its weaker counterpart, rather than consent to an avowedly neutral alien ruler? Evidently, the existence of power symmetry between clans was a condition for the emergence and sustainability of the podesteria.

Because the Genoese seized control of the selection of their own podestà, they designed their podesteria so as to maximize the neutrality and minimize the power of the alien ruler. The podestà in Genoa was a non-Genoese noble, given governance powers for the period of a year, and was supported by twenty soldiers, two judges, and servants that he brought with him. He was offered very high wages and a bonus if there was no civil war when he left office. To minimize his incentive to collude with a given clan, he was selected by a council whose members were chosen on a geographic basis (to prevent its control by any one clan). He – and all relatives to the third degree – was prohibited from socializing with the Genoese, buying property, getting married, or managing any commercial transactions for himself or others. Until permanent housing was built, he had to move his residence around the city – to prevent him from associating for too long with the members of any particular clan. The podestà and his retinue were required to exit the city at the end of his term and not return for several years, and his son could not replace him in office. Moreover, the system provided an administrator who controlled Genoa's finances, which limited the clans' ability to expropriate income as a means of increasing their military power. The Genoese podesteria – an ostensibly benign example of alien rule – lasted for about 150 years. That the Genoese continued to nominate alien rulers long after the emperor demanded that they do so provides strong evidence of the institution's legitimacy.

Hence the Genoese were able to design the podesteria to meet their specifications. Their twin goals, in this respect, were to avoid interclan conflict that threatened social order and to further economic growth. To accomplish these goals, the podesteria severely constrained the alien ruler, providing him with incentives to maintain the peace and limiting his ability to collude with either of the contending clans. We can infer that the design was successful because it was maintained long after pressure from the Holy Roman Empire had waned. Under these highly particular conditions elected alien rule can become legitimate.[25]

Alien Rule Imposed

When alien rule is imposed over the objections of the ruled, the picture changes radically. All of the examples of antipathy to alien rule mentioned are the result of its imposition. Generally, children do not elect to have stepparents; academic departments do not elect to be placed in receivership; well-established firms do not elect to be taken over; nations do not willingly surrender their sovereignty. The individuals who are subject to such outcomes are likely to regard them as malign and illegitimate.

Everyone knows that imposed alien rulers can overcome their governance dilemmas by dividing the natives whom they willingly exploit (*divide et impera*). In this case, artful governance serves as a substitute for legitimacy (Robinson 1972). It is less apparent that natives also may come to regard imposed alien rule as (at least somewhat) legitimate. In what follows, I try to explain how this rabbit was pulled out of this particular hat in an institution known as the Chinese Maritime Customs Service (CMCS).[26]

The CMCS was an international, predominantly British-staffed bureaucracy under the control of successive Chinese central governments from its founding in 1854 until 1950.[27] Established by foreigners during the Taiping Rebellion to collect taxes on maritime trade when Chinese officials were unable to collect

---

[25] Clark (2007: 739–740) points out, however, that other Italian city-states also developed podesterias during this period, but these institutions had quite different outcomes from Genoa's. The Florentine podesteria, for example, was unable to quell violence between Guelfs and Ghibbelines, and Pisa's podesteria cemented the dominance of one clan over others. Further research is necessary to determine if these different outcomes reflect variations in the incentives provided by these various podesterias.

[26] Until 1912, the CMCS was known as the Imperial Maritime Customs Service.

[27] The origin of the Qing dynasty, which was established in the seventeenth century and persisted until 1911, was Manchu rather than Han, and as such, itself constituted an example of alien rule. The Manchus adopted nearly all of the governance institutions used in the preceding Ming dynasty, which had been dominated by the Han. And Han filled the vast majority of government positions. "When 'barbarian' conquerors such as Mongols and Manchus adopted Confucian culture, the Chinese people could accept them because their primary loyalty was to a culture rather than to a particular nation" (Zhao 2004: 42). Antipathy to the regime was based more on its ineptitude than its alien origins (Welch 1980: 97). The notion that the Qing somehow tolerated the CMCS because they too were alien rulers seems inconsistent with the persistence

them, it soon came to provide a panoply of collective goods, including domestic customs administration, postal administration, harbor and waterway management, weather reporting, and anti-smuggling operations. It mapped, lit, and policed the China coast and the Yangzi. It was involved in loan negotiations, currency reform, and financial and economic management. It even developed its own military forces (Lyons 2003; Tikhvinski'i 1983: 255; Tung 1970: 107–110). In time, the CMCS evolved into one of the most effective bases of Qing government support (Fairbank 1953: 462).

The CMCS owed its existence to the weakness of Chinese central control. Like the Genoese, the Qing Empire found itself threatened by foreign powers (Franke 1967: 66–92). For centuries, the center had maintained order by rotating its agents among the various provincial units, much as if they had been French *intendants*. The bulk of its revenue came from taxing the inland trade, mostly in agricultural products. The manufacturers of the rapidly industrializing European countries – led by the (British) East India Company – eagerly sought export markets for their textiles and other manufactured goods. To that end, they aggressively pursued free trade with China. Because the Chinese economy was largely self-sufficient, there had traditionally been little domestic interest in foreign trade.[28] All that changed, however, with the British-instigated importation of Indian-produced opium. This was an import that created its own demand. As ever more Chinese became addicted to opium, the Qing outlawed it. Even so, the Europeans still managed to smuggle large quantities of opium into China (Hart et al. 1986: 55; Franke 1967: 68).

The vast amounts of money associated with the opium trade had two important consequences for the Qing regime. On the one hand, it led to a large export of currency, depleting the Chinese supply of silver. On the other, it altered the balance of power between Peking and the landed gentry (Wakeman 1966). The gentry gained at the expense of the center's agents. At the same time that central government control was enfeebled, widespread corruption and banditry siphoned tax revenue away from it and disrupted trade. In addition to the gentry, the drug trade fostered a number of other domestic contenders for power – a rising merchant class, highland bandits and smugglers, and the Taiping rebels. Just as in Genoa, social order was breaking down in Kwangtung. Social disorder threatened overseas trade, alarming both the Qing government and the imperialist powers.

China's military defeat in the Opium Wars revealed that the regime was no match for the Western powers (Hart et al. 1991: 2–7; Tung 1970: 7). Nor could it effectively deter rebellion at home (Tikhvinski'i 1983: 240–241; Teng and

---

of the CMCS until 1950. Despite this, the ethnic boundary between Manchu and Han remained salient prior to the 1911 Revolution (Rhoads 2000).

[28] From the mid-eighteenth century until 1830, China restricted imports and exports to the port of Canton; the Qing granted the Cohung (a group of private Chinese entrepreneurs) monopoly rights over trade (Chesneaux et al. 1976; Morse 1961).

Fairbank 1954: 125; Costin 1968: 159–205). The Qing were induced to accept a series of treaties that eroded aspects of Chinese sovereignty at the point of a gun (Horowitz 2004; Brown 1978: 177; Tung 1970: 19–21). The CMCS was a by-product of these treaties, providing alien control over the maritime customs service, which was responsible for collecting revenue derived from overseas trade.[29]

With respect to foreign trade, Peking wanted to accomplish two principal tasks: to control smuggling and to maximize its tax revenue. By surrendering taxing authority to the CMCS, however, the Qing regime made itself vulnerable to exploitation by foreigners. Under normal circumstances (as discussed earlier) alien rulers should have responded by skimming at least some of the revenues they collected.

Why did the CMCS not take advantage of this opportunity? There are at least two reasons. On the one hand, because a good part of the Qing's revenue reverted to Western countries to pay for war debt, skimming the receipts would have been robbing Peter to pay Paul. More fundamentally, the CMCS was devoted to the Chinese because it was in their best interest to do so (Chesneaux, Bastid, and Bergère 1976). The treaties that the Western countries had signed with China were very advantageous to them. Because the Qing regime committed to these treaties, the foreigners had a stake in the success of the Qing. As the Service's farsighted inspector general Robert Hart appreciated, any hint of corruption on the part of the CMCS would have created friction between China and the Western powers (Wright 1950).

On the other hand, Hart instituted controls providing transparency to the Chinese government and deterring his own employees from corruption (Wright 1950). In an era characterized by robust Western discrimination against the Chinese,[30] the CMCS employed both Chinese and Westerners. To facilitate their cooperation, it hired Chinese linguists. Customs stations were supervised by Chinese superintendents, who collected customs dues and duties, whereas Western commissioners acted as assessors and accountants of duties on foreign trade. Because the commissioners never collected duties, they had no incentive to cheat, let things slide, or arbitrarily punish a trader. Commissioners were given an allowance for their port's operations, and expenditures had to be approved by the inspector general. The Chinese superintendents held the purse

---

[29] China had a long tradition of employing aliens in government: "One secret of the efficiency of China's imperial government had been its longstanding custom of co-opting alien chieftains on the frontiers to become servants of the empire" (Hart et al. 1991: 13). This was referred to as *i – i chi-I*, or "using barbarians to control barbarians."

[30] "Many Chinese writers mention the public gardens laid out in the [treaty ports], with bandstands, flower-beds and notice-boards inscribed with regulations. 'No dogs or Chinese' has become a stock phrase denoting the insulting existence of these municipal parks. Whilst it is not true that there was ever a sign bearing that bald prohibition – municipal councils in China were as long-winded as anywhere else – the hundreds of rules and regulations governing these tiny scraps of land did indeed exclude most Chinese people." (Wood 1998: 2).

strings of local customs and were privy to the internal workings of the Service. All funds (in theory, at least) were accounted for (Wright 1950: 282).

In the Service's early years, Hart traveled from port to port inspecting each one; an audit secretary also visited the ports on a regular basis to carry out inspections. Offenders were instantly dismissed and required to forfeit their pay and retirement allowance. These controls proved highly effective: during Hart's fifty-year career the cases of reported malfeasance could be counted on the fingers of one hand (Wright 1950: 287).

Chinese nationalism first arose in reaction to the unequal treaties – and treatment – imposed on the country by the Western powers in the nineteenth century (Zhao 2004). Following the revolution of 1911, the old state apparatus was destroyed and the new one had yet to solidify. Many regions fell under the sway of warlords; there was a profound disintegration of the political order (Fairbank 1986: 1308). The CMCS's gunboats policed the coastal cities, providing a haven from warlord conflict. And its capital provided the new government with sorely needed international credit. Despite the nationalist goals of the revolution, the CMCS prospered (Hu 1955: 176–204; Brunero 2006). Indeed, this nationalist political transformation actually *increased* the influence of the CMCS (Clifford 1965: 18). In 1932, for example, the CMCS was generating 60 percent of central government revenues, a much greater proportion than before (Anderson 1998: 30).[31]

Implications

In the midst of intense interclan conflict that threatened the economic development of Genoa – and under the pressure of an external threat – the Genoese elected to have an alien ruler. Because an Italian from another city-state could easily be made dependent on one of the two contending groups (for example, he could marry into either faction), thereby destroying the mutual deterrence equilibrium that provided the rationale for alien rule in the first place,[32] they designed an elaborate series of incentives and constraints to motivate the podestà to provide social order in a bitterly divided polity.

---

[31] A strikingly similar story can be told about another key alien-dominated institution during this period of Chinese history: the Sino-Foreign Salt Inspectorate (Strauss 2008). From 1928 through 1937, for instance, this British-dominated agency collected an average of 25% of Chinese central government receipts. It enacted rigorously fair and effective policies and, in so doing, generated legitimacy in an extremely nationalist environment.

[32] "In mutual-deterrence equilibria, each clan is deterred from attacking the other by the self-enforcing belief that an attack will not pay, given the other clan's military strength, the cost of the attack, and the implied loss from forgoing future joint piracy" (Greif 2005). The podesteria is an example of what Gellner (1983: 15) terms *gelding* – a practice that denies governors links with particular kin groups, "whose interests are then liable to sway the officers from the stern path of duty, and whose support is, at the same time, liable to endow them on occasion with too much power." Court Jews and Ottoman eunuchs were similarly gelded in their own societies (Coser 1974).

As an imposed form of alien rule, the CMCS was initially greeted with hostility (Chesneaux et al. 1976: 1301). Despite this, however, it proved to be effective at collecting taxes, attacking piracy, and minimizing corruption (Fox 1940: 143–186; Morse 1961 63). On the heels of these notable successes, the CMCS soon began to provide a wide range of collective goods in coastal China. The institution persisted for over a century, even surviving the nationalist revolution of 1911.

Given these conditions, the alien ruler was preferred to a native one because the alien could be relied on to be a neutral third party, rather than a partisan who would upset the delicate balance between rival clans. Note that this explanation differs from the old sociological bromide – made popular in H. G. Wells's *War of the Worlds* and countless other science fictions about alien invasion – that an external threat unites previously conflicting groups (Coser 1956). In the present case, the external threat does not bring the parties closer together. Quite the contrary: the impetus for the election of an alien ruler hinges on the intractability of intergroup conflict.

Yet the mechanisms responsible for the adoption of alien rule do not explain its persistence. Alien rule is best able to persist over the long run when it provides subjects with efficient outcomes – those that maximize the key native groups' expected returns. By eliminating disruptive clan conflict, the podesteria fostered Genoese prosperity. Although it was established at the behest of a foreign power, the Genoese continued to use the podesteria long after it was demanded of them. By maximizing revenue from foreign trade and providing key collective goods, the CMCS provided similar returns for the Qing regime, if not for the Chinese people as a whole.[33] Significantly, its influence actually increased after the nationalist revolution of 1911.[34]

The institutions used to control the alien rulers and the rival subjects differ markedly in the two cases, however. Because they effectively elected alien rule, the Genoese could craft much greater constraints on the podestà than the Qing

[33] "Given the Western domination of China after 1860, the Customs was useful both to Western traders and to Chinese administrators, enabling the Chinese government to meet some of its immediate problems and Western merchants to exploit their Chinese market more effectively" (Fairbank 1953: 463). Because Fairbank's assessment was based on the records of the CMCS rather than the Qing archives, which were unavailable to him, the possibility that this conclusion suffers from a pro-Western bias cannot be ruled out. The overall Chinese assessment of the CMCS remains to be determined (note that this will be a difficult task, indeed, in the absence of reliable survey data). Note that a similar kind of alien rule in Siam that was established in the same period has been held to have enhanced the monarchy there (Trocki 1992: 93).

[34] A European-run institution, the Ottoman Public Debt Administration (OPDA), played a similar role in the Ottoman Empire from 1881 to 1918 (Blaisdell 1929; Clay 2000). Like the CMCS, the OPDA was able to produce greater tax revenue for the central government by reducing bureaucratic corruption. Moreover, by raising the confidence of Western investors in the regime's fiscal responsibility, the OPDA also contributed to the development of the territory's infrastructure, especially with respect to railroads. Unlike the CMCS, however, the OPDA did not survive the rise of nationalism in Kemalist Turkey.

could on the CMCS. Despite this key difference, this chapter therefore suggests that if it is both effective and conducted according to bureaucratic norms emphasizing merit-based allocation and procedural justice,[35] even imposed alien rule can gain legitimacy in time.

The Legitimation of Alien Rule

The concept of legitimacy was invented to help account for social order in large societies (Weber 1978; Zelditch 2001). Because it is usually assumed that it is too costly to attain order in the long run on the basis of sanctions derived from incentives or naked coercion,[36] political stability must also rest, in part, on some normative basis. Agents who have internalized the relevant norms can be relied on to control themselves. Legitimacy provides a means of referencing this normative basis of social order.

In legitimate regimes established rules will be honored even in the absence of sanctions for noncompliance. Acceptance of the rules as a result of the anticipation of sanctions may well yield compliance, but if so, this owes to considerations of power rather than legitimacy. As discussed previously (Chapter 1), the measurement of legitimacy poses a formidable challenge. Although compliance is often observable, the motivation driving it – that is, whether it is due to the anticipation of sanctions – is difficult to discern absent reliable subjective evidence. By the same token, anything less than full compliance with the rules reveals some decrement of legitimacy. Whereas compliance may be a result of either legitimacy or the threat of sanctions, noncompliance indicates some degree of illegitimacy.[37]

What then determines the legitimacy of a government in a given society? There are two different views of the matter. On one view (Parsons 1960), the principal determinant of legitimacy is a consensus among rulers and ruled about values, norms, and beliefs. Because aliens – by definition – do not share values, norms, and beliefs with natives, alien rule can never be legitimate on this view.

Opposed to this is an instrumental theory of legitimacy that has gained force since the rise of liberalism. On this view, a regime is legitimate to the degree that it provides valued collective goods – including procedures and policy outcomes – to the ruled. With respect to procedures, legitimation occurs

---

[35] However, the CMCS was far from a perfect bureaucracy: it had no formal criteria for recruitment, no rules for promotion and little predictability of postings, and the inspector general ran the Service with virtually no accountability (Anderson 1998: 7).

[36] This may not be true in the short run, however. For example, Liberman (1996) argues that the Nazi occupation of Western Europe on balance profited Germany and encountered relatively little in the way of resistance and much in the way of collaboration.

[37] Thus legitimacy implies an obligation to abide by established rules. If I accept the legitimacy of the Internal Revenue Service, then I will pay the taxes that are due even if I know I could free ride with impunity. What if the rules themselves are deemed to be illegitimate in the eyes of the governed? Then – absent coercion – compliance will suffer apace.

to the degree that governments legislate and enforce the law fairly. In Western societies, at least, this means according to due process (Gamson, Fireman, and Rytina 1982). So long as these procedures do not put any category of individuals at systematically greater disadvantage or risk than any other, rational people (acting, as it were, behind a Rawlsian veil of ignorance) will grant legitimacy to the government (Rogowski 1974; Coleman 1990: 288).[38] The emphasis on procedure has a key strength, for it can account for compliance among both the losers and winners of particular government programs and policies. This is a defining characteristic of legitimate rule (Linz 1978). Losers continue to grant legitimacy to the government because they believe that they might be winners in the next rounds of government activity. The importance of procedures is supported by a range of experimental (Tyler 2006) and historical (Levi 1997) research. From this perspective, the success of the CMCS probably is owed in no small part to the existence of deeply rooted Confucian bureaucratic norms.

There is, however, another instrumental consideration. Substantively, at least since the rise of liberalism and its emphasis on individual rights, governments are judged by the outcome of their policies as well as the procedures that generate them.[39] This suggests that legitimacy is also a by-product of the government's effectiveness in producing collective goods (Lipset 1960: 38–71; Beetham 1991: 109; 237).[40] To some extent, this effectiveness is in the eyes of the beholder. The citizens of many less developed countries might regard a new regime as highly effective if it managed to substantially curtail corruption, for example, even in the face of poor economic growth. The same reaction would not be expected to hold for the citizens of highly developed countries.[41] Thus the effectiveness of a regime is a judgment that is highly context dependent.

---

[38] Note that this conception of fairness does not imply that government policies must lead to an equality of outcome among individuals or social groups, but it does strive toward the attainment of equality of opportunity.

[39] Huntington (1991) suggests that the legitimacy of democratic regimes rests on both procedures (which guarantee contestation of rule) and the effectiveness of public goods provision, whereas nondemocratic regimes must rely solely on the latter consideration.

[40] Thus, alien rulers may produce bundles of public goods that natives regard as suboptimal. Because one of the requisites of effective governance is accurate information about the conditions and desires of individuals embedded in localities (Scott 1998), alien rulers are likely to be too distant from natives to govern effectively. Even the native central rulers of large societies have difficulty attaining this kind of information; Hayek's (1973) attack on central planning is based on this premise, as are most arguments on behalf of federalism and political decentralization. This informational obstacle is that much more severe for alien rulers, for they may be subject to the deliberate withholding of information by natives (Scott 1985). Current conflict over immigration policy in the advanced societies reveals that cultural distance strongly attenuates voters' willingness to devote their taxes to provide for the welfare of others (Alesina, Baqir, and Easterly 1999).

[41] Indeed, the theory of retrospective voting (Fiorina 1981) suggests that the only information that individuals need to vote for or against incumbents is a calculation of the changes in their own welfare since the last election. This can be a misleading criterion because changes in individual

Nevertheless a regime whose provision of collective goods *decreases* over time cannot credibly claim to be effective.[42]

Yet if legitimacy is nothing but the quo of some government quid, then every time a social group deems itself the loser from a given policy, it will withdraw legitimacy from the regime. Regimes can tolerate the withdrawal of legitimacy by small, socially isolated groups, but as the numbers and pervasiveness of the discontented grow, chances of political instability increase apace, although their mobilization hinges on their capacity to resolve the collective action problem (Olson 1965).

The instrumental view of legitimation has garnered substantial empirical support. Thus, the greater the relative income of ethnoregions, the less likely they are to demand sovereignty (Sambanis 2006; Siroky, Dzutsev and Hechter 2013). The prevalence of immigration in the modern world provides further evidence: after all, immigrants voluntarily trade native but (presumably, in their eyes) relatively ineffective rule in their homelands for more effective rule by aliens.[43] The growing popularity of city managers in the United States, many of whom are alien to their communities and on this account perceived as less beholden to native interest groups, may also be a testament to the link between effectiveness and legitimacy (Nalbandian 1991).[44] A study of nineteenth century American cities suggests that voters were willing to cede the political autonomy of their local governments to join larger metropolitan areas when the perceived costs of their existing sewers, water supply, lighting, and street systems exceeded their perceived benefits (Dilworth 2005). There is even some evidence that an occupying power that rules impartially and effectively provides collective goods can win over subject populations.[45] Because

welfare may be a result of events that are quite beyond the control of rulers. For example, the incumbent president, Woodrow Wilson, was significantly punished by voters in seaside communities that experienced a series of shark attacks in New Jersey in 1916 (Achen and Bartels 2012).

[42] In George Orwell's fictional *1984*, Oceania – that oppressive regime ruled by Big Brother – manages simultaneously to lower the chocolate ration but to deceptively report that it has been raised. The saps who mostly inhabit Oceania are thereby persuaded that their lives have been bettered. This kind of chicanery might be possible in a society in which information is monopolized by the rulers, but thankfully this option still seems to be rather remote at the present time in societies with a free press and open access to the Internet.

[43] I am grateful to Deven Hamilton for alerting me to this point. This statement presupposes that the higher level of economic development in immigration societies owes, at least in part, to their more effective governance. This is not to suggest that immigrants are indifferent to their native cultures; only that their desire for effective governance often trumps attachment to their native culture.

[44] Whereas American city managers are formally no more than the agents of elected decision makers (e.g., city councils), in reality these principals often fail to exercise much oversight (Selden, Brewer and Brudney 1999). Thus despite the distinction between politics and administration, city managers – like Genoa's podestà – tend to exercise much independent authority and set policy (Svara 1999).

[45] See Gavrilis (2005) for an account of American rule in the Iraqi city of Ar Rutbah; Smooha (2004) on Israeli Arabs' acceptance of the state of Israel prior to the Intifada, and Lammers

there is no contradiction between the emphasis on procedure and that of sub-stance, they can be combined to provide a more robust instrumental account of legitimation.

Conclusion

This discussion has implications for determining the source of the strong pref-erence for native rule. By treating this preference as unconditional, Orwell's epigraph at the beginning of this chapter implies that the source of the pref-erence for native rule is universal, at least since the emergence of the norm of national self-determination, rather than instrumental and, hence, contingent. Nonetheless this implication may not be warranted.

Consider the following relationship between legitimacy, the types of rule and the fairness and/or effectiveness of governance:

Legitimacy of Government, by Type of Rule and Level of Fairness/Effectiveness of Rule[46]

Type of Rule

		Native	Alien
Fair/Effective	High	**Type I** *High legitimacy* OECD countries	**Type II** *Intermediate legitimacy* Genoese *Podesteria*, CMCS
	Low	**Type III** *Low legitimacy* Kibaki's Kenya Mugabe's Zimbabwe	**Type IV** *Illegitimacy* Belgian Congo

In the modern world, the prevalence of types I and III is far greater than types II and IV.[47] Why is it more difficult for alien rulers to attain legitimacy? People

(1988, 2003) for a more general analysis. Commenting on the willingness of states to accept foreign troops on their native soil, Lake (2007: 76) notes that "countries subordinate to the United States in security affairs enjoy lower defense expenditures as a proportion of national in-come." These countries therefore are willing to trade off some degree of military sovereignty for increased protection by an alien power. Need it be pointed out that the recent popular success of movements – like Hamas and Hizbollah in their respective territories – also lends support to the idea that groups that provide effective governance often come to be regarded as legitimate? After all, this is what originally fueled Mao's Chinese Communist guerillas (Popkin 1979).

[46] Note that the two dimensions in the table are correlated – at every level of efficient and fair gov-ernance, native rulers can attain more legitimacy than alien rulers *ceteris paribus*.

[47] As the history of Western European state formation reveals, however, the prevalence of types II and IV has often been self-canceling in the long run. Invariably, these states crystallized around

may prefer native to alien rulers simply because native status is an observable predictor of superior governance. In contrast to the noninstrumental explanations advanced earlier, the widespread antipathy to alien rule may derive from the weakness of alien rulers' incentives to govern fairly and effectively. Alien rulers generally have few incentives to provide fair and effective governance.[48] Absent such incentives, there is nothing to restrain rulers from engaging in outright predation. Because natives tend to be more accountable to the ruled than aliens for the multiple reasons discussed earlier, they are likely to produce fairer and more effective governance than alien rulers.

The examples in this chapter, however, show that given the appropriate incentives, alien rulers indeed can be motivated to provide fair and effective governance – and, hence, to earn some measure of legitimacy.[49] This outcome is least problematic in the case of elected alien rule. The Genoese provided these incentives themselves because they were able to design an institution that tied the podestá's compensation to his ability to secure social order in the Republic. This provided him with ample motivation to rule fairly and effectively.

Imposed alien rule is quite another story. These incentives are usually weak, if not altogether absent, in the case of classical colonialism. Yet even imposed alien rule can become sustainable under some conditions. Alien rulers can be motivated to provide fair and effective governance when aliens impose rule on native territory to augment their own security (for which they are prepared to incur some cost) or to share in the profits of increased trade and commercial activity. Thus it was in the vital interest of the CMCS to prop up a shaky Qing regime so as to profit from favorable foreign trade treaties. This similarly motivated the British inspector generals of the CMCS to exercise fair and effective rule. Profit from trade and commercial activity likewise provided an incentive for good governance in the case of British rule in Hong Kong. Many Hong Kong natives preferred alien (British) rule to Chinese rule at the time of the handover (Scott 1989: 13). Moreover, support for the legitimating role

core areas that expanded into culturally distinct peripheries (Hechter 1998). Core rulers initially were regarded as alien – they often met with armed resistance – but in the course of centuries many of them were reframed as native. In peripheries that were consistently subject to unfair and ineffective rule, however, rulers from the core continued to be regarded as aliens. This helps account for the prevalence of nationalist movements in these kinds of peripheries.

[48] Even if their desire to provide fair and effective governance is sincere, cultural differences between aliens and natives make it politically difficult for alien rulers to sustain the high level of funding necessary to promote social order and economic development in native societies. Such failures of political will have doomed colonial regimes, contemporary peacekeeping operations, and nation-building efforts alike: in all of these situations, aliens have a strong tendency to rule on the cheap (Marten 2004; Doyle and Sambanis 2006: Hodge 2011). Despite this, some have argued that there is a strong argument for the imposition of alien rule in the form of neo-trusteeship in the case of failed states (Fearon and Laitin 2004).

[49] Likewise, the authority of nongovernmental organizations, which have increased rapidly in the postwar world, therefore rests largely on their Otherhood and their lack of petty self-interests (Meyer 2010: 7).

of alien rule comes from the record of United Nations's peacekeeping operations. Recent analyses demonstrate that these operations have often succeeded in reducing intergroup conflict over the long run (Doyle and Sambanis 2006; Fortna 2008).

Alien rule is not an all-or-nothing phenomenon. It can be partial as well as total. The CMCS did not usurp the role of the Qing Emperor: its rulership was confined to specific sectors of governance in China. Likewise, Christians and Jews in the Ottoman Empire who obtained the protection of Western representatives were free to do business under the laws of a Western country, rather than those of the Empire (Kuran 2004).

An international market in governance services would offer alien rulers ample incentives to provide fair and effective governance (see Chapter 7). The role of competitive markets in disciplining the producers of goods and services is powerful. Moreover, the effects of market discipline are culturally universal. Contemporary exemplars of successful alien rule are likely to hasten the advent of such an international market. This is good news for those seeking to improve the performance of governments in an era in which cultural politics has achieved exceptional salience.

3

The Failure of Legitimate Rule in Iraq

Colonies do not cease to be colonies because they are independent.
— *Benjamin Disraeli*

If alien rule can only be legitimated by effective and fair rule, then it follows that the absence of either or both of these conditions should result in an illegitimate regime that is likely to face resistance and social disorder. Such has been the fate of modern Iraq. Modern Iraq was initially ruled by aliens: first by the Ottomans and then by the British. Thereafter the territory – divided as it is into predominantly Sunni, Shi'i, and Kurdish territorial zones – was ruled by native Sunni Muslims.[1] None of these various regimes attained much legitimacy, however, and as a result modern Iraq has had a turbulent history.

In their attempts to contain this turbulence, the different rulers of Iraq experimented with various forms of rule. Sometimes, they granted native Arabs substantial authority within their localities. At other times, they wrested authority from natives and tried to rule localities from central locations such as Istanbul or Baghdad. The strategy of granting natives local authority is known as *indirect rule*. The alternative strategy – which is akin to alien rule – is known as *direct rule*. Neither strategy was particularly effective, however, and this chapter explains why.

The Dilemma of Governance in Iraq

In 1918, Arnold Wilson, acting civil commissioner of the territory now known as Iraq, faced a dilemma. A self-confident British colonial officer, Wilson was

---

[1] This is not to claim that sectarian distinctions in Iraq are, or have been, monolithic. The terms *Shi'i* and *Sunni* describe groups made up of individuals with many other attributes – such as class and political ideology – that in certain situations and for certain purposes may become politically salient and thus allow the members of different sects to unite (Haddad 2011: 8).

charged with the task of establishing social order in a well-armed, culturally heterogeneous population that had been liberated from centuries of Ottoman rule. As is often the case in the modern world, British governance was made more difficult by the population's hostility to its new alien masters. The dilemma, as the colonial officer later recounted, was whether to govern Iraq directly or indirectly:

> Ought we to aim at a "bureaucratic" form of administration, such as that in force in Turkey and in Egypt, involving direct control by a central government, and the replacement of the powerful tribal confederation by the smaller tribal or sub-tribal unit, as a prelude to individual in place of communal ownership of land, or should our aim be to retain, and subject to official safeguards, to strengthen, the authority of tribal chiefs, and to make them the agents and official representatives of Government, within their respective areas? The latter policy had been already adopted, in default of a better one, in Basra wilayat, and especially in the Muntafiq division: was it wise to apply it to the Baghdad wilayat? Both policies had their advocates. (Wilson 1931)

After due deliberation, Wilson chose direct rule. Two years later there was a massive rebellion and he was out of a job.

Today, the Iraqi state faces an uncannily similar situation to that of Britain at the end of World War I. Following the toppling of Saddam and the establishment of a constitutional regime, the Iraqi government finds itself ruling a culturally divided and notably unruly territory. Surprisingly, the answer to Wilson's question – Is social order in societies such as Iraq best attained by direct or indirect rule? – is as elusive now as it was at the end of World War I. If anything, the question is even more pressing today, for the increasing prevalence of civil war, state failure, and terrorism has sharply underlined the problem of social order in many parts of the world. Critics of the American occupation have lamented that the Bush administration had adopted no coherent plan for administering the peace before invading;[2] the result was a weak interim state that was either unwilling or unable to maintain order at the local level (Ricks 2006).[3] Paul Bremer's solution was to implement direct rule, a strategy that was criticized for fueling sectarian violence (Diamond 2004: 3). Likewise, the new Iraqi government appears incapable of maintaining order in the absence

---

[2] Experts on nation building and Middle Eastern affairs presented the Bush team with possible postwar strategies before the occupation began, but the administration neglected to seriously consider their recommendations. Thus Jay Garner, the initial American official in charge of postwar reconstruction, merely had eight weeks between the announcement of his appointment and the start of hostilities to organize a government in Iraq. As one American ex-general (Barry McCaffree) has pointed out, this is far too little time to set up a new Safeway supermarket, let alone the government of a sizable country (Traub 2004: 62).

[3] Some argue that because U.S. troops did not stop the looting that occurred immediately after Saddam's removal, Iraqis were left with the impression that the United States would tolerate acts of violence. In some cases, U.S. troops encouraged disorder: rather than stop lootings, troops egged the looters on. What was perceived (rightly) as disorder for Iraqis was considered an acceptable by-product of freedom to U.S. military men and women (Packer 2005).

of American and coalition forces. Whatever might be said about the various regimes in modern Iraq, they did not turn their backs on some received theory of governance. No such tried-and-true theory exists. To promote political legitimacy and social order in Iraq, one must understand how different governance structures affect the probability of unrest given the country's specific characteristics and circumstances.

For social engineers intent on attaining order and legitimacy, the choice of a system of governance is a dilemma because there continue to be advocates for both of the positions outlined by Wilson. Indirect rule allows the state to pass the high costs of rule to local (e.g., native) groups. But indirect rule sometimes has its downside: for example, some writers have blamed ethnofederalism for the fragmentation of the Soviet Union (Beissinger 2002; Bunce 1999; Roeder 1991). Although direct rule is often a hedge against fragmentation, it is not a sufficient guarantor of social order, either. On the one hand, some stateless societies (such as traditional tribal societies in the Arabian peninsula as described by Ibn Khaldun) manifested a good deal of social order. On the other, sultanistic regimes (such as Duvalier's Haiti) – the *ne plus ultra* of direct rule – are often visited by disorder (Chehabi and Linz 1998).

Evidently, the relationship between social order and these types of governance is complex. In some situations, an increase in direct rule can instigate resistance in a polity, fostering disorder. Indirect rule is no necessary panacea, however: it too can hinder social order. Because governance structures are pivotal for attaining social order – in contemporary Iraq as well as elsewhere – this chapter aims to explore their general effects.

Indirect and Direct Rule

Before the advent of contemporary communications, transportation and military technology, large polities – such as empires and big states – were faced with severe problems of governance. Enforcing directives emanating from the center over large distances is difficult, to put it mildly (Hechter 2000: Ch. 4). Take the problem of expansive territory. Once an order is promulgated from the center, what assurance can there be that it will be complied with in the periphery? How does the center know if compliance is ever really attained? And how long does it take such assurance to reach central authorities? Consider taxation, which is the lifeblood of the modern state. Central rulers can demand that residents cough up a fixed proportion of their income to the treasury, but how can they make sure that they receive the amount they are owed (Kiser and Schneider 1994)? Analogous problems arise in the case of justice. How can central rulers enforce the law of the land throughout their realm?

These problems are serious enough in a culturally homogeneous territory. But large polities are almost always culturally heterogeneous. Consider the implications of the projection of central rule in territories made up of distinct cultural – ethnic, linguistic, and racial – groups. How can central rulers make sure that their laws can be understood, let alone complied with, by the members of distinctive cultural groups (Scott 1998)?

The only way the center can gain these assurances is by monitoring behavior in the periphery. Monitoring is a very costly activity, however, and both geographic and cultural distance sharply increases its costs.

As a result of the expense of monitoring, large polities could only be maintained until recently on the basis of indirect rule. In a system of indirect rule, the central ruler exerts direct control only in the ruler's own domain (Gerring et al. 2011). To simplify an admittedly complex picture, spatially distant territories were controlled by traditional – that is, local – authorities, who pay tribute (or taxes) to the central ruler in exchange for guarantees of their security and the right to rule within their local sphere (Bendix 1964: Ch. 2). What this means is that, for the most part, the members of peripheral regions and distinct cultural groups within empires and large states were ruled by their own kind.

For reasons that need not concern us here, *direct rule* made great strides on the European Continent following the French Revolution (Tilly 1990; Hechter 2000).[4] Direct rule enables central authorities to exert their control over the totality of their territory. It fosters economic growth by standardizing coinage, weights, and measures. It removes interregional barriers to trade and migration. It facilitates communications, thereby extending the reach of markets. Urbanization and industrialization are spurred in its wake. At the same time, direct rule brings about significant political changes. Unlike wealth, authority is a zero-sum commodity. The center can only gain control by wresting it from local authorities. Because large territories tended to be culturally diverse, these local authorities often have different ethnicities, languages, or religions from those of central rulers. Thus, at its inception direct rule often implies rule by aliens. By shifting dependence from local to central authorities, direct rule challenges the legitimacy of the center in two separate ways. It encourages local authorities to persuade their rural dependents that central (alien) rulers

---

[4] "How did France sustain this effort? The explanation surely lies with the excellent provisions of the *Loi Jourdan*, promulgated in 1798, and beyond that the entire administrative apparatus which was geared to enforcing it. This apparatus, created in its essentials by the law of 28 Pluviôse VIII (17 February 1800) and supplementary consular decree of 17 Ventôse VIII (8 March 1800), reinforced the centralization of power through a strict hierarchical chain that ran from Paris (ministers) to the departments (prefects), districts (sub-prefects) and municipalities (mayors), and along which instructions supposedly sped with the rapidity of an 'electric current'" (Rowe 2003b: 8). As Rowe points out, however, this top-down view of command and control was only imperfectly realized at the local level – even in post-Revolutionary France. For this reason, some writers (Chatterjee 1993: 14) justifiably claim that all nation building is an inherently colonial enterprise. Likewise, Napoleonic government in foreign territories, such as the Rhineland, was more pragmatic and more dependent on local elites than most historians have assumed. Although Napoleonic administrative reforms in the Rhineland were impressive on paper, they "underwent modification when confronted with the challenges of governing a recently annexed peripheral region with a largely alien culture" (Rowe 2003a: 282–283). Attempts to impose direct rule persist to the present day in Russia, China, and Brazil, among other countries.

are illegitimate as a means of preserving the locals' traditional privileges. And it encourages newcomers to the cities to form distinctive cultural groups to contest resources controlled by the center. Yet indirect rule is no panacea either. Under indirect rule local authorities may be tempted to secede and opt out of the regime. After all, why should they settle for half a loaf when secession would provide them with the whole thing (Riker 1964)? This temptation can only be mitigated when the center has sufficient resources to earn the loyalty of local authorities. By the same token, any decrease in centrally controlled resources threatens to erode local authorities' loyalty to the regime.

As direct rule progresses, one typical scenario takes place in the countryside. By usurping the power to tax and administer local justice, and by extending public education, direct rule weakens traditional authorities.[5] The more literate a peasantry is, for example, the less dependent it is on local leaders, for literacy lowers its cost of migration. Direct rule is also often associated with the denigration of its new subjects.[6] In culturally distinctive regions, therefore, traditional authorities are very likely to play the alien card in resisting the incursions of the central state. Even in culturally distinct regions where local rulers assimilated to the culture of the center, direct rule spurs resistance, for it permits the emergence of new leaders who could mobilize the culturally distinct peasantry against the alien rulers of the center.

A bottom-up type of resistance is more likely to emerge in cities where massive shifts in social conditions produce new levels of uncertainty, particularly among the increasing number of displaced persons (Vail 1989; Anderson 1998). Once people migrate into urban areas, they face competition for scarce resources such as jobs, spouses, placement in educational institutions, residential space, and government services. The lion's share of these resources is likely to go to individuals who organize effectively and act cooperatively. This gives people an incentive to join groups in which the members act to favor one another in the battle for resources. These incentives hold across a wide variety of arenas. How do individuals decide what sort of group to join? They are likely to join the group that maximizes their expected benefits. The expected benefits of group membership, at least in part, are an increasing function of the

---

[5] As this account should make plain, both direct and indirect rule are not constant, but variable. A given ruler may employ more or less direct rule, and hence more or less indirect rule. By the same token, a territory may be subject to more or less alien rule. Thus, whereas full-fledged direct rule implies alien rule, alien rulers can also adopt some degree of indirect rule. For example, Japanese governance in Taiwan was more indirect than it was in Korea (see Chapter 4).

[6] Thus, following the Anglo-Norman invasion of Ireland, Gerald of Wales (1126–1223) opined that the Irish natives are "a filthy people, wallowing in vice. They indulge in incest, for example in marrying – or rather debauching – the wives of their dead brothers" (Gillingham 1987: 19). Similar sentiments were expressed following the Cromwellian conquest of the island in the seventeenth century. Only a century later, however, the Anglo-Irish nobility led an Irish nationalist rebellion against English rule. Direct rule often takes the form of alien conquest. What separates it from previous forms of conquest is its ability to impose its culture on its new subjects as a result of the vastly expanded capacity of the modern state.

size of the group, up to a point that is nearly half the size of the entire population (Chai 1996). In any large population center, the optimal size of a group therefore will be considerably larger than the number of migrants from any single community of origin (cf. Hannan 1979; Cederman 1995).

Yet groups cannot act effectively unless members share interests. In the absence of such shared interests, actions that help some members of a prospective group may hurt other members, and there will be little incentive for members who will be hurt to engage in the collective action. One way that a group of individuals can have shared interests in a particular outcome is if they have a common position in the division of labor (Hechter 1978). This gives them an interest either in raising the returns for the occupational roles commonly held or in opening up opportunities for entry into other, more rewarding occupations.

Social Order and Forms of Governance

To the degree that a society is ordered, its individual members behave both predictably[7] and cooperatively. Mere predictability is an insufficient condition for social order, however. The denizens of the state of nature (think of the inhabitants of Rio's *favelas* as portrayed in the Brazilian film *City of God*) are quite able to predict that everyone will engage in force and fraud whenever it suits them. Hence they are accustomed to taking the appropriate defensive – and offensive – measures. But none of the fruits of social and economic development can occur in the absence of a cooperative social order. Thus, in a viable social order, individuals must not only act in a mutually predictable fashion; they must also comply with socially encompassing norms and laws – rules that permit and promote cooperation.

Social order is not a constant but a variable; it exists to the degree that individuals in a given territory are free from the depredations of crime, physical injury, and arbitrary justice. Perfect order is an ideal, so it cannot be attained in Iraq, or anywhere else for that matter. By any reckoning, present-day Iraq falls far short of this ideal: Iraqis are facing the perils of gunfire, kidnapping, murder, and bombings on a daily basis. Despite this, there is a greater amount of order in certain Iraqi regions (such as Kurdistan) than others.

How can this woeful amount of order in today's Iraq be increased? This question is an instantiation of the general problem of social order that has dogged social theorists at least since ancient times. The most popular solution dates from the seventeenth century (Hobbes [1651] 1996): it implies that social order is the product of direct rule, a multidimensional variable composed of at least

---

[7] Hayek (1973: 36), for example, defines order in opposition to entropy. For him it is "a state of affairs in which a multiplicity of elements of various kinds are so related to each other that we may learn from our acquaintance with some spatial or temporal part of the whole to form correct expectations concerning the rest, or at least expectations which have a good chance of proving correct."

two independent dimensions: *scope* and *penetration*.[8] The scope of a state refers to the quantity and quality of the collective goods it provides. Welfare benefits, government jobs, state-sponsored schools and hospitals, and a functioning system of justice are examples of such goods. Socialist states have the highest scope; neoliberal ones the lowest. Scope induces dependence: where state scope is high, individuals depend primarily on the state for access to collective goods.

In contrast, penetration refers to the central state's control capacity – that is, the proportion of laws and policies that are enacted and enforced by central as against regional or local decision makers. Penetration is at a maximum in police states in which central rulers seek to monitor and control all subjects within their domain. Polities relying on local agents to exercise control (municipal police forces, for example) have lower penetration. Scope and penetration often covary, but not necessarily. For example, federal states with similar scope have less penetration than unitary states.

Just how direct rule may foster social order is a matter of some dispute.[9] On one view, high scope and penetration foster order by instituting a common culture that provides the shared concepts, values, and norms – or in game-theoretic language, the common knowledge (Chwe 2001) – required for cooperation to emerge and persist. Intuitively, cultural homogeneity is essential for social order. However, the stability of culturally heterogeneous societies that have adopted indirect rule – such as Switzerland, the United Kingdom, and Finland – calls this conclusion into question.[10] On another view, social order rests not on cognitive commonality, but rather on the power and authority of central rulers. Indeed, the popular concept of state failure implies the loss of this central authority.[11]

Although direct rule maximizes rulers' income, revenue, and power, it has two distinct liabilities. First, it engenders the opposition of local rulers (and their dependents), whose power is threatened as the state advances. Second, it is costly, for direct rulers must assume the financial responsibility of pervasive policing[12] while simultaneously providing the bulk of their citizenry's collective

---

[8] For a more extended discussion of direct and indirect rule and their effects on patterns of group formation, see Hechter (2004).

[9] For a discussion of the major theories of social order and their limits, see Hechter and Horne (2009).

[10] To say nothing of the attainment of social order in countries of immigration such as the United States, Australia, Canada, and New Zealand.

[11] Nearly forty years ago, two eminent comparativists made the same point, albeit a bit differently. Nettl (1968) insisted that the state was hardly to be conceived as an institution carved out of marble and granite but rather a variable that he termed *stateness*. And Huntington (1968: 1) assured us that "the most important political distinction among countries concerns not their form of government but their degree of government."

[12] The costs of policing are political in addition to pecuniary. In occupied Iraq, for example, the American administrations, unwilling to add more military boots on the ground, contracted out an increasingly large proportion of the security responsibility to an international mercenary force. Although this added considerably to the bottom line, it avoided domestic political costs.

goods.[13] Moreover, the idea that social order is produced in a top-down fashion by resourceful central authorities leaves a fundamental question begging: Just how can this power ever manage to be concentrated in the first place? To this question, top-down theorists have little in the way of an answer, save for the (often valid) idea that it is imposed by conquest on fragmented territories by more powerful states. Beyond its inability to account for primary state formation, this answer underestimates the difficulty that modern states have had in attempting to impose order on less developed societies.[14]

The nature of this difficulty becomes apparent when we recall that the emergence of the modern bureaucratic state in Western Europe was long drawn out and arduous to boot (Elias 1993; Ertman 1997; Gorski 2003). Feudal landholders who managed, against all odds, to secure a preponderance of political power were, for a time, invariably overcome by jealous rivals, rapacious invaders, or intrusive agents of the church. In consequence, the concentration of power oscillated around a highly decentralized equilibrium. This equilibrium persisted for centuries until new military, communications, and industrial technologies allowed more power to be concentrated in the modern centralized state.

At the same time, an increase in state scope and penetration can have perverse effects. Direct rule can fuel the mobilization of both traditional and new groups that carry potential threats to order, as well as to the state.

When a state extends its scope – when it becomes the primary provider of collective goods – it increases individuals' dependence on central rulers. Yet state-provided collective goods, such as education, welfare benefits, and government jobs, are costly to produce and limited in supply. Not everyone receives as much as they wish, and not everyone gets an equal share of them. Direct rulers become the principal target of redistributive demands by new or traditional groups that can threaten to disrupt the social order.[15] Moreover, to the degree that state-provided goods are culturally specific, such as national education in a given language, they are likely to dissatisfy groups that have distinctive preferences regarding such goods.

---

[13] Whereas legitimation reduces the policing costs of direct rule, it does not reduce the cost of providing collective goods. Of course, attaining legitimacy in Iraq and other Arab societies is no easy task: "The central problem of government in the Arab world today is political legitimacy. The shortage of this indispensable political resource largely accounts for the volatile nature of Arab politics and the autocratic, unstable character of all the present Arab governments" (Hudson 1977: 2).

[14] These difficulties are perhaps the single principal concern of historians of the former colonies in Africa and Asia (Beissinger and Young 2002; Cooper and Stoler 1997). Rulers' demand for direct rule is subject to constraints, of course. As a result of those constraints, rational rulers of democratic regimes are forced to settle for the much more modest goal of reelection.

[15] The existence of spatially-concentrated groups with divergent, if not opposing, demands on the central government is one of the principal rationales for the policy of fiscal federalism (Oates 1972).

Consider the recent shift from class- to culturally based politics in advanced capitalist societies (Hechter 2004). By providing the bulk of collective goods in society, the direct-rule state reduces dependence on class-based groups (such as trade unions), thereby weakening them. To the degree that state-provided goods are distributed unfairly to individuals on the basis of cultural distinctions, however, the legitimacy of the state in the eyes of these constituents is challenged. This provides such individuals with an incentive to mobilize on the basis of factors such as race, ethnicity, and religion. As a result, social disorder may increase. The rise of nationalist violence has been attributed, in part, to just this mechanism (Hechter 2000).

An increase in penetration may also spur disorder. As the state extends its control apparatus, it infringes on the traditional self-determination of social groups, particularly culturally distinctive ones. This imposition of a single set of norms on a culturally diverse population may motivate the leaders of disfavored groups to oppose the state. In pre-invasion Iraq, for example, the Ba'athist regime prevented Kurds from speaking Kurdish in public and pressured them to adopt Arab names and identities in official documents (Human Rights Watch 1995). In addition, throughout Iraq, it implemented a highly invasive system of surveillance by recruiting a network of spies that constantly monitored Iraqis. This Orwellian system of control, coupled with severe punishments marked by physical torture, created a culture of terror that encouraged Iraqis to seek refuge in more protected social spheres such as extended families and religious groups (Makiya 1998). In spite of their relative lack of visibility before the American invasion, such groups likely formed the social bases of sectarian conflicts.

Effective governance need not reside exclusively with central rulers, however. Recall that in a system of indirect rule, authority is distributed among a number of local groups. Distributed authority is especially likely to occur in culturally heterogeneous societies. Indirect rulers delegate substantial powers of governance to traditional authorities in return for the promise of tribute, revenue, and military service. Although both direct and indirect rule foster dependence, direct rule results in individuals' dependence on central rulers, whereas indirect rule entails the dependence on their local counterparts. Because there is no compelling reason to believe that centralized rule is inherently more effective in promoting order than its more decentralized counterpart, bottom-up explanations of social order – which date at least from the time of Althusius ([1614] 1964) – have recently been gaining greater attention. These theories explain how social order is enhanced when a variety of social groups and voluntary associations mediate between individuals and central rulers.

Theories explaining the relationship of indirect rule and social order come in two varieties. In one, intragroup relations are critical for the attainment of order. On this view, the internal solidarity of groups contributes to social order either by promoting pro-social norms and orientations to action (Tocqueville [1848] 1969; Putnam 2000) or by subjecting group members to heightened levels of social control (Fearon and Laitin 1996; Hechter, Friedman, and Kanazawa 1992; Weber [1919–1920] 1958).

The second theory suggests that the key to social order lies in the nature of intergroup relations. Societies that foster intergroup relations tend to have groups composed of socially heterogeneous individuals. In such societies, cross-cutting ties attenuate loyalty to any one group by providing individuals with a stake in many different groups (Simmel [1922] 1955). By contrast, socially seg-regated patterns of group affiliation strengthen group loyalties and foster inter-group competition. The first pattern of group affiliation should produce strong ties, few bridges between groups (Granovetter 1973), and low social order; the second should produce weak social ties, many bridges between groups, and high social order. Whereas there is evidence that crosscutting ties and network bridges indeed do promote social order (Blau and Schwartz 1984), too little attention has been paid to the difficulty of establishing such bridges in tra-ditional societies characterized by strong ties.[16]

But indirect rule also has its liabilities. Its reliance on solidary groups is only justifiable if these groups do not set out to subvert social order or threaten the state. Lacking adequate incentives, solidary groups may attempt to subvert the social order, however. There is a large literature on failed states (Kohli 2002), which attributes disorder to a variety of solidary groups that act as hindrances to, and substitutes for, central authority. Moreover, such groups need not be perennially subversive; they can sustain social order at one time and subvert it at another.

Because each form of rule has strengths and liabilities, choosing an optimal form of governance is anything but child's play. Direct rule may quell insur-gent activity in some contexts, but in others it may stimulate the emergence of social groups that threaten the regime. Under indirect rule, groups may use their autonomy to challenge state authority. Evidently, there is no universally optimal choice of governance structures for the attainment of order.

Nonetheless, insight into the problem of order in today's Iraq can be gained ·by examining the effect of varying forms of governance on social order in the history of this territory. Since the late Ottoman period, people in this region have experienced varying types of rule. Indirect rule was implemented in some time periods, direct rule in others. Occasionally, the Iraqi state simultaneously adopted different governance structures for different regions. The following discussion of Iraqi history focuses on the relationship between alien rule, gov-ernance structures, and order. It suggests that none of these forms of rule man-aged to attain legitimacy in this culturally divided land.

---

[16] For example, Kurdish immigrants in Sweden have been known to employ honor killing as a means of preventing their daughters from having liaisons with Swedish males (Lyall 2002; see, however, Ahmadi 2003). Imagine how difficult it is to establish social networks composed of Catholics and Protestants in Northern Ireland, Serbs and Kosovars in Kosovo, Jews and Israeli Arabs in Israel, or Shi'i, Sunni, and Kurds in Iraq.

Iraq under Alien Rule

Iraq under the Ottomans

Ottoman Mesopotamia – the territory now known as Iraq – was born of conflict between the Ottoman and Safavid empires during the early seventeenth century. The Ottomans finally conquered Baghdad in 1639 (Sluglett and Sluglett 1990: 2). Iraq's strategic position between these two rival empires destined it to be a frontier buffer zone. Because of their limited interest in the territory and its distance from Istanbul, the Ottomans ruled Iraq indirectly.

Centuries of famine, flooding, Mongol invasions, and the collapse of irrigation systems had left much of the land unsuited to agriculture. Two distinct social structures emerged: the urban provinces of Mosul, Baghdad, and Basra, and the outlying tribal territories (Tripp 2000: 18). Urban and tribal Arabs were so different that they comprised almost separate worlds (Batatu 1978: 13). Istanbul could not exert as much control over rural areas as urban ones (Nieuwenhuis 1981: 120). As was customary throughout their empire, in 1702 the Ottomans initially delegated governance in the urban provinces of Iraq to local authorities known as *Mamluks* – highly educated slaves who were trained specifically to be indirect rulers (Hourani 1991: 251; Nieuwenhuis 1981: 14).

Although the Mamluks were ostensibly under the Sultan's thumb, Istanbul wielded very little actual control over them. The Mamluks recognized the Ottoman Sultan symbolically (in religious services and on coinage, for example) and obtained formal confirmation of their governorships from the Sultan, but they retained considerable autonomy de facto (Tripp 2000, 9). Ottoman Janissary troops were dispatched to Baghdad, but the Mamluks kept them under their tight control. The government of Baghdad was largely self-sufficient, consisting of military, administrative, financial, and judicial branches (Nieuwenhuis 1981, 27). Mamluks provided what collective goods there were and funded their own local armies, enabling them in some cases (as in Mosul) to successfully maintain the Ottoman frontier (Khoury 1997: 188). Mamluks in the Iraqi region were obliged to send tribute to Istanbul, but did so only irregularly. Because Istanbul did not demand much of the Mamluks, they had little cause for complaint.

Mamluk power, however, did not extend into the bulk of arid rural lands. Most rural inhabitants adapted to the desert ecology by embracing pastoralism.[17] Unlike agricultural crops, livestock are easily stolen, and in the absence of a strong state, pastoralists could rely only on their tribal affiliations for protection of their herds and families. Clans forged alliances based on the notion that "anyone who commits an act of aggression against any one of us must expect retaliation from us all, and not only will the aggressor himself be likely to suffer retaliation, but his entire group and all its members will be equally

---

[17] That all tribes were nomadic is an overgeneralization. Some tribes settled in small sedentary areas. Nonetheless, these sedentary groups were organized much as their nomadic counterparts, through (fictive) kinship relations (Nieuwenhuis 1981).

liable" (Gellner 2003: 311). This principle led to a system of strong, self-policing tribal groups that defended themselves by threatening to retaliate, and often retaliating, against individual members of aggressor groups.[18] Because these tribes relied only on themselves for protection from outside threats, they had to develop effective means for self-defense: they amassed enough weapons and knowledge of warfare to become ministates (Jabar 2003).[19]

Given their military capacity and acumen, the tribes often attacked settled areas, but they were held in check in two ways. First, the Mamluks could rely on their own military strength to resist tribal threats. Strategies of tribal warfare rested primarily on surprise attacks by small groups, as this was the most effective means for engaging in conflict with other tribes. Because their weapons were relatively primitive, the tribes were largely incapable of defeating large provincial armies. Second, Baghdad lured some tribal leaders into the provincial government, providing them with wider-scale governance rights in exchange for their fealty.

Indirect rule, however, came to an abrupt end in the mid-nineteenth century – and with it, the autonomy of the Mamluks (Nakash 1994, 32). Reacting to the threat of rising European nation-states and the nationalist secession of Greece in 1828 (McDowall 1992: 14), the Ottomans attempted to increase their authority in Iraq. They consolidated their military forces and sent an army to capture the Mamluk leaders in Baghdad, Mosul, and Basra (Tripp 2000: 14). Under the Tanzimat reforms initiated by Sultan Abdulmecid, the three provinces fell under the direct rule of Istanbul. The increased presence of the Ottoman army and officials augmented Istanbul's penetration in the Iraqi region.

As direct rule progressed, the Ottomans favored Sunnis over other groups. Government jobs were given primarily to Sunnis, and schools provided by the state were hardly attended by Shi'is, who had their own schools (Sluglett 2003: 8).[20] Meanwhile, Kurdish tribal chieftains, fearing a loss of autonomy, organized a series of revolts – some aiming for complete independence, others for the control they exercised before direct rule was implemented (McDowall

---

[18] Tribes are not necessarily pure kinship groups. "The concept of tribe is unclear and controversial. The word is used to refer to a kinship group, an extended family, or a coalition of related families. It may refer to the elite family from whom some larger confederation gets its name, to a cultural, ethnic, or other non-familial social group, or to conquest movements of pastoral people without regard for the internal basis of cohesion" (Lapidus 1990: 26). Whether blood relations are real or fictive, the bond helps create group solidarity.

[19] "Each strong tribe was a miniature mobile state, with its patriarchal headship usually head by a warrior household; its own military force; its customary law, which was preserved by the 'arfa (literally, 'the knowledgeable', actually tribal jurists or adjudicators); its non-literate culture; its territoriality in the form of dira (tribal pastures) or, later, arable lands; and its mode of subsistence economy, i.e. pastoralism, commerce, and conquest" (Jabar 2003: 73).

[20] "In general, religious Shi'is tended to view the state, whether the Ottoman Empire or Qajar Iran, as a sort of necessary evil; for this and other reasons, they were not inclined to press for bureaucratic, educational, or military employment" (Sluglett 2003: 9).

1992: 14). Ottoman direct rule created resentment along these ethnic and religious lines, foretelling the emergence of contemporary ethnic and religious
political cleavages.[21]

All told, enhanced direct rule reduced social order in the urban provinces.
In addition to encroaching on Mamluk rule, for the first time the Ottomans
sought to bring the tribes in the countryside under their control. They did so
by investing in irrigation,[22] altering the region's ecology, and thereby attach-
ing tribesmen to the land.[23] For the most part, Ottoman efforts to domesticate
tribal nomads were successful. In southern Iraq, for example, the percentage of
nomads decreased from 50 percent in 1867 to 19 percent in 1905. Meanwhile,
the rural settled population increased from 41 to 72 percent during these years.
New cities emerged, as well (Nakash 1994: 5).

At the same time, the Ottoman Land Law of 1858 altered the tribal land-
scape by creating a new type of relationship between Istanbul and the Iraqi
tribes. Although land was deemed the property of the Ottoman Empire, title
deeds, which were handed to anyone who already possessed or occupied parcels of land, granted their holders virtually complete rights of ownership.
Because these deeds could be handed only to individuals, tribal shaykhs were
the most common recipients (Tripp 2000: 15–16). By offering landownership
benefits only to shaykhs, the Ottomans effectively bought their loyalty. The
shaykhs became landowners – indirect rulers of their tribesmen who now
assumed the status of tenant farmers. Because landownership still resided
in the state, the Ottomans could revoke land rights as easily as they could
grant them.

The new land laws transformed tribal social structure. Under the new system, the state was no longer just a tax-extracting agency. As differential rights
to land created tension and social conflict, landowners relied on the state to
enforce their land rights and maintain order.[24] Conflict over land rights aided

---

[21] Although opposition to the state can often be framed in terms of ethnic or religious discourse,
organization, and not the mere existence of ethnic or religious diversity, is required for collective
action (Brubaker 2002). Ethnic and religious groups are politically salient only in so far as they
are internally solidary (Hechter 1987).

[22] "Unlike Mamluk efforts to break the tribes by occasional blows without providing an alternative way of life, the new Ottoman governors encouraged the tribesmen to settle down and
take up agriculture. The governors' effort reflected Istanbul's desire to settle the tribes so as to
increase agricultural production and tax revenue to sustain the Empire's growing involvement
in world capitalist economy" (Nakash 1994: 32).

[23] "The Ottomans considered settlement the means by which they could 'civilize' the nomads....
In seeking to settle the tribes and bring them under strict government control, the governors
attempted to restructure tribal society. They sought to break the great tribal confederations and
to undermine the status of their paramount shaykhs as 'lords' who controlled large dominions.
In this struggle over taxes, and the control of food and trade routes, the governors attempted
to reduce the power of the shaykhs, partly by conferring their position to others" (Nakash
1994: 33).

[24] Indeed, rebellions against the Ottomans broke out in 1849, 1852, 1863 to 1866, 1878 to 1883,
and 1899 to 1905 (Nakash 1994: 34).

the regime, for it spurred competition between tribal shaykhs.[25] The Ottoman strategy of divide and rule weakened ties between tribes and principal shaykhs as well as those between shaykhs and their tribesmen. A classic form of inter-dependence – characteristic of indirect rule – resulted between tribes and the state. The landowners' stake in state law made them complicit in the new polit-ical order (Tripp 2000: 17).

Resistance, including widespread revolt, grew among tribesmen who were disadvantaged by the new system, however. In geographically accessible ter-ritories the Ottoman forces crushed the rebellions militarily. Elsewhere, they increased their exploitation of tribal shaykhs, becoming more adept at dividing the tribes. Only belatedly did the Ottomans recognize that tribes were essential for maintaining social order at the local level and that the indirect rule of tribes was essential for quelling disorder.[26]

Direct rule was fomenting social disorder. The Young Turk movement in the late nineteenth and early twentieth centuries increased direct rule as well as hardship for the majority of the region's rural population. Arab reactions against "Turkification" erupted as the Young Turks augmented state scope by bringing schools and other cultural organizations to Iraq. These were venues where like-minded individuals and intellectuals from different provinces could recognize their common interests. At the same time, the movement created social spaces for individuals dependent on and loyal to Arab cultural institutions to organize against the state. Secret societies emerged to challenge Ottoman hege-mony and to resist what they deemed to be encroachments on Arab culture. An estimated sixty newspapers and journals appeared in the early twentieth century, as did a number of clubs, groups, and societies. Among the groups that flourished during this time was the National Scientific Club of Baghdad, whose members promoted knowledge of Arab language and culture. This club attracted both Sunni and Shi'i intellectuals. Groups such as the Reform Society of Basra, which organized to regain provincial autonomy, became crucibles of Arab nationalism. Despite Ottoman attempts to suppress them, these secret societies grew stronger (Tripp 2000: 22–28).

In sum, the Ottoman Empire's indirect rule seemed well adapted to the region's social structure. The tribes and Mamluks were self-sufficient and self-policing, and neither directly challenged the authority of the state. Low pen-etration afforded both groups a high degree of autonomy, giving them little reason to resist state authority. Because Istanbul's scope was low, individuals

---

[25] The Ottoman practice of pitting shaykh against shaykh "so changed the conditions of life in the affected regions as to attenuate the old tribal loyalties or render them by and large ineffectual" (Batatu 1978: 22).

[26] In 1910 a Baghdad deputy to the Ottoman Empire wrote, "To depend on the tribe is a thousand times safer than depending on the government, for whereas the latter defers or neglects repres-sion, the tribe, no matter how feeble it may be, as soon as it learns that an injustice has been committed against one of its members readies itself to exact vengeance on his behalf " (Batatu 1978: 21).

were generally not dependent on the empire for their livelihood. Mamluks supplied the bulk of the collective goods in the urban provinces, and tribal members provided one another with collective goods in the countryside. The Ottomans relied on shaykhs to control the tribes, but no tribe was permanently favored by Istanbul. Uncertainty about the prospect of receiving favored treatment encouraged the shaykhs to toe the Ottomans' line. No tribe was permanently denied the opportunity to receive the few favors the state provided, therefore, in the long run, all of them were in the same boat. Neither Mamluks nor shaykhs had much reason to challenge Istanbul for a larger share or a more preferable bundle of collective goods. Indirect rule worked.

When the Ottoman Empire began to institute direct rule, however, new bases of opposition arose both in the cities and in the countryside. This analysis of the Ottoman period suggests that only when indirect rule is maintained by a strong central state can it be effective. To the degree that local groups have high autonomy and are not perpetually disadvantaged by the state, they have little incentive to challenge central authorities. Moreover, when individuals have low dependence on the center, they are unlikely to regard it as a target of collective action. An increase in direct rule, however, carries with it the potential for disorder. As direct rule impinges on previously autonomous groups, they are more likely to become restive.

Iraq under British Rule

World War I brought with it the end of Ottoman governance in Iraq. British troops took Baghdad in March 1917, and the British occupation of Mosul and Kirkuk followed shortly thereafter (Sluglett and Sluglett 1990: 9; Atiyyah 1973: 151). Interested in controlling a land bridge to India and becoming increasingly aware of the importance of oil, the British initially opted for a sharp increase in direct rule. Considering the Iraqis incapable of managing their own country, they abolished Ottoman-governing institutions (such as the elected municipal councils) and installed British political officers in their stead (Tripp 2000: 37).[27] In August 1915, the Ottoman Penal and Criminal Procedure Code was removed; its replacement, modeled on the Indian civil and criminal codes, was called the Iraq Occupied Territories Code.

Direct rule displaced former Iraqi officers and government officials with British counterparts. By August 1, 1920, the civil administration consisted of 534 high-ranking officers and personnel, however, only 20 of these were Iraqi (Atiyyah 1973: 214). The British military presence was also pervasive. One American observer of the British occupation noted in March 1917 that "the British meant to show the native population that there would be no trouble in the city while they were running it. Every man on the street had his rifle and bayonet" (Mathewson 2003: 54).

---

[27] This was not done in the Kurdish territories, which were least amenable to direct rule because of the mountainous terrain (Kocher 2004).

The British increased the scope of their rule by providing Iraqis with the bulk of their collective goods. Funding for education and medical services, although meager, increased almost threefold from 1915 to 1918. The British Army and civil administrations employed Iraqi laborers to build roads as well as railway and irrigation systems (Atiyyah 1973: 219, 224).

In some respects – particularly regarding tribes – British rule remained indirect, largely because their initial efforts at direct rule spurred resistance. Initially, the British miscalculated the tractability of tribal shaykhs, only to discover that they could pose serious threats to social order. For example, when the British took Qurna in 1914, they relied on the support of Shaykh Khaz'al, known to command obedience from a number of different tribes in the area. However, most tribesmen soon deserted Khaz'al, causing him to demand aid from the British lest the tribes rise up against him. The British faced similar experiences with other tribes. When force was used to subdue the tribes, tribesmen readily declared their support for the occupiers, but as soon as the British forces retreated, the tribesmen turned against them (Atiyyah 1973: 109–112). The British eventually gave generous amounts of money to shaykhs to secure order indirectly (Atiyyah 1973: 219). They also enacted the Tribal Civil and Criminal Disputes Regulation, which gave shaykhs the authority to adjudicate disputes within their tribe as well as to collect taxes for the government (Tripp 2000: 37).

The initial reaction to British occupation varied by region. Leading figures in Basra, for example, first accommodated British authorities, as reflected in the words of an Expeditionary Force commander, who telegraphed, "We were cordially welcomed by the inhabitants, who appeared eager to transfer their allegiance to the British Government" (Atiyyah 1973: 87). This acceptance arose because leading figures in Basra had preexisting economic relationships with British merchants desiring access to the Persian Gulf. Because the British were at war with the Turks, this appeased Arab nationalists (Atiyyah 1973: 86–87; Tripp 2000: 32).

At first, Kurdish tribal authorities welcomed the British as well. Leaders in Sulaimaniyya handed control of the region to Britain, which shortly thereafter granted Shaykh Mahmud Barzinji, believed to be influential among the Kurds, the governorship of Lower Kurdistan. By passing its control capacity to a local notable, the British hoped to rule the region indirectly. They miscalculated the scope of Shaykh Mahmud's influence, however. Conflicts between Kurdish shaykhs, as well as Shaykh Mahmud's ambitions, resulted in a series of revolts. When Shaykh Mahmud declared Kurdistan an independent state in May 1919, the British dispatched a military unit to reclaim Sulaimaniyya. Although it successfully suppressed Shaykh Mahmud, this increase in state penetration nonetheless stirred new opposition against British intrusion into Kurdistan (Tripp 2000: 34).[28]

---

[28] "Often local in nature, these could be aimed against neighbors as much as against the British authorities, but they stemmed from a similar desire, even compulsion, on the part of the Kurdish

In other areas, however, resistance to the occupiers appeared almost immediately. In early 1918, a group of clerics, shaykhs, and other influential persons
in Najaf and Karbala formed the Society of Islamic Revival to defend Islam
against the British (Tripp 2000: 33). When a British officer in Najaf was killed
in 1919, the British blockaded the city and responded with sweeping arrests
and executions. Shi'i clerics and civilians also opposed the British, some even
forming alliances with Sunni groups who shared their sense of frustration over
losing jobs and status under direct rule (Yaphe 2003). By April 1920, resistance
to the British became increasingly organized. Shi'i Ayatollah al-Shirazi issued a
fatwa against employment in the British administration. Shi'is and Sunnis met
to formulate strategies for obtaining Iraqi independence, as did Shi'i 'ulama
and tribal shaykhs of the mid-Euphrates region (Tripp 2000: 41). A number
of secret organizations and parties also emerged, including Haras, the leading
nationalist party of the time, whose success can largely be attributed to a rare
instance of Sunni–Shi'i cooperation. At this point the effect of British direct
rule was to put Sunni and Shi'i in a similar structural position: both groups
faced the loss of jobs and status. This kind of external threat typically fosters
intergroup cooperation (Coser 1956).[29]

Much of the response to British direct rule therefore was framed in terms of
Arab self-determination. A goal of Iraq's major political parties, for example,
was to obtain Iraqi independence for Basra, Baghdad, and Mosul. The British
reacted to these developments by strengthening direct rule: they increased the
number of security forces and intelligence officers in the cities, making public
protest virtually impossible. Iraqi resisters were forced to meet in mosques,
which quickly became forums for stimulating Arab nationalism. With 130
mosques in Baghdad, 35 in Basra, and 51 in Mosul, anti-British propaganda
was easily spread throughout the Iraqi population (Marr 2003: 23; Atiyyah
1973: 275–280). By 1920, therefore, most of Iraq was resistant to British rule.
Despite this, in April 1920, the League of Nations awarded Britain the mandate to rule Iraq (Dodge 2003: 5). This fueled even more anti-British sentiment
and two months later culminated in outright revolt. An estimated 130,000

---

tribal chieftains to exploit any perceived weakness of central power and to assert their own
autonomy. They resented any attempt by outside powers to curb their own freedom of action"
(Tripp 2000: 34).

[29] In similar fashion, the first Swiss federation was established when the Habsburg Empire threatened to wrest control over the so-called Devil's Bridge over the Saint Gotthard Pass, the key
North-South trade route between German principalities and the Italian city-states, from the cantons that originally controlled this territory. This external threat provided an incentive for three
previously autonomous cantons – Uri, Schwyz, and Unterwalden – to band together in hopes of
retaining their control over the route and the revenue deriving from it (Finer 1997: 957–958).
As is well appreciated, the same principle also came into play under colonialism. Perhaps the
only thing that the various indigenous groups in the colonies could agree on was the desirability
of self-determination. Once this was realized, intergroup conflict, which had been submerged in
the nationalist effort to end alien rule, resumed anew.

Iraqis rebelled, but the movement was not effectively organized; it lacked the support of some Sunni groups who feared the movement would undermine their traditional dominance in the region (Tripp 2000: 44; Marr 2003). Even so, the British only managed to quell the rebellion by the end of October. Thus direct rule fared no better under the British than it had under the Ottomans.

After the revolt the British abruptly changed course, abandoning direct rule. The subsequent government included Iraqis and adopted a variety of once spurned Ottoman institutions. Iraqi officials replaced British political officers in the provinces. To further economize on control costs, the Royal Air Force (RAF) was enlisted to pacify rebellious tribes in the countryside by bombing them (Dodge 2003: 154; Sluglett 2003: 7).[30] In 1921, the annual military budget for Iraqi operations was reduced from £25 million to £4 million (Mathewson 2003: 57).

In 1921, the British installed the Hashemite Amir Faisal as King, marking the beginning of a period of indirect rule in Iraq that lasted thirty-seven years under three different Hashemite monarchs. Despite Faisal's exalted title, the British maintained much control over Iraqi politics. British "advisors" functioned behind the scenes, while Britain maintained control of the country's foreign relations as well as veto power over military and financial matters (Sluglett and Sluglett 1990: 11). Faisal – a non-Iraqi Arab widely perceived as a British puppet – had little legitimacy among the Iraqi people (Bengio 2003: 16). Because he was too weak militarily to withstand tribal opposition, Faisal was largely dependent on the British, and specifically the RAF, to enforce order.

Indirect rule under the Hashemites was unsuccessful primarily because the British failed to recognize that its effectiveness rests on the basis of fair and equitable treatment of tribal and religious groups. Because Iraqi society was so culturally diverse, and the Hashemite monarchs favored one cultural group over all others, legitimacy and social order were never attained.

Faisal was far less tractable than the British had hoped. The tension between Faisal and the British reflects a fundamental problem with indirect rule: local autonomy often spurs noncompliance with central state authority. From the start, Faisal insisted on playing the key leadership role in Iraq, a demand that the British conceded to only to avoid any resistance that might have emerged were the government seen as illegitimate (Dodge 2003: 20). Given the abysmal failure of their experiment with direct rule, however, the British were willing to take this risk.

Faisal's strategy for ruling the tribes was shaped after the Ottomans' – namely, the parceling out of land rights, and similar to the Ottomans, he used it to bind the shaykhs to his regime. In 1933, the monarchy passed the Law Governing

---

[30] Winston Churchill, the responsible minister, chose the air force because planes could "police the mandated territory of Mesopotamia for less cost than the traditional method of military occupation (Omissi 1990: 16). Arthur Harris, the strategist who devised the bombing strategy to control the tribal areas of Iraq, later employed the same tactics in the bombing of Dresden.

Rights and Duties of Cultivators. This law protected and increased the land-owning rights handed to shaykhs during the Ottoman Empire, but afforded the cultivators fewer rights. Peasant tribesmen were required to pay money rents and shares of their crops to their shaykhs. If they did not have enough money or crops, they were required to remain on the land and work until their debts were paid off (Tripp 2000: 47–52).[31] This strategy bound tribesmen to their local rulers; as a result, they became more dependent on their shaykhs than on the state for goods and control.

Faisal also attempted to build an Iraqi army, at first consisting of Sharifian officers and Sunni tribesmen. The Sharifian officers held strong pan-Arab ideologies that left Shi'i and Kurdish elements in Iraq feeling marginalized; for them, the military was an arm of the Sunni-dominated government and not a mechanism for national integration (Kelidar 2003: 31). Later, the army consisted largely of Kurdish and Shi'i conscripts, antagonizing members of these communities who were not inclined to fight for a country that did not afford them much political representation (Kelidar 2003: 31; Tripp 2000: 87).

Faisal's rule was a balancing act: while reigning in potential challengers he also tried to keep British interference at bay. Although the monarchy was a retreat from direct rule and a response to the liabilities of direct rule, indirect rule proved no panacea for the British either because the Sunni-dominated state was anything but evenhanded in its distribution of collective goods. Government jobs were provided primarily to Sunnis, and although the Iraqi educational system preached Arab nationalism, this message rang hollow to many non-Sunnis (Tripp 2000: 95). The Kurds were incensed when, despite British promises to grant Kurdish autonomy, the 1930 Anglo-Iraqi treaty failed to even mention minority rights, much less Kurdish self-determination (Natali 2001: 263). Dissatisfaction with these policies led to the formation of new political and potentially threatening organizations among underrepresented cultural groups.

Despite a series of military coups in the mid-1930s, British hegemony remained unchallenged.[32] In 1941, however, a coalition of nationalists and constitutionalists raised the stakes when they tried to topple the monarchy, end British control, and open the territory to Axis influence. The British responded by increasing their military assets in Iraq, thereby ramping up direct rule. Anti-government protests were violently repressed. By creating a highly personalized

---

[31] By the late 1950s, 55% of cultivable land was held by only 2,500 people, mostly Sunni. Further, 70% of Iraq's arable land consisted of 3,400 large haciendas. By 1957, a large proportion of the rural population was landless. In short, augmented indirect rule immiserated the peasantry. The law also reduced urban migration, effectively tying many peasants to their shaykhs' lands (Cole 2004).

[32] Although both Kurds and Shi'is rebelled, these actions were largely confined to specific tribal groups rather than a grand coalition of Kurds or Shi'is. Whereas some Shi'i tribes revolted, others either sided with the state or remained neutral, unwilling to risk their own arms and tribesmen without first witnessing the outcome of other uprisings.

and generous central governing body – now enriched by the growth of oil revenues – the monarch was for the most part successful in pitting groups in civil society against one another. Consider the state's response to Shi'i demands for greater representation in government. In the 1920s the state hired only twenty-one Shi'i ministers, but by the 1950s, this number had risen to seventy-six. This increase in Shi'i representation is misleading, however, because it does not take into account the growth of the state apparatus. Despite the doubling of Shi'i representation in government from 18 to 36 percent between the 1920s and 1950s, Sunnis continued to hold the key positions, and the Shi'i remained underrepresented (Nakash 1994: 127).

Demonstrations and uprisings continued to pose challenges for the British-backed government. Many demonstrators were killed in al-Intifada in 1948. Courts-martial led to the imprisonment of hundreds of agitators. Oppositional groups gained more ground; the Iraqi Kurdish Democratic Party (KDP), for example, held its founding congress in Baghdad in 1946 (Tripp 2000: 117; Natali 2001: 263). The Shi'i disseminated literature attacking pan-Arabism and the state and submitted petitions to the government demanding freedom of expression and a greater share of various collective goods (Marr 2003: 42; Nakash 1994: 119). Moreover, class-based oppositional groups emerged for the first time; various artisan associations began to coalesce and form the Iraqi Communist Party (ICP) (Sluglett and Sluglett 1990: 22). The class divisions fostered by indirect rule – and an upsurge in Arab nationalism in the Middle East – set the stage for a violent military coup in 1958 led by 'Abd al-Karim Qasim (Tripp 2000). So ended British domination in Iraq.

To some extent, the era of British rule recapitulates the fate of direct and indirect rule under the Ottomans. Although the British imposed direct rule to strengthen their control of Iraq, the strategy backfired. Direct rule fostered Iraqi nationalism and increased the solidarity of different religious and ethnic groups. When the British reverted to a more indirect form of rule, order was restored, but only temporarily.

Why was indirect rule under the Ottomans more successful? Although the Ottomans also played favorites, they did not allocate collective goods on a cultural basis. Nor was any particular tribe *persistently* favored over its rivals. The Ottomans provided goods such as land rights to different tribal leaders, but they did not hesitate to rescind them, as well. Preferential treatment was so short-lived and indeterminate that no local group felt permanently disfavored. Moreover, under British rule, the military was afforded more freedom to mobilize against the occupation; this helped bring about the coup that ended British rule in Iraq altogether.

Iraq under Native Rule

In 1958, Abd Al-Karim Qasim, an Iraqi nationalist general, seized power in a coup d'état that eliminated the monarchy. Qasim's regime marked the beginning of an era of an unprecedented growth in direct rule. He transformed himself into the personification of Iraq, a tactic later adopted by Saddam Hussein. Qasim dramatically increased state penetration, repressing rebellious groups more vigorously than his predecessors.

This repression is exemplified by Qasim's relationship with the Kurds. Qasim initially provided the Kurdish population with its own cultural space: Kurds were awarded positions in government, opportunities in education, and even some cultural rights. For a brief time Kurds and Arabs experienced a sense of unity, and the KDP even publicly recognized Qasim for acknowledging Kurdish cultural rights. By 1959, however, the Kurds began to use their autonomy to distinguish themselves from Arabs. Despite regarding themselves as Iraqis, they insisted on being recognized as members of a distinct culture with a non-Arab language and heritage. For a short while, a Kurdo-Arab state seemed possible, and Kurdish relations with Qasim were positive (Natali 2001: 267–268).

External influences (not least those emanating from the United States) convinced Qasim to change his policies toward the Kurds. Ultimately he arrested Kurdish nationalists and bombed Kurdish rural areas, fueling greater Kurdish resistance to the regime (Natali 2001: 269). Qasim's policies toward the ICP – similar to those toward the Kurds – ran hot and cold. At the outset, Qasim lent some support to the ICP, which reached the height of its power between 1958 and 1959. The ICP grew rapidly, building a people's army of up to 11,000 volunteers, as well as organizing a number of protests, student movements, and trade unions (Sluglett and Sluglett 1990: 53–54, 63). However, Qasim later withdrew his support from the communists, and toward the end of his rule the state banned ICP newspapers, broke up communist unions, and even shut down other leftist groups such as the Youth Federation, the Partisans for Peace, and the Women's League (Sluglett and Sluglett 1990: 75–76; Batatu 1978: 948; Yousif 1991: 187).

Whereas Qasim's increasing penetration of the North spurred the Kurds' demands for cultural autonomy, heightened state scope undercut the ICP by replacing it as a source of collective goods. Qasim increased state scope dramatically. Similar to other Third World nationalists of that era, Qasim extended direct rule by nationalizing Iraq's oil, increasing state welfare, and distributing land to the impoverished peasantry (Al-Eyd 1979: 41). His efforts were only partially successful, however. The oil industry, the major source of foreign exchange, remained in private hands.[33] Nonetheless Qasim was able to divert

---

[33] Although Qasim tried to nationalize the oil companies, he first had to settle a number of old disputes and work toward self-sufficiency in production and the market. The government attempted to negotiate with the Iraq Petroleum Company (IPC) for control of unexploited areas of oil resources. When negotiations failed, the state passed a law that withdrew the IPC's concession rights to the area. The state also imposed cargo dues and port charges on IPC shipments through Basra (Al-Eyd 1979: 19). The IPC did not accept the law, and in an act of defiance cut production to penalize the country and put pressure on Qasim. This move ultimately cost Iraq $550 million between 1950 and 1970. The state responded by establishing the Iraqi National

funding from infrastructural projects to public housing schemes and housing loans in the cities. Educational investment trebled, and many new schools and hospitals were built (Tripp 2000: 167). Qasim imposed ceilings on individual holdings (618 acres in irrigated areas and 1,236 acres in rainfall areas) and promised that the sequestered land would be redistributed to landless peasants in plots of about 20 to 40 acres each (Dann 1969: 57; Sluglett and Sluglett 1990: 138). As a result of inadequate enforcement, however, little redistribution actually occurred (Khadduri 1970: 117; Sluglett and Sluglett 1990: 38). Even so, Qasim's concerns for the poor won him much popular support.

Because direct rule is so costly to implement, how did Qasim fund this increased state largess? Half of the new funds came from appropriation of revenue from oil wealth, and half from loans offered by the Soviet Union and Czechoslovakia. The increased scope provided by these resources was successful in muting much class-based opposition to the regime (e.g., by the ICP). However, the increased level of penetration stimulated opposition among disadvantaged cultural groups. The Kurds were particularly eager to see Qasim overthrown, so much so that they looked to pan-Arab groups – such as the Ba'ath – for support (Tripp 2000: 168). In fact, it was the Ba'ath who staged a coup against Qasim. The Ba'ath Party ruled for only a few months before being overthrown by members of the armed forces. Five years later it reemerged to overthrow the existing regime.

The Ba'athists – and Saddam Hussein in particular – continued to increase direct rule. Saddam completed Qasim's mission against class-based opposition by emasculating the country's trade unions (Dodge 2003: 160). Following a huge increase in the price of oil in 1973, he used oil revenues (which increased eightfold from 1973 to 1975 [Tripp 2000: 314]) to substantially increase state employment, the size of the military, and the quantity of state-provided welfare benefits. State employment rose from 20,000 to more than 580,000 from 1958 to 1977 (Dodge 2003: 160). The army and security services grew rapidly as well. In 1967, the ratio of military manpower relative to population was 10 per 1,000 people; by 1984, this ratio was 42 per 1,000 (Makiya 1998: 34).[34]

All told, the civilian arm of the state is estimated to have employed 21 percent of the working population, with 30 percent of Iraqi households dependent

---

Oil Company (INOC); however, this venture failed to remove the state's dependence on the IPC. In ensuing years, the IPC and the INOC collaborated on joint ventures.

[34] "The army that carried out party policy in the second half of the 1970s was different from the one that waltzed in and out of governments in the 1960s. It had metamorphosed into a creature of the Ba'ath party. Three things account for this. The first change was the comprehensive series of purges of all influential high-ranking officers.... The second change ... was the establishment of a new system of accountability in which party men could thwart the orders of their senior non-Ba'athist officers if they suspected them.... The third change was to separate ideology from the military. Comprehensive party organization robbed officers of the opportunity to see themselves as surrogates and guardians of a national identity otherwise in jeopardy" (Makiya 1998: 25–26).

on government payments in 1990 through 1991. These revenues also enabled Saddam to establish a patronage system that divided potential rivals.[35]

He invested heavily in schools, hospitals, food subsidies, and housing projects. In 1968, Saddam also implemented land reform: "Tribal Shaykhs were no longer paid off for their expropriated land. The government helped form a large number of agricultural cooperatives and became the primary distributor for agricultural surplus, and there were genuine improvements in rural standards of living" (Khadduri 1970: 119). These measures laid the foundation for a high degree of social order by increasing dependence on the state and by aligning personal and state interests.

Saddam's state immensely increased its penetration. On assuming power, Saddam expanded the party militia and restructured the secret police to forestall political opposition. Saddam established three separate secret police agencies, each independently responsible to the Revolutionary Command Council. The *Amn*, designed with the help of the Soviet KGB, was responsible for internal security. The *Estikhbarat* was set up to root out dissidents operating outside of Iraq. And the *Mukhabarat* – or Party Intelligence – was the most powerful and feared agency among the three (Makiya 1998: 14). The Mukhabarat penetrated every aspect of Iraqi life to the extent that Iraqis never knew when or by whom they were being spied on. Members of Saddam's regime were themselves spied on (Roberts 2000). Spying created a heightened sense of fear and paranoia that kept dissent and political unrest at a minimum. Saddam also resorted to torture and execution to keep people in line (Makiya 1998).[36]

Although Saddam's access to oil revenue and foreign aid funded the growth of direct rule, his resources were hardly sufficient to counter the opposition of disfavored groups. Resistance principally emanated from two directions. Tensions between the state and the Kurds had been escalating, as Ba'ath promises for Kurdish autonomy were only honored in the breach. When oil production in Kirkuk was nationalized in 1974, the Kurds demanded a proportionate share in oil revenues. Saddam refused, and a Kurdish revolt broke out with Iranian support. When this support dried up, the Kurds were defeated. Far from

---

[35] Thus, "the capacity of certain Shi'i figures to command respect and to exercise authority within the community clearly unnerved a regime based on narrow circles emanating from the Sunni lands of the north-west.... It was the hidden potential of these forms of social solidarity which worried … Saddam Husain. Consequently, similar to previous rulers of Iraq, they tried to undermine that solidarity, channeling resources towards the Shi'i community at large, whilst ensuring that certain groups, families and individuals were more favored than others. In this way, a patronage network was established, drawing many Shia into the widening circle of those who were in some sense complicit in the order being established in Iraq" (Tripp 2000: 204).

[36] "As the terror struck deeper into the population – and no longer solely at its margins – withdrawal, cynicism, suspicion, and eventually pervasive fear replaced participation as the predominant psychological profile of the masses.... The post-1968 stratification of Iraqi society, unlike that of other Third World countries, evolved by compromising people in the violence of the Ba'ath, by sucking them into the agencies of the secret police, the army, and militia. The inordinate role of fear in Iraq can only be understood from this standpoint" (Makiya 1998: 58).

securing stable order, however, increased penetration encouraged the creation of a new Kurdish party – the Patriotic Union of Kurdistan (PUK). Whereas the PUK opposed the regime, its competition with the KDP gave Saddam political leverage to divide the Kurds (McDowall 1992: 27–29).

The secularism of the (now much more effective) central government encouraged greater Shi'i solidarity, however. Saddam's secular clientelism harassed the Shi'i population. For example, in the course of a 1969 territorial dispute with Iran, the Ba'ath regime demanded that the Shi'i Ayatollah Muhsin al-Hakim condemn the Iranian government. Al-Hakim refused, and Saddam responded by shutting down a university in Najaf. Demonstrations by the Shi'i followed, as sermons turned into political protests. The state arrested high-ranking religious leaders and shut down Islamic schools, spurring riots and demonstrations – the violent oppression of which only furthered the cycle of protest and violence. The Safar intifada of 1977 was soon followed by the expulsion of the Shi'i leader Ayatollah Khomaini (Tripp 2000: 202–203), and the Iranian Revolution fostered more Iraqi Shi'i Islamist resistance. To counter this threat, Saddam initiated the Iran-Iraq War with the tacit support of the United States and the Soviet Union (both alarmed by the Shi'i takeover of Iran). Finally, the failure of Iraq's Kuwaiti occupation opened the door for a series of spontaneous revolts in the Shi'i south (Cockburn and Cockburn 2002: 188). The increase of state penetration was only effective in the short term. The imposition of direct rule stimulated opposition among culturally disadvantaged groups, especially those, such as the Shi'i, which already had an organized base. Thus, as had occurred under Qasim, Ba'ath Party direct rule favored some groups and severely repressed others.

The Iran–Iraq War (1980–1988) lasted far longer than anyone had anticipated, not least Saddam. At the war's end, Iraq faced a severe recession. Because direct rule is costly to maintain, the downturn in the country's economic fortunes posed a grave challenge to the regime. To forestall the possibility of a military coup, Saddam purged and divided the officer corps and killed high-ranking political officials then replaced them with members of his clan, transforming the regime in a sultanistic direction. Last, he attempted to overhaul the economy through economic liberalization; the failure of this policy motivated his invasion of Kuwait.

Following the Gulf War, many anticipated that the no-fly zones and United Nations sanctions would significantly weaken Saddam's regime. This did not occur, however. By allowing for indirect rule in the northern part of the country, the no-fly zones compromised Iraq's territorial integrity.[37] Ironically, the no-fly zone shored up the regime by relieving the resource-poor center of much of the cost of controlling Kurdish territory. Although the United Nations sanctions severely affected the Iraqi economy and the standard of living, Saddam

---

[37] In contrast, Iraqi helicopter gunships were permitted in the southern no-fly zone, substantially reducing Shi'i autonomy.

also found a way to use these to his advantage. He created a government food-rationing system to dissuade dissent in the general public and rewarded his supporters in the party and military by giving them privileged access to food. Moreover, Saddam and his immediate circle profited handsomely from kick-backs in the United Nations Oil for Food Program (Alnasrawi 2002: 100). For these reasons, invasion was arguably the only means of toppling the regime.

Whereas Saddam's use of direct rule did not fully succeed in quashing the opposition – both Kurds and the Shi'i Marsh Arabs caused him trouble – it provided the greatest level of social order in Iraqi history. High scope – in the form of welfare benefits and government employment – left much of the population dependent on the state and unwilling to challenge it. At the same time, high penetration instilled such fear in the country that merely to express disapproval of the regime was to court the prospect of the harshest of punishments.

However, this level of direct rule could only be sustained in Iraq by exogenous windfalls derived from oil revenues and foreign aid. Neither of these revenue streams depended on the economic productivity of the population, which was hampered by the use of direct rule in Iraq.[38] Direct rule hindered productivity in two different ways: first, as a result of the state's increasing intervention in the economy, and second, as a result of its increased coercive power – as indicated, for example, by the enhanced role of the secret police.

Following 1973 the price of oil soared, and after 1979 both the Soviets and Americans turned a blind eye on Saddam's efforts against the Iranian revolutionaries. Once the center lost these sources of exogenous financial and political support, however, direct rule should have been imperiled. Paradoxically, foreign intervention – in the form of United Nations sanctions and the no-fly zones – helped Saddam economize on control costs and maintain a higher-than-expected level of direct rule.

Implications

The establishment of direct rule was one of the ultimate goals of the modern state. However, because it shifts dependence – for jobs, security, insurance, education, and other collective goods – from traditional authorities and intermediate social groups to the central state, it is extremely costly to implement.[39]

The center has but three means of providing the requisite largess. First, it can do so by its capacity to generate revenue and collective goods endogenously

[38] By contrast, indirect rule is well suited to advanced multicultural societies because it can simultaneously satisfy the demand for cultural diversity (for example, in the form of federalism) and economic growth.

[39] The USSR and its Warsaw Pact allies probably represent the apex of direct rule in modern history. Given their level of economic development these states did attain high levels of social order – especially when compared to the more liberal successor regimes. However, maintaining socialism in a global economy proved to be infeasible in the medium run (see Przeworski 1991: 51–99).

on the basis of robust economic development. This is difficult to accomplish in less developed countries (and no option in the near term for Iraq), but the examples of the four Asian tigers, China, and India reveal that it is indeed possible.[40] A second means of doing so is by assuming central control over the revenues provided by the export of key resources, such as oil. Were it not for Iraqi oil wealth, it is highly unlikely that Saddam would have been as effective as he was in implementing direct rule. Absent these means, direct rulers must rely on foreign sources of aid.

In addition to its manifest costs, direct rule can stir opposition. Competition over collective goods and resistance to encroachments on autonomy can result in challenges to state hegemony by ethnic, religious, or tribal groups. In response to British direct rule, for example, new political parties emerged in Iraq, Sunni and Shi'i groups collaborated, and traditional tribal affiliations were strengthened. Extreme direct rule, as occurred under Saddam, was more effective because it combined extensive welfare benefits with the harshest of sanctions for noncompliance. Although indirect rule imposes considerably fewer costs on central authorities, it too is costly.[41] In addition to agency costs, which substantially cut into potential central government revenues (Kiser 1999), indirect rule is only effective when it devolves decision making to groups that are willing to comply with central authorities. What determines whether a given group will be compliant? This question is akin to the classic problem of federalism (Riker 1964), and the solution resides in the center's ability to render the groups (and subunits) dependent on it for access to vital resources. To the degree that groups are dependent on the center, their leaders' interests will be aligned with those of the state, and they will therefore be motivated to curb their members' oppositional proclivities. This dependence derives from, but is not limited to, financial, kinship, military, and welfare relations with the center.[42] Indirect rule of Iraq by the Ottoman Empire, for example, was largely enforced by the looming threat of an Ottoman invasion. British indirect rule during the first Hashemite monarchy also hinged on the RAF's ability to subdue subversive elements in Iraq.

What implications does this analysis have for the current Iraqi state? How can it bring order to this perennially unstable land? Absent a massive influx

---

[40] Likewise, Ireland's entrance into the European Union initially spurred rapid investment-led economic growth.

[41] In the physical world, the second law of thermodynamics states that systems spontaneously change toward greater entropy. The cell, for example, does not exist in isolation: "It takes in energy from its environment in the form of food, or as photons from the sun … and it then uses this energy to generate order within itself. In the course of the chemical reactions that generate order, part of the energy that the cell uses is converted into heat. The heat is discharged into the cell's environment and disorders it, so that the total entropy – that of the cell plus its surroundings – increases, as demanded by the laws of physics" (Alberts et al. 2002: 71). To the extent that these laws also apply in the social world, this would explain why all forms of social order are costly to attain.

[42] Group dependence is maximized in hierarchical societies such as Japan (as reflected in Japan's keiretsu, headed by large financial institutions (Gerlach 1992) and minimized in loosely integrated warlord societies such as contemporary Afghanistan (Fairbanks 2002).

of oil revenues, direct rule appears to be an unlikely option. It has resulted in social disorder throughout Iraqi history, save during the Ba'ath regime when Saddam's rule was absolute. Just as the British did in the aftermath of World War I, the Americans banked heavily on direct rule in post-invasion Iraq. As the British before them, however, this attempt was hampered by inadequate military and economic commitment by the Bush administration (Ricks 2006; Bremer 2006; Diamond 2005).[43] American failure at securing order has left Iraqis with a mess to contend with. A poorly functioning Iraqi economy and insufficient financial support from other countries doom any effort at direct rule. Iraq's cultural and ethnic diversity also poses grave challenges to central-ized rule. Previous to the coalition's withdrawal, attacks on American troops and Iraqi police have emanated from tribal, ethnic, and religious organizations. Members of the Iraqi state are themselves so divided along ethnic and religious lines that it is hard to imagine them reaching a consensus on how to directly govern their culturally fractured society.

Indirect rule has been effective in Iraq only when a resource-rich center has refrained from systematic differential treatment of cultural groups. The British, Qasim, and Saddam all played favorites, and when they did, revolts ensued. Indirect rule of the tribes under the Ottomans, however, was most successful because it did not perpetually favor one tribe over another. The likelihood of obtaining state-provided goods was just as great for one tribe as the next; ditto for the likelihood that such goods would be withheld. Because local leaders in such regimes were always on edge, challenging the regime was seldom in their long-term interests.

Some writers have claimed that disorder could have been reduced if the American occupiers rejected centralization in favor of some kind of federa-tion (Galbraith 2006). On this view, the Coalition Provisional Authority (CPA) could have relied on solidary intermediate groups to control their own mem-bers, thereby reducing the cost of state scope and penetration. Presumably, this strategy would have provided Iraqis with more legitimate rulers (Diamond 2004). But this view is mistaken. The CPA did not take this course because it worried about placing power in the hands of leaders who could very well use their enhanced position to disrupt the nascent state (Bremer 2006). Given that the strongest local rulers, such as Muqtada al-Sadr, were the most significant threats to order, these concerns were well founded.[44]

---

[43] Paul Bremer states that he requested more troops from Rumsfeld on several occasions, only to be rejected. Bremer also claims to have told Bush, Rumsfeld, and Rice that free and fair democratic elections required a voting infrastructure that Iraq lacked, and installing it would take months. However, faced with pressures at home, particularly by an upcoming election and the need to re-present the occupation as successful and brief, the Bush administration repeatedly urged Bremer to administer Iraq as though speed was of the utmost importance (Bremer 2006).

[44] Further, the more that membership in these groups crosscuts the major axes of conflict, the greater the resulting order (Varshney 2002). However, at the present time, prospects for the es-tablishment of socially integrated intermediate groups in Iraq seem slim.

What should the Iraqi state do now? The effectiveness of indirect rule hinges on the resources available to the center as well as the solidarity of local groups. Therefore, the Iraqi state should rely on groups that would be most solidary in each of the territory's many regions. Unfortunately, over the past few years, some of the most solidary local Iraqi groups, such as al-Qaeda's Organization in Mesopotamia, other Sunni groups, and al- Sadr's Mahdi Army, have proven the most threatening to state stability. It would be difficult for the Iraqi state to see eye to eye with these insurgent groups, much less to make them dependent on its largess. But not all local solidary groups threaten the state. For example, the Grand Ayatollah Ali al-Sistani denounced involvement in sectarian violence (International Crisis Group 2006). Where other solidary groups (such as tribes) exist, the state can nurture them and rely on them to establish order. These groups' bases of affiliation are not ultimately significant; what matters is the state's ability to create interdependent and evenhanded relationships with them. The state could also invest in reinvigorating civil society such that new groups can emerge, groups bound by a common interest in quashing violent insurgent organizations.

The prospect of accomplishing these goals in a cost-effective manner is dubious at best; moreover, it cannot occur overnight. In the meantime, an increasingly vigorous resistance consumes resources that could otherwise be used for vitally important civil investment. In the elections of 2005 and 2010 most Iraqis voted on the basis of sectarian identification (Ottaway and Kaysi 2012: 4). Power is now highly fragmented, and the new constitution is controversial. One of the central issues is whether the central government has the right to exploit oil and how the resulting revenues should be shared among the regions, many of which are segmented by sect. Whereas the constitution grants the central government control over the old oil fields and revenues, it is mute about who controls the new ones. When Kurdistan began signing contracts to develop new fields, other provinces, especially Sunni ones, were spurred to demand equal powers to those granted the Kurds. The upshot is that Iraq continues to be beset by significant sectarian strife. Similar to Saddam Hussein, Prime Minister Nouri al-Maliki has attempted to adopt direct rule, but he lacks sufficient resources to pull it off. The following assessment made in February 2012 should by now sound familiar:

Maliki's stubbornness in maintaining a highly centralized system at a time when the government was clearly unable to cope with Iraq's problems is difficult to understand unless it is seen in the context of his quest for greater power and his concern that decentralization could undermine national unity. From the point of view of improving conditions for Iraqi citizens, and as a result helping the government increase its legitimacy and maximizing chances that those currently in government would be reelected, greater decentralization would have been the rational choice, since Baghdad was clearly unable to deliver services effectively. But the issue that concerned Maliki was different, namely the possibility that decentralization would be the undoing of the country.... The issue of decentralization became a symbol of Sunni resistance. (Ottaway and Kaysi 2012: 14)

Instead of responding to Sunni demands, the government initiated a new, countrywide policy of de-Ba'athification, which was used as a means of disqualifying opposition electoral candidates. In the last two months of 2012, Sunni bombers attacked a political party, a military headquarters, a busy marketplace, and a university campus (Ghazi and Hauser 2013). These events hark back to the 1920 revolt against British rule. As the baseball player Yogi Berra would have expressed it, this is déjà vu all over again.

Multicultural societies lacking high state capacity are compelled to employ indirect rule, which places authority in the hands of local – thus, native – elites. Whereas the native status of local elites generally enhances their legitimacy, the fragility of these societies increases as state capacity decreases. Under these conditions civil war or secession therefore become more likely.

Direct rule – which in a multicultural society is always alien – can only come about when there are sufficient resources to create high state capacity. These resources can come about either from the conquest of a superior power or from endogenous economic growth. The legitimacy of direct rule, however, does not merely flow from high state capacity. It depends instead on the center's effectiveness in producing demanded collective goods, on the one hand, and its fairness in allocating these goods, on the other. The greater the legitimacy of direct (alien) rulers, the less resistance they are likely to face.[45]

For much of its history Iraq was ruled indirectly because state resources were lacking. Yet even during those relatively few periods when state capacity increased – allowing for the effective production of collective goods – central authorities faced considerable resistance because these goods were never distributed fairly. The Sunnis were favored by the Ottomans, the British, and Saddam Hussein; nowadays in post-occupation Iraq the Shi'is are favored. Hence, it can be no surprise that political stability in Iraq has remained elusive.

---

[45] This conclusion has implications for the burgeoning literature on the causes of civil war. In their influential article, Fearon and Laitin (2003) claimed that state capacity (as proxied by GDP per capita) was the principal cause of civil war onset. In contrast, this analysis suggests that state capacity has no necessary effect on political instability. Whereas state resources indeed are a precondition for direct rule and its heightened social control capacity, what matters more is the legitimacy of central authorities, which is affected by variations in effectiveness and fairness of the production and allocation of collective goods.

4

Resistance to Alien Rule in Taiwan and Korea

> *The use of force alone is but temporary. It may subdue for a moment; but it does not remove the necessity of subduing again; and a nation is not governed, which is perpetually to be conquered.*
>
> *– Edmund Burke*

The problematic American-led occupation of Iraq reinforces the scholarly consensus that the effects of alien rule on native populations are usually damaging. These days the idea of alien rule is a dead letter. But is this really the case? After all, as Chapter 2 argues, some modern instances of alien rule have met with notable success. Further, self-determination evidently has not worked its wonders in many parts of the world. The list of egregious native rulers in the contemporary world is depressingly long. Some writers have advocated the imposition of alien rule, in the form of neo-trusteeship, as a solution to the growing problem of failed states and the threat they pose to international order (Fearon and Laitin 2004). Others have claimed that by offering access to modern institutions and technology, colonialism often provided the colonies with net benefits (Ferguson and Schularick 2006; Lal 2004; Mitchener and Weidenmier 2005). These considerations suggest that any blanket condemnation of alien rule is likely to mislead.

This chapter analyzes; the conditions responsible for resistance to alien rule by comparing the reactions to Japanese rule in Taiwan and Korea from the late nineteenth to the mid-twentieth centuries. This comparison is instructive because these countries have many common features and were colonized by the same power in the same historical era, but experienced markedly different levels of nationalist resistance.

Explaining Resistance to Alien Rule

In any given society resistance to alien rule is an outcome that is a result of both historically specific and general factors. This chapter applies a general theory of collective action to the problem of resistance; as such, it cannot hope to do justice to the idiosyncratic factors at play in either Taiwan or Korea. Whereas analyses rooted in general theory lack fine-grained historical detail, they are also much more generalizable to other cases of alien rule. For present purposes this is a worthwhile trade-off.

Resistance to alien rule is affected by the supply of participants and the demand for regime change. Supply factors consist of the conditions that affect individuals' capacity to engage in collective action. Most resistance to rule is not spontaneous; it flows from organizations and their leaders. As the previous chapter reveals, one part of the native population is particularly able and prone to mobilize resistance – native authorities who have been displaced by an occupying power. These individuals, and the groups that depend on them, generally engage in the most violent forms of resistance to alien rule (Petersen 2002). In the case of Taiwan and Korea, the supply of participants was affected both by initial differences between the two countries and by Japanese colonial policies that determined the strength of native elites and the recruitment of collaborators.

By contrast, the demand for regime change is determined by the quality of a regime's governance.[1] To the extent that a regime is legitimate, it reaps compliance without resort to repression. Recent attempts to devise a positive theory of legitimacy (Hechter 2009; Jennings and Van Deth 1990; Lake 2007; Tyler 2006) conclude that the legitimacy of any regime – whether it is native or alien – is enhanced by governance that is fair, characterized by procedural justice and due process, and that effectively produces an appropriate basket of collective goods. This chapter explores the economic, cultural, and political consequences of Japanese rule in Taiwan and Korea and explores the motives for collective action against the alien ruler.

In its initial phase, military occupation is feared by natives because it augurs pervasive uncertainty and the risk of significant loss. Because individuals are highly sensitive to the prospect of loss (Kahneman and Tversky 1979), many people flee the approach of an occupying army. They fear that the alien's justice will rule their land, much to their detriment. For native elites, occupation often implies a loss of authority. On this account, resistance to military occupation is likely to peak in the initial stage of occupation. After some time much of this uncertainty is resolved for better or worse, and the individuals who advance themselves by collaborating with the alien ruler (including, but not limited

---

[1] The use of the term *demand* is crucial here. In addition to providing universally valued public goods such as defense and sanitation, states provide collective goods – such as education in a specific language – that may not be universally valued by all groups in a culturally heterogeneous society (Laitin 1992).

to, the indirect rulers discussed in Chapter 3) may provide a base of support within the native community.

On theoretical grounds, therefore, one expects that (1) resistance to alien rule should be high in the initial phase of occupation, except when preceded by the surrender of a national army, (2) the greater the opportunities afforded to native elites by the new regime, the weaker the resistance to alien rule,[2] and (3) the less effective and fair the alien regime is, the lower its legitimacy and greater the resistance to its rule.

To assess these propositions, I first examine the differing levels of resistance between Taiwan and Korea to Japanese colonial rule. This analysis leads to the conclusion that such resistance was greater in Korea than Taiwan. Following this discussion, I assess alternative arguments accounting for variation in resistance to Japanese colonial rule between Korea and Taiwan. Then the discussion turns to factors affecting the supply of participants for collective action, paying particular attention to elite collaborators in Taiwan and Korea. Next, I turn to demand factors, examining the effects of alien rule on the respective social structures, cultures, economies, and governments of the two territories. The conclusion summarizes the reasons for greater Korean resistance.

Resistance to Japanese Rule

Following the Treaty of Shimonoseki (1895) ceding Taiwan to Japan, the new Japanese colonial rulers faced an armed resistance by remnant military forces from the Chinese mainland.[3] After five months of effort, this armed resistance was neutralized (Lamley 1970: 25), but the fighting was not over. Guerilla bands led by a congeries of prominent civilians, criminals, and outcasts (Lamley 2007: 207) challenged Japanese authority. From 1895 to 1902, there were more than 8,000 confrontations between locals and the colonial troops (Chou 1989: 285). For the most part, this resistance was not couched in nationalist terms; many of the leaders of these groups simply opposed any state, be it Chinese or Japanese, which sought to penetrate their redoubts (Katz 2005: 55).

The Japanese colonial administration overcame these challenges with brutal force. More than 6,000 (and as many as 14,000) Taiwanese were killed in the

---

[2] Note, however, that this relationship may be non-monotonic, depending on the existing social structure of native society. In countries (such as Korea) having an educated and politically active elite, the lack of opportunities under alien rule is likely to spur resistance. In less developed countries having no such elites (such as British and French colonies in Africa, as well as in Taiwan), the openness of the system to native elites is less likely to do so. The Japanese government sponsored native elites to a much greater degree than the British and French.

[3] As discussed earlier, measuring the resistance to alien rule is no mean task. A wide range of resistance activities varies from exit, to the establishment of clandestine newspapers and radio stations, to full-fledged insurgency (Michel 1972; Scott 1990). Systematic data on this range of activities simply does not exist for Korea and Taiwan. Hence this chapter gauges levels of resistance from reports of actual contentious events.

first six months of occupation (Roy 2003: 35), and some 12,000 were slain from 1898 to 1902 (Lamley 2007: 207). By the end of 1897, the Japanese government brought in additional manpower from Japan, including 250 police officers; 3,100 policemen; 664 military officers; and 3,375 soldiers (Chou 1989: 122). More than 4,600 Taiwanese were deemed to be bandits and received the death penalty, and thousands of others were killed without due process (Chou 1989: 180).

The Taiwanese gradually learned the futility of violent resistance and the importance of bargaining with the Japanese colonial administration (Fulda 2002: 364; Roy 2003: 47). Much Taiwanese resistance to alien rule eroded: from 1900 to 1910, there were only ten major disturbances (Kerr 1974: 107–108). The final two guerilla uprisings occurred in 1915. Aside from a violent aboriginal uprising against the Japanese occupation in 1930 (the Wushe Incident), all organized armed resistance to the occupying authority ceased (Lamley 2007: 220, 224).

In the 1920s, newly formed Taiwanese political organizations began to demand racial equality and home rule (Chen 1972: 477), but the Taiwanese never pressed for independence from Japan. These political organizations merely called for a separate and equitable standing for Taiwan within the Japanese Empire (Lamley 2007: 233). Throughout the decade of the 1930s, Taiwan was so peaceful that the British Consulate's annual reports repeatedly remarked that "there is absolutely no reason for imagining that there is any degree of discontent, which could possibly be dangerous" (Annual Report on the Island of Formosa 1997: 610–611).

Korea proved to be a very different story. The Japanese military murdered the Korean queen in 1895 sparking the formation of the Righteous Army – an armed, anti-Japanese movement. This initial resistance was put down by the Japanese troops, but after the Korean emperor was dethroned in 1907, resistance reemerged and grew into a broad-based movement that included the elites, the intelligentsia, and the local peasantry. In 1908, there were 1,451 armed engagements involving 69,832 men; two years later following ruthless repression by the Japanese military, there were only 147, totaling 1,892 men. By August 1910, when Japan officially annexed Korea, armed resistance had already been effectively quelled (Ku 1985: 3). Resistance to Japanese colonial rule was forced underground: secret societies and private schools became important venues for nationalist activity (Lee 1963: 97).

Korean resistance to alien rule boiled over in 1919. Nationalists took advantage of the funeral of the former emperor to stage a major demonstration in Seoul (Brudnoy 1970: 169). On March 1, 3,000 copies of a Korean declaration of independence, signed by thirty-three leaders from a variety of religious and underground nationalist groups, were distributed to a crowd (Ku 1985: 65–66). Korean flags, fashioned in secret, were waved, and thousands of Koreans took to the streets. Concurrent demonstrations were organized in seven other cities, including Pyongyang (Ku 1985: 68–69). Mass protest continued on a countrywide scale throughout the month of March (which came to be known as the March First Movement). These demonstrations became truly national in character and lasted into April, with an average of fifteen protests a day throughout the peninsula. At least 460,000 Koreans participated in the movement in these two months, despite arrests. Korean estimates suggest that there were two million participants; Japanese estimates place it at one million (Ku 1985: 72–73; Lee 1963: 114). The movement was only finally subdued when the Japanese government sent 6 battalions of infantry and 400 gendarmes to Korea. They resorted to measures including torture and flogging (Ku 1985: 103–109), and Japanese colonial authorities killed and arrested thousands from all regions of the country (Lee 1963: 115–118).

The brutal repression of the March First Movement sent a powerful message to the Korean nationalists. Nearly all of the movement's leaders were imprisoned or exiled. Japanese authorities suppressed all lectures, publications, and street demonstrations that they deemed to be anti-Japanese. Aside from a few isolated violent incidents, the two most important uprisings against the Japanese colonial rule after the March First Movement were the Six Ten and Kwangchoo incidents. The first uprising emerged out of an imperial funeral procession of over 400,000 Koreans, which morphed into a nationalist protest (Dong 1965: 289). The uprising was suppressed before it could spread to the rest of the country, however. The second incident lasted for five months and involved as many as 54,000 Korean students who were outraged by Japanese policies in Korea and motivated more by resentment than nationalist demands (Dong 1965: 290–291).

Despite this repression, Japanese colonial policies under the new mandate allowed for alternative means of mobilizing resistance through newspapers, radio, and voluntary associations. Nationalists concentrated their efforts in education, stressing the importance of maintaining Korean culture and national consciousness in the face of increasing assimilation attempts by the Japanese authorities (Lee 1963: 238–246).

The Korean Communists were most successful at organizing internal resistance. Emboldened by the Bolshevik Revolution, they helped organize more than 330 large strikes and many smaller ones involving tens of thousands of workers between 1920 and 1925, and 900 strikes involving 70,000 workers between 1931 and 1935. These strikes are particularly impressive because nearly 453,000 Korean strikers were arrested between 1932 and 1935 (Simons 1995: 140, 144). The Communists also engaged in insurgency, such as Kim Il Sung's raids against Japanese outposts on Korean's northern border (Simons 1995: 142–144; Buzo 2002: 46)

Korea's greater resistance to alien rule is further borne out by considering evidence on trends in policing (see Figure 4.1).

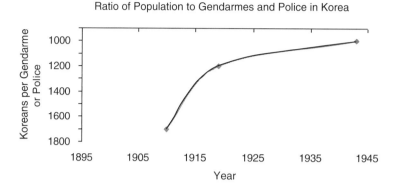

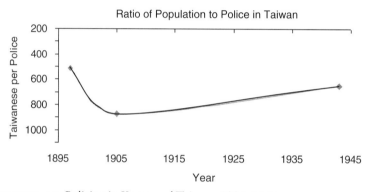

FIGURE 4.1 Policing in Korea and Taiwan, 1895–1945.

Figure 4.1 reveals a sharp drop in the ratio of police per capita in Taiwan from
1895 to 1905, and a very modest upswing thereafter. The Korean pattern is
quite different: the ratio increases steadily until 1945. This expansion of policing is an indirect measure of resistance to Japanese colonial rule. Likewise,
the number of Koreans convicted for political offenses rises consistently from
1922 to 1931 (Dong 1965: figure 8), and the number of such cases brought to
trial rises from 1936 to 1943 (Dong 1965: figure 9).

Although Taiwan experienced twenty years of guerilla insurgency, the conflicts were local rather than national in scale. The absence of an aboriginal state
in Taiwan meant that no treaty could be signed between the Japanese government and the aboriginal population. The political disunity of the aborigines
compelled the Japanese colonial administration to engage in counterinsurgency against each group resisting central control. Once the local insurgencies
were subdued in 1915, there is little further evidence of resistance to Japanese
rule in Taiwan.

Rates of military volunteering are consistent with this assessment of differential resistance to alien rule. Whereas 15,000 Koreans volunteered for service

in the Japanese armed forces in 1938 (Kim 2005:138), hundreds of thousands of Taiwanese had volunteered by 1942 (Lamley 2007: 241).

Finally, the present-day reaction to the collaborators of yore is quite different in the two countries. Under a special law enacted in 2005, the South Korean government established an Investigative Commission on Pro-Japanese Collaborators' Property. On May 3, 2007, the government confiscated property (worth $3.9 million) of the descendants of nine Korean collaborators who had received court titles and money from Tokyo (*New York Times* 2007). So far, the Commission has listed 452 collaborators, and more confiscation is planned in the future. No comparable action has been taken by the Taiwanese government.

Overall, therefore, resistance to Japanese colonial rule was markedly greater in Korea than Taiwan. What accounts for this differential response?[4]

Alternative Explanations

Admittedly, the comparison falls far short of the requirements of a crucial experiment. To some extent, stronger Korean resistance to Japanese rule may stem from differences between the countries at the onset of Japanese rule. First, because of *geography* and *topography*, Japan had distinct strategic interests in Taiwan and Korea. Whereas Korea was a beachhead for military expansion in Asia, Taiwan had less strategic importance. Although this led to somewhat different governance policies, for the most part both countries suffered similar levels of political repression at the hands of the Japanese. Thus, geographical differences alone cannot explain why resistance to Japanese rule was stronger in Korea than Taiwan.

Second is the issue of *duration*. Japan's occupation of Taiwan began fifteen years before Korea's, and this too might have weakened resistance by affording greater scope to Japanese colonial efforts to assimilate the Taiwanese. However, there is less to this argument than meets the eye. Although Korea only became an official Japanese colony in 1910, Japanese involvement began well before that date. Japanese troops were spurring resistance in the peninsula as early as 1895 (Schmid 2002: 44). By 1905 Japan declared Korea a protectorate, assuming control of its foreign affairs. Prior to annexation, the Japanese government forced the Korean emperor to abdicate, installed his son as emperor, and disbanded the Korean army (Robinson 1988: 37). So the duration of alien rule cannot be the answer.

The most popular explanation for the variation in resistance levels is that Korea's history of statehood and consequent *national identity* provided

---

[4] In this respect, it is important to note that Taiwan experienced yet another bout of alien rule following Japanese colonization. When Chang-Kai Shek and the *Kuomintang* assumed control of the island in 1950, their regime was so brutal and corrupt that it made the Japanese look good by comparison.

organizational and ideological bases for the development of a nationalist movement.[5] Unlike Taiwan, Korea had been an independent state for millennia. The Joseon Dynasty, overthrown by the Japanese government, had been established in the late fourteenth century. In contrast, Taiwan had already experienced bouts of alien rule at the hands of the Chinese, Dutch, and Spanish. There can be no doubt that Korean national identity was stronger than Taiwanese (McNamara 1986). However, a Taiwanese identity was beginning to emerge at the end of the nineteenth century.[6] The Han Chinese, by this period the majority in Taiwan, were beginning to identify as Taiwanese, and the emerging school system had Taiwanese, not Mandarin, as the teaching language (Fujii 2006: 67). Further, Korean nationalism only emerged at the end of the nineteenth century (Eckert 1991; Robinson 2007; Shin 2006; Wu 2003); initially it was primarily a reaction to Western imperialism (Eckert 1991: 226; Lee 1963: 47, 51; Schmid 2002: 5).[7] Nationalist antipathy to Japan did not crystallize until the Japanese Empire assumed full control of the peninsula (Rhee 2001: 142, 201; Robinson 1988: 3; Schmid 2002: 32).

All told, initial conditions account for neither the timing nor the intensity of resistance in these countries. In both Taiwan and Korea, resistance peaked soon after the Japanese colonial administration assumed control. To account for the temporal variation in the intensity of resistance, the demand for regime change and the supply of nationalist leaders must be considered independently.

Supply Factors: Rebels and Collaborators

Resistance to alien rule is a function of the supply of participants and the demand for regime change. In the case of Taiwan and Korea, supply factors played a major role in determining resistance to the Japanese rule. Two particular factors stand out: the difference in the native social structures during the period of alien rule and the varying levels of native collaboration.

Social Structure

The gentry class in Taiwan was small and weak relative to its Korean counterpart, and many Taiwanese elites emigrated to China immediately after Japanese takeover. The Treaty of Shimonoseki stipulated that for two years

---

[5] Indeed, Chen (1968) argues that the legacy of Korean statehood – and the absence of statehood in Taiwan – is the fundamental cause of these different reactions to Japanese rule.

[6] Tse (2000: 157) suggests that when China ceded Taiwan to Japan through the Treaty of Shimonoseki, the creation of a sense of national identity was spurred.

[7] By 1874, the Korean regime aimed "to preserve Korea's defenses against the more distant but more insidious Western menace. Western missionaries, Western merchandise, and Western ideas were regarded as the real danger to Korea, not the Japanese. Japan would be converted from enemy to friend by adherence to civilized standards of courtesy and by treating Japanese demands for changes in protocol as curiosities peculiar to the special domestic problems of the Japanese nation" (Palais 1975: 270).

the ethnic Chinese residents of Taiwan had the option of leaving the island and immigrating to mainland China or remaining on the island and becoming Japanese subjects. Some estimates put the number of emigrants at a few thousand (Chu and Lin 2001: 106); others suggest that about a quarter of the Taiwanese population took advantage of the exit option (Lamley 2007: 208; Roy 2003: 34).

Taiwanese emigrants were primarily wealthy and from the upper gentry (Lamley 2007: 208; Chou 1989: 308). Their exodus deprived Taiwan of much of the potential leadership of a nationalist movement. The status of the remaining gentry – who by virtue of their degrees, titles, and classical education had enjoyed high privilege under Qing rule – declined under Japanese rule (Chou 1996: 44).[8] In contrast, at the onset of Japanese colonial rule Korea was highly polarized; it boasted a well-entrenched landed elite – the *yangban* – with centuries of aristocratic legitimation (Cumings 2005: 151). As in feudal Europe, these landed aristocrats fought against the Crown's attempts to centralize power in Korea (Palais 1975: ch. 14). To cement their control of the land the yangban, consisting of the top 10 percent of the population, occupied key positions in the government and the military establishment (Breen 1998: 87).

After the abdication of Emperor Kojong in 1907, a group of yangban-led guerillas formed to repel the impending Japanese colonial conquest (Breen 1998: 103). By the time Japan assumed control in Korea in 1910, most of these insurgents had fled to Manchuria (Cumings 2005: 146). The remaining Korean elite had nowhere to go without suffering an enormous loss of status. Whereas the majority of Taiwanese elite could maintain their privileged status by emigrating to China, the bulk of the Korean elite stayed on the peninsula where they became subject to the will of the Japanese colonial administration. This difference in patterns of elite exit had major consequences for the course of resistance to alien rule in these two lands.

Collaboration

To the (usually very real) degree that alien rulers are resented by native populations, their costs of control are correspondingly higher than those of native rulers. How can these surplus costs ever be borne? The answer lies in the use of native intermediaries who collaborate with the alien power to govern the native population (Lammers 1988; Robinson 1972). Collaborators are essential because occupation regimes, similar to their colonial counterparts, always aim to rule on a shoestring. Because alien rulers in part depend on collaborators to provide social order, it is generally not in their interest to denigrate these collaborators.

Why do natives collaborate with an oft-hated alien ruler? As Max Weber (1994: 93) suggests, many government bureaucrats continue to work for alien

---

[8] Some of the native elites that fled to China later returned and helped establish the *Kuomintang* regime in Taiwan (Cheng 2001: 21).

rulers because they see their jobs as apolitical and have no desire to deprive their fellow citizens of access to essential services (health, sanitation, utilities, and so forth). Alien rulers thus seek to employ native leaders for their specialized skills – in realms such as governance, security, and cultural production – and because they are usually endowed with legitimacy. Both assets are valuable for the maintenance of order under the new regime. In the best of circumstances, collaborators can serve as indirect rulers (Hechter 2000). If native elites are not sufficiently rewarded by the new regime, however, they are likely to foment opposition to it. Accordingly, the leaders of nationalist movements often come from the ranks of discontented elements of the native elites and intelligentsia (Hroch 1985).

The Japanese colonial administration sought to build an elite-driven regime in Taiwan that provided social order at minimal cost (Chu and Lin 2001: 105). At the onset of Japanese colonial rule, a motley group of local leaders and others cooperated with the regime primarily to protect their neighborhoods and villages from armed conflict (Lamley 2007: 215). After the first few months of turmoil, some merchants and gentry joined the ranks of collaborators. By rewarding these Taiwanese notables on the basis of their wealth, social status, or community service, the Japanese colonial officers gradually succeeded in inducing more reputable and ambitious Taiwanese to collaborate (Lamley 2007: 215–216). By the end of the Japanese colonization, at least 36,000 Taiwanese officials were employed in the Japanese colonial bureaucracy (Chao and Myers 1998: 21).

The Japanese also provided a variety of incentives to foster collaboration. These included a conference inviting the Taiwanese gentry to participate in the cultural transformations and the "new learning" promoted by Japan (Lamley 2007: 216) and the awarding of gentleman's medals to cooperative elites (Roy 2003: 45, Chu and Lin 2001: 106). The gentry were given economic incentives and business privileges (Roy 2003: 45), and many Taiwanese were allowed to enroll in universities in Japan (Fulda 2002). Some of the Taiwanese educated under Japanese colonial rule joined voluntary associations to end customs, such as foot binding and queue wearing, that the Japanese regarded as retrograde (Lamley 2007: 218). Despite their initial clashes with the hill peoples, the Japanese regime eventually also helped the aborigines obtain education and jobs, turning them into some of the most loyal warriors of the Japanese Empire (Chu and Lin 2001: 110–111).

On assuming power in both countries, the Japanese colonial administration instituted land reform (Myers and Yamada 1984: 428–429). The impact of this land reform, however, was different in Taiwan than Korea. In Taiwan, Qing rule between 1684 and 1895 had led to a relatively even distribution of land among peasant small holdings (Ka 1995: 16). This system gave rise to a class of perpetual tenants. The Japanese colonial administration gave *ta-tsu* holders long-term bonds in exchange for their tenants, mollifying some who lost large holdings (Myers and Yamada 1984: 429). The resulting Taiwanese social structure was relatively flat: large farms were exceptional; for the most part the land was held in small parcels (Ka 1995: 148–149). The upshot was that land reform in Taiwan did not fundamentally change the Taiwanese social structure (Chu and Lin 2001: 106).

Prior to annexation, all land in Korea was officially the property of the crown, but it was controlled by the yangban who collected rents from peasant tenants (Lee 1963: 93). To encourage yangban collaboration with the new regime, the Japanese colonial administration granted exclusive land ownership rights to its members following a land survey intended to create a modern system of private land ownership (Kang 1994: 100). The yangban registered ownership claims over the common property of villages and claims by independent farmers to their own lands. As a result, a huge Korean tenant class, burdened by high rents and taxes, had its traditional hereditary rights to land replaced by short-term contracts (Lee 1963: 94). The Japanese government attempted to further entice yangban collaboration by offering eighty-four members titles and stipends. Only eight refused, and the Japanese colonial officers pensioned off thousands of others (Henderson 1968: 77).

Even so, many of the yangban resented Japanese colonial rule. Their privileges had never rested on landownership, but on access to high government and military offices. However, the Japanese government ended all statutory distinctions among Koreans (Lee 1963: 96) and reserved virtually all government offices for themselves.[9] Because many Korean landlords who were unable to pay their taxes had their lands confiscated (Lee 1963: 94–95), Japanese landownership increased fourfold between 1910 and 1923. When the emperor died in 1919, a large proportion of the mourners who came to Seoul to mourn his death – many of whom were arrested in the subsequent March First Movement – were former yangbans (Lee 1963: 96). Demonstrators complained about the loss of yangban privileges and property (Lee 1963: 96). Although the elimination of class distinctions was meant to appease the lower classes, it mostly succeeded in estranging the elites from the new rulers.

Ironically the Japanese colonial authority managed to alienate the peasants as well. The gifting of private land ownership to the yangban met with increasing resistance from the peasantry. They accused the landlords of collaborating with the alien ruler (Cumings 2005: 152). Peasant protest was so severe that the Japanese government enacted a radical land reform that established tenants' rights, giving long-term security to their leases. By raising the cost of labor, the land reform also led many Korean landowners to invest in industry rather than agriculture. The small Korean business class was nurtured by the Japanese colonial administration to encourage their collaboration. This small elite received financial support and direct subsidies for selected land

---

[9] The number of Japanese in the peninsula rose rapidly, reaching 708,448 in 1940. In 1937, 41.4 percent of the Japanese population in Korea was in government service; the corresponding percentage for Koreans was 2.9 (Henderson 1968: 75).

reclamation, mining, and industrial projects (McNamara 1989: 311). During the period of Japanese colonial rule major economic expansion was impossible without state-controlled credits or subsidies. Thus Korean entrepreneurs had very strong incentives to collaborate with Japanese state officials (McNamara 1989: 315).

These differences in the interaction of native elites with the alien ruler attest to the importance of supply factors in understanding varying resistance to Japanese alien rule. Taiwan was an agrarian economy characterized by small farms and a relatively weak native elite. At the onset of Japanese alien rule, landlords with the strongest Chinese loyalties and Taiwanese who stood to lose most from the occupation were allowed to escape to the mainland. This enabled the Japanese colonial administration to rid Taiwan of most of the leaders of a potential nationalist opposition and helped establish new elites who were dependent on the Japanese government and thus willing to collaborate with the new rulers.

Korea was a much more polarized society having a strong and well-entrenched elite that had little opportunity to exit on its own terms. Its traditional stranglehold on Korean society was threatened by the Japanese occupation, and its class privilege was soon eliminated by egalitarian policies and by its removal from government offices. Only a very small segment of this elite collaborated with the Japanese alien ruler. As a consequence, Korea had an ample supply of leaders who had reason to mobilize a nationalist resistance movement against Japanese rule.

Because the grievances resulting from occupation ultimately motivate nationalist collective action, we next consider other factors affecting the demand for change in these two countries.

Demand Factors: The Effects of Japanese Rule

Economy

At the turn of the nineteenth century, both Taiwan and Korea were primarily agricultural societies. Taiwan opened several ports to foreign trade by the 1860s, but its harbors were in poor condition. Taiwan had neither strong banking institutions nor a reliable currency system. Poor sanitation and public health caused high rates of plague and disease.

By contrast, with a market economy on the rise, Korea had already begun to undertake economic growth decades before Japanese rule (McNamara 1986). The Korean infrastructure was much more developed than the Taiwanese with small manufacturing and mining sectors (Haggard et al. 1997: 869). Last, disease and epidemics were less endemic than in Taiwan because of Korea's continental climate.

The Japanese colonial administration largely invested in agriculture in Taiwan and in mineral extraction and industrial development in addition to agriculture in Korea. Beyond this, the Japanese occupation brought important infrastructural investments into both territories. Yet the vividness of these investments was greater in Taiwan than Korea because of its much lower level of development and differing social structure at the outset of Japanese occupation.

Overall, the economies of both Taiwan and Korea grew under Japanese rule. The gross domestic product (GDP) increased at 3 percent annually in Korea, and 4 percent in Taiwan (Liberman 1996: 103). Moreover, mortality was reduced by a better diet, increased availability of modern medical services, and a general improvement in public health.[10] These aggregate indicators suggest that alien rule increased overall welfare levels in both countries, one of the key determinants of political legitimation.

During the first decades of Japanese rule, the government sought to increase agricultural production in both colonies. The Japanese colonial administration encouraged more specialization and the adoption of improved seeds and fertilizers, leading to better techniques and higher productivity (Myers and Yamada 1984: 432; Han-Yu and Myers 1963). However, because of its more favorable subtropical climate, this effort was more actively promoted in Taiwan.

In Taiwan, both arable and irrigated land more than doubled. *Hsiao-tsu* holders compensated for their higher taxes by increasing land productivity by an impressive 81 percent by 1938 in cooperation with Japanese rulers (Ka 1995: 61). Agriculture was also more diversified in Taiwan. Korean farmers depended solely on rice as the main source of income and planted coarse grains and vegetables for subsistence (Ho 1984: 441).

In Korea, however, agriculture gradually fell behind construction, commerce, and services. The greatest growth of GDP was consistently in manufacturing and mining (Haggard 1997: 869). Whereas growth in Taiwan occurred without much change in the social structure (Ho 1975: 423), Korea witnessed some of the most dramatic social changes of any agrarian society undergoing an industrial revolution, incurring large-scale population shifts and high levels of dislocation and urbanization (Cumings 2005:175).

Korea's industrial development served mainly to expand the Japanese home market and to supply the government with the resources needed for expansion and war mobilization. Some small firms benefited from cooperation with the Japanese colonial authorities, but overall Japan discouraged Korean-owned industries. The average size of Korean-owned factories decreased during Japanese rule (Haggard et al. 1997: 871). Japanese entrepreneurs owned all the large financial and commercial firms, and, particularly in the private sector, the ranks of Korean white-collar workers in 1940 was an exceptionally low 4 percent (Eckert 1996: 22–27). Japanese workers comprised about 20 percent

---

[10] Taiwanese death rates decreased from 33 per thousand in 1906 to 19 per thousand in the 1935–1940 period, and Korean death rates also declined from 35 per thousand to 23 per thousand in the 1935–1940 period. It should be noted that caloric consumption decreased in the late 1930s (Ho 1984: 352, 398).

of the workforce in manufacturing employment. Most Koreans were clerks and lower level functionaries (Haggard et al. 1997: 873), although by the end of the occupation Koreans comprised 30 to 36 percent of the higher ranks (Eckert 1996: 25).

In sum, Japanese alien rule resulted in greater disruption of the Korean than the Taiwanese social structure (Cumings 2002: ch. 3), and the benefits of development, although substantial in both countries, were more visible in Taiwan. Natives owned a greater proportion of the productive forces in Taiwan than their counterparts in Korea, and Japanese colonial policies stripped Korean elites of much of their power.

Culture

From the late 1930s onward, Japanese cultural policy in both Taiwan and Korea was relentlessly assimilationist.[11] To induce compliance with alien rule, the regime had the overweening ambition to replace Korean and Taiwanese identity with Japanese (Aziz 1955: 11). This goal was reflected in new directives in education, religion, and language.

The Japanese government sought to assimilate the Korean population by stressing their geographical proximity, linguistic similarities, and common Buddhist and Confucian roots (Rhee 1997: 153–154; Kang 1994: 149, 152). At the same time, it enacted harsh policies with the aim of eradicating all vestiges of Korean culture. New education policies were one cornerstone of this attempt (Kang 1994: 150; Lone and McCormack 1993: 65). The Educational Ordinance of 1911 established a unified schooling system throughout Korea designed to develop industrial, agricultural, and commercial skills (Chen 1968: 146). Koreans' education on the peninsula was limited to elementary, vocational, and technical schools (Kang 1994: 151–152). Less than one-third of school-age Koreans attended school (Lone and McCormack 1993: 66–67).[12]

Subjects of study, textbooks, and proper teaching procedures were controlled by the governor-general (Chen 1968: 147). Ethics courses designed to instill loyalty to the Japanese emperor were required. The use of textbooks printed before Japanese annexation was prohibited (Kang 1994: 151–152).

Education was regarded as critical for the assimilationist project in Taiwan as well (Tsurumi 1979: 617). Although Taiwanese students could study

---

[11] Prior to this, the Japanese state – which was convinced of the country's ethnic purity – had excluded Koreans and never imagined that they were on the same footing. Japan's shift in cultural policy in the late 1930s was a result of the war with China and subsequent labor shortages that occurred throughout the empire (Bruce Cumings, personal communication). During this period, the Japanese attempted to draw lessons in nation building from Britain's experience with the Celtic Fringe and France's with Algeria. They misinterpreted the British and French historical experiences, however, and thus failed to draw the correct conclusions. For an intriguing comparison of Japanese and European policies toward internal colonies, see Caprio (2009: 198–212).

[12] Elites, however, often sent their children to study in Japan (Lone and McCormack 1993: 68).

engineering, science, technology, and medicine, the subjects of law, politics, and the social sciences were forbidden for their allegedly disruptive potential (Copper 1996: 31; Morris Wu 2004: 53). As in Korea, many Taiwanese elites sent their children to Japan to be schooled (Phillips 2003: 21). The Taiwanese emerging literati class was strategically interacting with the Japanese rulers, collaborating with the regime, while also opening the space for expressing political grievances and demanding political concessions. In Korea, however, to be educated was to be anti-Japanese throughout the entire colonial period (Tsurumi 1984: 307).

Taiwanese education policy differed from Korean in two key respects: it was initially less centralized and a far greater proportion of students were educated in Taiwan. First, whereas the Japanese colonial administration took central control over Korean education immediately after annexation, this did not occur in Taiwan until twenty-four years after annexation. As a result, the shift in Taiwan's education system was gradual rather than instantaneous, and the gradualism of this shift reduced the resistance to Japanese assimilation (Chen 1968: 146–148). Second, whereas only a small proportion of the Korean population received any education at all, the Japanese regime greatly expanded educational opportunity in Taiwan.[13] The low level of student enrollment in Korean primary schooling was an obstacle to cultural assimilation.

Japan's colonial linguistic policies were closely wed to its educational policies. One of the Japanese government's colonial goals was the dissemination of the Japanese language in both Taiwan and Korea (Kang 1994: 151). Japanese became the official language of Korea (Breen 1998: 105; Lone and McCormack 1993: 66), and Korean became a second language in schools. The Japanese administration responded to the nationalist uprisings of 1919 by easing its policy of cultural repression: it allowed the use of the Korean language in magazines, newspapers, radio, and other communication media (Robinson 1999). This policy shift had the unintended consequence of stimulating Korean nationalism (Robinson 1988: 4).

In the 1930s, restrictions against the use of the Korean language mounted heavily as Japan prepared for war. Korean newspapers were closed (Kim 2005: 137), and the instruction of Korean – even as a secondary language – was prohibited in 1938 (Rhee 1997: 74). All classroom instruction was to occur in Japanese (Breen 1998: 114). Students received harsh punishment for speaking Korean in class (Breen 1998: 114), and it was expected that they would speak Japanese at home (Kim 2005: 137). Whereas the Taiwanese might have encountered sporadic inhibitions against speaking their native language in public, Koreans were subjected to severe punishments, such as the imprisonment in 1942 of thirty-three leading members of the Korean Language Society (Chou 1996: 54).

---

[13] By 1943, 81 percent of males and 61 percent of females were enrolled in primary school in Taiwan (Phillips 2003: 21). Korean school enrollment reached only 33.8 percent in 1940 and approximately 50 to 60 percent by 1945 (Park 1999: 147).

By the 1930s, the use of Chinese in Taiwan in most publications and public fora was prohibited (Jones 1999: 82; Mendel 1970: 21). Yet, despite the rough similarity of language policy in the two countries, there was considerably more linguistic assimilation in Taiwan than Korea. Whereas more than 57 percent of Taiwanese knew Japanese by 1941, the corresponding figure for Korea was 17.6 percent (Chen 1968: 173; Tse-Han et al. 1991: 45).[14] Further, Koreans were forced to discard their ancestral names and adopt Japanese ones (Breen 1998:105). Those who did not comply were fired, expelled from school, denied mail and train service, and given decreased rations (Kim 2005: 138; Rhee 1997: 74). Unlike in Korea, however, the shift to Japanese names in Taiwan was optional (Jones 1999: 82) – indeed, a permit was required to change names in Taiwan (Hicks 1994: 41). By 1942, only about 10 percent of the population had done so (Tse-Han et al. 1991: 32); in Korea, where the policy was compulsory, 80 percent of the population had adopted Japanese names (Kim 2005: 138).

At first, the Japanese colonial administration encountered few problems with religion in Korea. Because Buddhists had faced discrimination in Confucian Korea, Japanese colonial policies redressed this and thus encouraged the bulk of the Buddhist population to be amenable to alien rule (Lone and McCormack 1993: 54; Kang 1994: 156). Whereas Christian missionaries were initially supportive of the Japanese annexation of the peninsula, they soon came into conflict with Japanese policy (Kang 1994: 156–157). Religion was among the only forms of permissible social activity, and Christian churches took a strong leadership role in the March First Movement (Kang 1994: 156–157; Lone and McCormack 1993: 54). Christians provided most of the signatures to the Declaration of Independence and also bore much of the brunt of Japanese colonial retaliation (Lone and McCormack 1993: 56).

The regime's introduction of Shintoism, which became the official state religion, created pervasive discontent. Shinto shrines were built throughout Korea's major cities as symbols of Japan's conquest and as a means of instilling reverence for Japanese alien rule (Rhee 1997: 63). Koreans were forced to worship at Shinto shrines beginning in 1935 (Kang 1994: 158). In 1940, more than 2,000 Christians were imprisoned for refusing to worship at these shrines, and 200 churches were closed (Kim 2005: 137).

In Taiwan, Chinese monks maintained strong relationships with the Japanese colonial regime until it enacted tougher assimilation policies in the 1930s. Because dissident groups, such as the Taoists, began to use Chinese temples, shrines, and meeting halls under the cover of Buddhism (Morris Wu 2004: 54), the Japanese colonial administration responded by announcing a campaign to raze and burn these sites throughout Taiwan (Jones 1999: 37, 62,

---

[14] The Japanese authorities may have had differing standards for evaluating Japanese linguistic assimilation. Wan-Yao Chou still concludes that the percentage of Japanese speakers in the two colonies varied greatly (Chou 1996: 52–53).

81–83). Students were forced to worship at newly constructed Shinto shrines, and Chinese families were asked to replace their Buddhist ancestral shrines with Shinto shrines (Tse-Han et al. 1991: 29). These measures, however, were enforced less stringently than in Korea. In Taipei, for example, most Chinese Buddhist temples were well connected with the local governments and escaped Japanese restructuring efforts (Jones 1999: 83, 87).

Finally, no analysis of the cultural consequences of alien rule in these countries is complete without mention of the still volatile issue of comfort women. During World War II, between 100,000 and 200,000 women were conscripted to serve Japanese soldiers sexually on the front lines. Korean women apparently accounted for 80 to 90 percent of all comfort women (Chung 1995: 16); some 150,000 Korean women were enlisted (Breen 1998: 113) as they were preferred by Japanese soldiers for their skin color (Oh 2001: 10). Although the number of Taiwanese comfort women is in dispute (Hicks 1994: 241), there were significantly fewer than there were Korean women. As a result, there has been much less outrage over the treatment of comfort women in contemporary Taiwan than Korea (Hicks 1994: 239).

Despite the fact that Japanese colonial cultural policies were largely similar in Korea and Taiwan, they were imposed more centrally in Korea, although there was some variation across localities and time periods (Kang 2001). Cultural policies in Taiwan were enforced locally, were less harsh than in Korea, and some – such as the prohibition of foot binding and restriction of opium smoking – were even progressive (Morris Wu 2004: 54).

Governance
Whereas the Japanese government instituted a form of direct rule in Korea, its rule in Taiwan was more indirect. In general, indirect rule inhibits nationalism by fostering collaboration among native elites, which aids legitimacy and reduces the demand for sovereignty (Hechter 2000; Sambanis 2006). Direct rule, however, has the opposite effect: it fosters resistance to alien rule by antagonizing local authorities who then seek to mobilize their dependents. The most extreme form of direct rule is military. Korea had an autocratic military regime wherein supreme political authority was held by one person. In contrast, there was a fusion of military and civilian rule in Taiwan.

When Japan incorporated Korea into the empire in 1910, ultimate political authority was concentrated in the Office of the Governor-General (Ku 1985: 10). Until 1919, only generals from the army and navy could be appointed to it. Even though civilians were eligible to hold the office after 1919, none did. The governor-general controlled the political bureaucracy and all military and naval forces; he had the power to issue executive ordinances that carried the same weight as laws from Japan. The Korean governor-general was responsible only to the emperor. Many procedures and laws, including commercial laws, civil procedures, and taxation laws, were developed directly by the governor-general's office (Chen 1970: 132, 127–140). To conceal the extreme directness of Japanese rule, a Korean governing body, the Central Council, was created with an ostensibly consultative role. The Council's membership was selected by the Japanese colonial administration, and it was never consulted about matters of any significance (Brudnoy 1970: 166–167). In effect, therefore, the governor-general of Korea had dictatorial control over the peninsula with few domestic checks on his power.

Taiwan was governed more indirectly.[15] Similar to Korea, the governor-general of Taiwan was empowered to implement imperial policy. However, his power was limited in several respects. The governor-general of Taiwan was not solely accountable to the emperor; there was considerable oversight from the government in Tokyo. The governor-general was placed under the authority of the Japanese Ministry of Colonial Affairs and Home Ministry, whereas the Korean governor-general's office was not. Although the governor-general of Taiwan had command of military and naval forces, he was forced to accept the direction of the ministers of Army and Navy over defense mobilization projects and certain administrative personnel decisions. When he used the colonial garrison for purposes of public order, he was required to issue a report to the minister of Home Affairs and the chiefs of staff of the Army and Navy (Chen 1970: 127–135).

Following liberalization in 1919, Japanese civilians were permitted to become governor-generals of occupied lands. This occurred in Taiwan – nine consecutive civilian governors held the post of governor-general between 1919 and 1936 – but not in Korea (Lamley 2007: 221). Because the civilian governor-generals of Taiwan had no control over the military, they were more constrained than their Korean counterparts.

Local administration in Taiwan also differed from that of Korea in a crucial way. In Taiwan, social control filtered down to the local level via the *pao chia* system (Chen 1970: 142–144).[16] This system permitted policing in the smallest of localities under a model that had been previously established by Qing administrators (Chen 1975: 393, 402). Faced with a series of local insurgencies, the Japanese colonial administration created this form of self-rule police in which all members of a pao or chia were fined if any anti-Japanese activity took place within the group (Chen 1970:145). The pao chia system gave the Taiwanese much greater involvement in their local affairs then their Korean counterparts. Pao chia headmen were elected by Taiwanese household heads for their respective units. The head of each pao and chia assisted the police in taking the census, watching population movements, preparing for natural disasters, and preventing crime. Although the Japanese colonial regime exercised authority over the system (Chen 1975: 396), many headmen had

---

[15] See Footnote 5 in Chapter 3 on variations in alien rule.
[16] Ten households made up one chia (*ko*), and ten *chia* made up one pao (*ho*). The head of each chia and pao was chosen from among the village elders and was accountable for each pao chia (Han-Yu and Myers 1963: 439).

incentives to collaborate with the Japanese officials – including educational benefits, business opportunities, and appointments to government posts (Chen 1975: 394, 397, 399–400).

In Korea, the Japanese government instituted a system of strict social control based on extensive Japanese policing, rather than an analog of the pao chia system. The Japanese police force was an overwhelming presence (more than 9 policemen for every 10,000 people), and it employed lengthy detention, physical abuse, and torture (Lee 1999: 37).

Japanese rule in Korea was much more direct and militaristic than in Taiwan, leaving little room for native elites to participate in governance. The demand for change was weaker in Taiwan as a result, at least in part, of the legitimation efforts of native elites.

Conclusion

This chapter began by outlining three propositions about resistance to alien rule. How do these fare in light of the Taiwan/Korea comparison?

Resistance should be greater in the initial period of occupation. This is true for both Taiwan and Korea. The Chinese elite controlling Taiwan waged a short-lived war against Japanese forces before finally ceding the island away. Following their exodus, the Japanese colonial administration struggled to put down unorganized local insurgencies for the first fifteen years of rule. The Korean elite, likewise, organized armed resistance against the Japanese regime for several years before the island was officially annexed. In both cases, elites organized rebellion against an encroaching alien ruler to protect their status and privilege within their respective societies.

The greater the opportunities afforded to native elites, the weaker the resistance to alien rule. This is also confirmed in the comparison. Collaboration was more likely when native leaders were given prominent roles in the new regime. When the Japanese government took over Taiwan, most of the traditional Confucian elites fled to the mainland. On the one hand, this stripped any subsequent Taiwanese resistance movement of a supply of potential leaders. On the other, it elevated a group of Taiwanese to elite status, making them dependent on – and loyal to – the alien regime. These new elites had little to lose from the end of Qing rule, and thus their lack of solidarity to the old regime granted them attractive opportunities under Japanese alien rule. No such opportunity existed for the traditional Korean governing elites, who spoke a unique language and had operated in a unique culture. They largely remained in Korea while the Japanese colonial administrators took over their previously privileged roles as government officeholders, ended formal class distinctions, and acquired huge tracts of Korean land. Together with elements of the large landowning class, which suffered in the Japanese colonial government's imposed land reform, these thwarted Korean elites played a key role in the development of anti-Japanese nationalism (cf. Gould 1996).

The less fair and effective the regime, the lower the legitimacy and greater the resistance to alien rule. Here the picture is more complex. This proposition may be divided in two parts. Consider first the provision of economic growth – a key indicator of effective governance. Japanese rule spurred economic development in both Taiwan and Korea. In Taiwan, Japanese investment led to much greater output of rice and created a modern sugar industry. The effects of alien rule in Korea were in some respects even more dramatic. By the 1930s, the Japanese colonial administration had ended centuries of exploitative relations between landlords and tenants in the Korean countryside. This helped to foster the rapid industrialization of the peninsula. If Japanese rule was relatively effective in both countries, but resistance in Korea was much greater, then effectiveness evidently is an insufficient determinant of legitimacy in this comparison.

A key problem with the proposition linking effectiveness with legitimacy is that assessments of welfare are deeply subjective. This is not to say that welfare assessments are mere social constructions that have no determinate causes nor that we cannot make causal inferences about them. Our perceptions hinge, in part, on our experiences. At the onset of Japanese alien rule, Korea was considerably more developed than Taiwan. For an observer to have noticed perceptible improvements in welfare, the Japanese colonial regime would have had to produce far more collective goods in Korea than in Taiwan (McNamara 1986). For this reason, the Japanese colonial contribution to the economic development of Taiwan was more dramatic, more vivid, than its contribution in Korea.

Now turn to the fairness of rule. Here the differences between Korea and Taiwan are striking, and they are consistent with this volume's theoretical expectations. The practices that constitute what the Koreans have termed *cultural genocide* – to say nothing about the treatment of Korean comfort women – were a great deal less fair than those meted out to the Taiwanese. Hence, in this comparison fairness turns out to trump effectiveness as a determinant of legitimacy and lower resistance to alien rule (cf. Tyler 2006). Fairness matters most to the intermediaries between aliens and natives – that is, to the collaborators with the alien regime – because they are likely to have the greatest influence in the native population because of their resources and traditional standing. As such, they can either collaborate with the regime or rebel against it. As we have seen, here too there is an important difference between Korea and Taiwan.[17]

The effects of alien rule on native populations are far from universal. Whereas these effects are often malign, in other respects they are beneficent. The history of Japanese colonial rule in Taiwan and Korea reveals both kinds of effects. The legitimacy of alien rule hinges on the kinds of policies that alien

---

[17] Quite a different outcome occurred in post-World War II Okinawa, however. Whereas some Taiwanese look back to the period of Japanese rule with nostalgia, many native Okinawans preferred alien rule by the United States to Japanese governance (Fackler 2012).

rulers impose on native populations. Although alien rule spurred infrastructural development and economic growth in both countries, it was more destructive of Korean institutions and culture than of Taiwanese. Japanese colonial policies targeting traditional Korean elites helped provide the conditions responsible for the growth of resistance to alien rule. Combined with the loyalty of the Taiwanese elites, the more liberal policies enacted by the Japanese colonial administration yielded greater acceptance of alien rule in Taiwan.

Difficult as it may be to do, the effects of legitimacy must be disentangled from those of repression because both mechanisms could be responsible for any observed lack of resistance. In Taiwan and Korea, however, the Japanese adopted similarly repressive policies limiting civil liberties and substituting Japanese newspapers for native ones (Ku 1985: 11; Copper 1996: 30). These policies were relaxed in both countries during the 1920s and were reinstated a decade later (Kerr 1974: 125; Brudnoy 1970: 173–174; Lamley 2007: 235–239; Lee 1963: 260–263). Because repressive measures followed the same course in these lands, at least some of the variation in resistance is likely a result of the differential legitimacy of the alien ruler in Taiwan and Korea.

5

Dynamics of Military Occupation

The truth is rarely pure, and never simple.

– *Oscar Wilde*

The recent American invasion of Iraq and Afghanistan has revived interest in the outcomes of military occupation, which is the most extreme form of alien rule. In contrast to annexation and colonialism, in this chapter military occupation refers to a type of alien rule that is imposed on the native society by a foreign power and that the international community refuses to recognize as constituting permanent sovereign control.[1]

The histories of military occupation in country after country have often been unhappy. Occupation is derided because it entails a high risk of loss for the bulk of the unfortunates who are subjected to it. It also ushers in boundless uncertainty; this is why people flee the impending arrival of an occupying army en masse. It raises fundamental questions about whose justice will rule the land. The common expectation is that it will not be the native's justice. If alien soldiers confiscate or destroy native private property, will the alien rulers be motivated to seek justice? If occupying soldiers rape native women, will the occupying authorities step in to halt the practice?[2] If most people dislike

---

[1] This definition excludes all cases in which occupation is elected and occurs at the behest of the native society, often in response to its perception of external threat (cf. Edelstein 2004, which includes such cases). Even though such elected occupations may also engender some native resistance, this resistance is likely to be much less vigorous than when occupation is imposed. It also excludes cases such as that of Iceland, which, despite its declaration of neutrality, was invaded by the British in 1940 and subsequently by the United States, but whose existing government cooperated with the Allied powers for the duration of the war.

[2] After a number of years, when an occupation regime stabilizes and becomes routinized, much of this uncertainty will be resolved. Therefore, initial resistance to the occupation is likely to be relatively high. As seen in Chapter 4, this was true of the Japanese occupation of Taiwan and Korea.

uncertainty, they are also quite averse to the prospect of certain loss (Kahneman and Tversky 1979). Especially for native elites, occupation typically results in the certain loss of their authority.

At the same time, the official historiographies of countries that have undergone occupation often romanticize resistance to it. This results in a tendency to exaggerate the selflessness and heroism of the native population and to downplay its collaborationist proclivities (Kalyvas 2006: 37; MacKenzie 1997: 1–2).[3] This bowdlerization ignores the inconvenient truth that some military occupations (such as those in postwar Japan and Germany) evidently succeeded in fostering new legitimate and sustainable regimes, whereas many others (such as the Soviet occupation of Afghanistan) indeed did inspire fierce resistance and ultimately failed.

This chapter attempts to account for these varying outcomes. Because there are surprisingly few systematic studies of the effects of military occupations, it proceeds by dipping into the large and heterogeneous case-study literature. For heuristic purposes, this literature can be divided into macro- and microlevel accounts of military occupation.

Macroanalysis

At the macrolevel, domestic reactions to occupation are the outcome of characteristics of the occupier's regime and the native society, as well as of mediating and exogenous factors.

Regime Characteristics

In the first place, not all occupation regimes are the same. One cause of this variation emanates from the characteristics of the occupying power itself. An occupation regime imposed by one state is likely to vary from one set up by

---

[3] World War II offers numerous examples of this tendency: "[F]or much of the war ... Europeans fell into line and contributed what [Nazi Germany] demanded anyway. After 1945, this was conveniently forgotten. Those who had endured the German occupation hailed the heroic *résistants* and passed in silence over the fact that German officials in most of Europe had not been overly troubled by resistance until late in the day. That the Germans had managed to divert the resources of the continent to the benefit of their own war economy was attributed to coercion [not to willing collaboration]" (Mazower 2008: 6). "Compared with many aspects of the history of the Second World War, the phenomenon of cooperation by Soviet citizens with the German occupation authorities has received less critical attention by scholars and has not been systematically examined for various reasons. Whilst doggedly prosecuting and punishing those suspected of 'collaboration' as traitors in the postwar period, the Soviet government was reluctant to acknowledge publicly that this wartime phenomenon took place on Soviet territories during the occupation or sought to diminish the significance of this phenomenon. Since the existence of collaboration could raise the question of the legitimacy of the Soviet regime and also could question the allegiance of the population to the Soviet state, the government refused to divulge the real scale of this movement and to openly analyse its origins and reasons" (Baranova 2008: 114). Likewise, Esdale (2003) challenges the historiographical consensus about the heroic Spanish resistance to the Napoleonic occupier in the Peninsular War.

another if only because the institutions of the states themselves are different. Even though both France and the United Kingdom are considered to be full-fledged democracies, their state structures and policies are far from identical. Because the characteristics of the occupied territories also differ, the same state may also adopt different institutions and policies in its multiple occupation regimes in different territories. Thus because in part to ecological consider-ations, the British resorted to direct rule in some parts of the territory of a given colony and indirect rule in others (Boone 2003; Lammers 2003). The Nazis did likewise in their occupation of France: they ruled the North directly but relied on the Vichy government to rule the South. Finally, both institutions and policies of a given occupation regime may shift as circumstances – such as the occupying power's fortunes in war – change. For instance, it is less costly to produce goods that benefit the native population when the occupying power reckons victory is at hand than when it must devote greater resources to fight-ing an intractable enemy.[4]

At any given time, however, several key dimensions of any occupation regime will exert influence on native resistance. Two of these dimensions – the effectiveness of the regime's production of collective goods and the degree to which it enacts fair governance – are likely to affect native resistance via their consequences for the regime's legitimacy.

To the degree that alien rulers are resented by native populations, their costs of control will be correspondingly higher than those of native rulers. How can these surplus costs ever be borne? One answer lies in granting decision-making authority to a native elite through some type of indirect rule. Indirect rule employs native intermediaries who are induced to collaborate with the alien power to govern the native population. Collaborators are essential because they lower the control costs of the occupation regime (Robinson 1972).[5] Because alien rulers depend in part on collaborators to provide social order, which is a prerequisite for attaining any of their aims in occupying the country in the first place, it is not in their interest to undermine collaborators' authority.

The challenge of legitimation faces all native revolutionary regimes, as well as alien ones. In this respect, different strategies have been employed histori-cally. One strategy – taken by Mussolini's Fascist regime in Italy – is to seek the collaboration of established cultural authorities, whom the new rulers consider to be best suited to legitimate their ideologies:

---

[4] To take one example, Stalin's policies with respect to the Soviet occupation of Germany from 1945 to 1949 shifted suddenly and unpredictably (Naimark 1995: 9).

[5] Indirect rule makes it possible to govern without erecting, financing, and feeding a bulky admin-istrative apparatus, as well as providing economies of information (Hechter 2000: 50–51). For instance, Napoleon ruled Habsburg Lombardy and mainland Naples indirectly because "the Habsburgs and Neapolitan Bourbons possessed administrative elites intellectually prepared for Napoleonic rule," and "assumed direct responsibility for exactly those parts of the [Italian] pen-insula where [his] rule, and the culture it rested upon, would seem most alien, and where indig-enous intermediaries would be hardest to find" (Broers 2003: 55).

The Fascist cultural compromise was a negotiated system in which some of the regime's legitimation goals were met in exchange for meeting some of the interests of [cultural] producers and consumers. With a policy of relative tolerance for artists and styles, the regime won, for a time, the consent and participation of a large portion of the Italian community of artists and the assent of audiences. Contemporary celebrities, from Mario Sironi to Giuseppe Terragni to Enrico Prampolini, lent their formidable talents to the project of giving Fascism a cultural identity. The adhesion of prominent and unknown artists, in turn, gave the dictatorship a cultural legitimacy that further cemented its rule (Stone 1998: 253).

The Nazis took quite a different tack on their accession to power, proclaiming all modern art and artists to be degenerate and championing traditional art forms (Barron and Guenther 1991).

Sometimes, occupation regimes seek collaborators among the members of ethnic or religious groups that had traditionally been subject to discrimination, thereby upending a country's long-standing cultural division of labor. Thus under the Soviet occupation of Lithuania, Jews were given managerial and official jobs that had previously been denied them (Petersen 2002: 105). When the French controlled Syria, they did much the same for the Alawites, who later came to lord it over the Sunni majority in that country (Pipes 1989). Likewise, Shi'i were advanced over Sunni in the wake of the American occupation of Iraq (Chapter 3).

During the Nazi occupation of Europe, the Channel Islands stand out as the territories that had the least resistance (Bunting 1995). In contrast to much of Europe, the Germans made extensive use of indirect rule and did not change the islands' system of government. The island government took responsibility for food rationing and distribution, thereby shielding the Germans from criticism of these policies.[6] By contrast, in Holland, the Germans reneged on their agreement to merely supervise Dutch authorities and abolished local and provincial self-government, restructuring administration in line with that in Germany.

When devising the post-World War II occupation policy for Japan, American experts discussed whether the occupation should be run directly or indirectly, and Japan specialist Hugh Borton forcefully argued for indirect rule, as "the United States and her allies had insufficient trained men to administer Japan down to the smallest hamlet" and indirect rule, moreover, would minimize resentment toward the occupier (Daniels 1984: 161–162).

Likewise, the Nazi occupiers of northern France delegated authority over the South to the (French) Vichy regime, which was anxious to maximize whatever limited sovereignty it could. By 1942 its best hope in this regard depended increasingly on its hold over the police. The secretary general of the police in

---

[6] Yet, as the fictional Grenada television series *Island at War* shows in exquisite detail, even the comparatively mild occupation of the Channel Isles raised considerable anxiety in the native population, not least because the absence of young British males (as a result of their enlistment in the military) led a number of native women into controversial liaisons with German troops.

the Vichy regime, René Bousquet, cooperated well beyond what he was asked for on the deportation of Jews so that he could preserve a higher degree of autonomy for his police. The reasoning seemed to be that "we will accept subordination to the occupier, but whenever possible we will execute orders ourselves instead of letting the occupier's agents execute them directly; this way we will still maintain an appearance of sovereign control – since who patrols the streets seems to be the one in charge." Bousquet saw this as his only alternative to falling into "total subordination" (Mazower 2008: 437–440). Even when indirect rule was not enacted, many foreign occupiers have striven to create the appearance of self-government.[7]

Another answer concerns ideology and information control. Whereas all governments invest resources in persuading their citizens and subjects of their right to (and rightness for) rule (Weber 1978; Lasswell 1927), some invest more than others. If the occupier's ideology manages to be persuasive, then compliance with the regime will flow from internal sources rather than policing.[8] Moreover, the longer term the occupation will be, the more useful ideological investment will be (Carlton 1992). However, little is known about how to successfully instill a new ideology in occupied populations.

Despite this difficulty, occupation regimes have a more readily available cognitive tool that can be used to mute resistance to their rule – information control. Two kinds of information are particularly critical to control in this regard. In the first place if credible, information about the benefits deriving from the occupation can help reduce native opposition to it. In the second, because of bandwagon effects, information suggesting that the occupying power will be victorious in war will likewise mute resistance.

For this reason, the American occupiers of postwar Japan employed censorship – especially of information related to the atomic bomb – to advance their vision of "a Japan where everybody had free access to information ... where everybody could say and write what they wanted, where there was *no censorship*" (Braw 1991: 145, emphasis added).[9] Thus at the same time that the United States was dismantling the information control apparatus of the

---

[7] For further discussion of the appearance of self-government during military occupation, see Brook (2007: ch. 3).

[8] Orwell's [1949] 1984 famous story about the effects of a reduction of the chocolate ration in *1984* is illustrative.

[9] In September 1945, the Press, Pictorial and Broadcast Division (PPB) under the U.S. Civil Censorship Detachment (CCD) issued the *Manual on Censorship in Japan* (Braw 1991: 62), and that same month the Supreme Commander of the Allied Powers (SCAP) in Japan issued a Press Code warning the Japanese press, among other things, that "no false or destructive criticism of the Allied Powers" would be allowed and that it should not "invite mistrust or resentment of [the Allied] troops" (Braw 1991: 41). The Basic Initial Post-Surrender Directive issued by President Truman (which reached Japan on November 8, 1945) stated that censorship was to be "established over mail, wireless, telephone, telegraph and cables, films, and the press as may be necessary in the interests of the military security and the accomplishment of the purposes set forth in this directive" (Braw 1991: 32).

Japanese state in the name of democratic freedoms, the occupation authorities secretly adopted their own means of censorship.

Consider the information control policies in the American occupations of Germany and Iraq (Goldstein 2008). During the occupation of Germany, the U.S. authorities rigorously controlled the media to block pro-Nazi and, later, pro-Communist propaganda (Goldstein 2009). In contrast, during the American occupation of Iraq the occupying forces did not establish a monopoly of the media, which allowed the effective use of the press, radio, television, and Internet by the forces opposing the occupation, decisively contributing to the failure of the occupier's goals. One factor that contributed to success in media control during the German occupation was the use of officers (often émigré scholars) with extensive knowledge of the German language, culture, society, and history. In contrast, in Iraq the U.S. government outsourced propaganda tasks to private corporations with no experience in the Middle East.

These characteristics of the occupation regime affect differential resistance via their effects on its legitimacy.

Legitimating Occupation Regimes

To reiterate, this book claims that two factors are necessary, if not sufficient causes of, the legitimacy of *any* government. The first is the regime's effectiveness at producing an appropriate bundle of collective goods. The second is its fairness in allocating these goods and in instituting policy most generally. These two elements are part of any conception of good governance. Similar to native rulers, occupiers can attain legitimacy to the degree that they govern well.[10]

---

[10] In addition to these factors, legitimacy can be adversely affected by several disruptive effects that the occupying troops cause in the occupied society. Demographic effects can be troubling in small societies, especially in long occupations. Such was the case of Iceland, occupied by British forces in 1940 and by American forces in 1941 until 1947 – subsequently the Americans kept an air force base in Iceland between 1951 and 2006. The main problem of that occupation was that American troops (mostly unmarried males) outnumbered Icelandic marriageable females (Roehner 2009a). A high number of marriages between Icelandic women and American men would have been highly disruptive in a population of roughly 120,000, especially if many of these women subsequently emigrated to America. Aware of the tensions this was causing, in March 1942 the American command prohibited American soldiers from marrying Icelandic girls (Roehner 2009a: 10–11). A similar problem occurred during the postwar American occupation of Germany, sometimes with fatal consequences both to the occupying soldiers and their native girlfriends: "To German women, American soldiers appeared pretty attractive, if only because their income was between five to ten times higher than the income of an average German or Austrian. As this competitive advantage appeared unfair to many, it gave rise to an anti-fraternization movement … which brought about the murder of several military, sometimes together with their lovers" (Roehner 2009b: 10). Another factor that could potentially breed hostility to the occupier, and therefore negatively affect the occupation, especially in a small society like Iceland, was the disruptive effects that the greater purchasing power of the foreign troops could cause in local economies. Often this could create (localized) high inflation and/or the appearance of black markets, which might benefit a minority but be detrimental to most (Roehner 2009a).

In modern society government is responsible for supplying collective goods, including social order, public services (clean water, sanitation, electricity, and so forth), dispute resolution, education, and economic growth. To the degree that any government fails in producing some or all of these collective goods on a consistent basis, its legitimacy is compromised. This implies that the legitimacy of an occupation regime, and its ultimate viability, is heightened by the effectiveness of its provision of these collective goods.[11]

The establishment of social order – the most fundamental collective good, because it is a prerequisite for the provision of all others – is intimately bound up with legitimacy (Edelstein 2004). Social order enables individuals to go about their own business without fearing for physical injury or their very lives. If, at least after its onset, occupation disrupts expectations and invokes widespread uncertainty, the return of social life to normality, to the routine of everyday life, is a vital stabilizing factor. The Japanese understood this when they occupied parts of Central China (1937–1945). A document produced by Japanese Special Service officers advised, "To get the common people to return speedily to their rightful occupations, we have to guarantee their life and property. To first settle their minds, we have to restore order" (quoted in Brook 2007: 38). Ditto in Nazi-occupied France (Carlton 1992: 143).

There is a certain irony to be found when the agent providing order had recently been responsible for its demise in the first place. This irony was often present during the first months of the Japanese occupation of the Chinese Yangtze Delta in 1937–1938:

> The first concern of the pacification team had to be to project the appearance of stability and good government … even and especially when they did not exist. The pacification process must cause the violence by which the occupation authority was imposed to disappear and make the new arrangement appear to be other than abruptly imposed. It must project the idea that a state structure exists where it does not; it must construe nominal submission as engaged support. (Brook 2007: 62–63)

Although I am aware of no studies that directly test the proposition linking the provision of collective goods with successful occupations, a comparison of seven cases of U.S.-led nation-building efforts undertaken since World War II – in Germany, Japan, Somalia, Haiti, Bosnia, Kosovo, and Afghanistan – provides some supportive evidence. What principally distinguishes the relatively successful outcomes from the least successful ones

> is the level of effort the United States and the international community put into their democratic transformations. Nation-building … is a time- and resource-consuming effort. The United States and its allies have put 25 times more money and 50 times more troops, on a per capita basis, into postconflict Kosovo [a relatively successful

---

[11] During the Nazi occupation of France, André Gide acidly observed (in his journal on July 9, 1940) that "if German rule were to bring us affluence, nine out of ten Frenchmen would accept it, three or four with a smile" (Gide 2000: 30).

occupation] than into postconflict Afghanistan [in 2003, an utter failure]. (Dobbins 2003: xix)[12]

Legitimation does not flow from the mere quantity of collective goods provided by the occupation regime, however. The manner in which these goods are allocated also matters a great deal (Tyler 2006). To the degree that some social groups are systematically excluded from regime-provided benefits, this will breed resentment and delegitimate the regime in their eyes. It will also create new social divisions or reinforce existing ones. Indeed, the successful occupation of postwar Germany also hinged in no small part on policies that were explicitly designed to foster the legitimacy of the American occupation regime in German eyes. Unlike Paul Bremer, who led the American occupation of Iraq (Chapter 3), Lucius Clay, who was in charge in Germany, veered away from the kind of direct rule initially advocated by Washington to a system of indirect rule that quickly led to the establishment of democratic institutions (Madsen 2012).

The occupation regime therefore has two quite different cost-effective means of inhibiting native resistance.[13] It can do so by increasing its legitimacy, but this is a highly costly strategy. Alternatively, as will be discussed further, it can employ the much less costly strategy of fomenting social divisions in native society by systematically favoring one set of social groups over others.

Alien rulers' choice of a governing strategy largely hinges on the incentives that they face. Since *divide et impera* is a much less costly strategy than legitimation, this accounts for its greater prevalence. Yet given the appropriate incentives, alien rulers can be motivated to provide fair and effective governance – and, hence, to earn some measure of legitimacy. Alien rulers can be motivated to provide fair and effective governance when they impose rule on native territory to augment their own security (for which they are prepared to incur some cost) or when they share in the profits of increased trade and commercial activity (Chapter 2).

Microanalysis

All forms of alien rule pose a serious governance dilemma. To adequately govern the territory, a state and civil apparatus of roughly similar size to the previous regime must be established. Police have to be hired, electricity and water must be provided, roads must be repaired, hospitals have to be administered, public transport must be maintained, and judges have to be appointed to resolve disputes. Even in the unlikely event that an adequate supply of labor existed in

[12] Unfortunately, this study does not empirically disentangle the effects of collective goods provision from coercion as the cause of successful occupation. It is also possible that alien rulers put more resources into nation building into countries where they expect to succeed.

[13] The key modifier in this statement is "cost effective." Native resistance to occupation can always be tamped down by coercion, but this strategy is anything but cost effective.

the occupying country, the costs of creating such an administration de novo are simply astronomical. Large numbers of officials and workers would have to be imported, and these new arrivals would also have to be bilingual. Small wonder, then, that alien rulers' first imperative is to minimize their administrative costs. In practical terms, this means that they must obtain the services of native workers and officials who are willing to collaborate with the occupying regime by continuing to man their jobs.[14]

Similar to all behavior that is deemed to be deviant, not to say unpatriotic in the extreme, the rate of collaboration with occupying regimes is seriously underreported in national historiography and media. Marcel Ophuls' film *The Sorrow and the Pity* (1969), which documented extensive French collaboration with the Nazis during World War II, was kept off French television for twelve years after its debut. Likewise, it took an American historian, Robert Paxton (1972), to provide the first analysis of the depth of French collaboration under German occupation.

At the same time, collaboration is as ancient as alien rule. According to the book of Joshua, when the Hebrews were encamped outside of Jericho, Joshua sent two spies to assess the military strength of the city. The spies found a refuge in the house of the prostitute, Rahab. When soldiers of the city guard came to look for them, she hid them under bundles of flax on the roof. After escaping, the spies promised to spare Rahab and her family after taking the city if she would mark her house by hanging a red cord out the window.[15] Rahab told the spies (Joshua 2: 9–13),

I know that the LORD has given this land to you and that a great fear of you has fallen on us, so that all who live in this country are melting in fear because of you. We have heard how the LORD dried up the water of the Red Sea for you when you came out of Egypt, and what you did to Sihon and Og, the two kings of the Amorites east of the Jordan, whom you completely destroyed. When we heard of it, our hearts melted and everyone's courage failed because of you, for the LORD your God is God in heaven above and on the earth below. Now then, please swear to me by the LORD that you will show kindness to my family, because I have shown kindness to you. Give me a sure sign that you will spare the lives of my father and mother, my brothers and sisters, and all who belong to them, and that you will save us from death.

Rahab may be celebrated in the Torah, but she would have been excoriated, if not killed outright, by her own people.

---

[14] Where they cannot find an ample supply of collaborators, the occupying power is compelled to resort to direct rule. Thus during Napoleonic occupation of Italy, "those parts of the peninsula where the grip of the centre on the periphery was weakest fell directly under Paris: Liguria, the Duchies of Parma, the Papal States, Tuscany and Piedmont. The French assumed direct responsibility for exactly those parts of the peninsula where their rule and the culture it rested upon would seem most alien, and where indigenous intermediaries would be hardest to find" (Broers 2003: 55).

[15] This may have been the origin of the designation of red-light districts.

In the face of such strong sanctions, why do natives ever collaborate with the occupier?[16] To some degree, the supply of collaborators is a function of the characteristics of native society – particularly the nature and degree of its social divisions. The greater these are, the more difficult it is to create a resistance coalition and the easier it is for the occupier to employ *divide et impera*. Beyond their service to native residents, collaborators can help legitimize the occupation if they are influential in their communities. In this way, each influential collaborator has a multiplier effect on the process of legitimation – and, by implication, on diminishing the prospect of resistance. In general, the larger the proportion of collaborators, the smaller the potential resistance (for some supportive experimental evidence, see Yoon and Thye 2011).

What counts as collaboration? The question is tricky because it relies on motivational issues that are notoriously difficult to discern. Two broad types of collaboration have been distinguished: *collaborationism*, which is based on an ideological identification with the occupier, and *state collaboration*, a pragmatic decision to work with the occupier so as to maintain social order and a working economy (Hoffmann 1968).[17] This dichotomy leaves out a third important reason individuals collaborate: because it is in their self-interest to do so. For the purposes of this chapter, collaboration can be loosely defined as any kind of help *willingly* provided by the local population to an occupying power, and it is best understood in contrast to resistance to that same power.[18]

Recent research has pointed to a diverse mix of motivations for collaboration. The stronger the inducements the occupier offers, the greater its chances to recruit collaborators. Likewise, to the degree that an occupier raises the costs of compliance – for example, by enacting policies of forced labor, as the Nazis did throughout occupied Europe – the easier it is for the resistance to recruit followers. Thus, the Nazis' adoption of forced labor dragnets led many Frenchmen to join the resistance, an option that they had not previously considered (Kedward 1993: 190). Conversely, if a resistance movement can offer more compelling inducements, it will be able to outbid the occupier. Some of

---

[16] Because collaborators link two different social networks, they may usefully be compared with brokers. Whereas brokers in corporations and in the real estate, theatrical, and entertainment markets provide goods to both parties and thereby reap substantial rewards (Burt 1992, 2004), this is not true of collaborators. Similar to brokers, collaborators are rewarded for their efforts – at least during the occupation. Unlike brokers, however, they are simultaneously likely to be looked down on by their masters and hated by their fellow nationals.

[17] An example of state collaboration is when government bureaucrats and firms continue to serve the occupying regime.

[18] This definition excludes forms of passive collaboration such as sexual liaisons between native women and occupying troops. Between 1943 and 1946, 20,000 French women who were accused of such liaisons had their heads shaved and were subjected to public humiliation (Virgili 2002). (See the photographs in this chapter.) The roughly 200,000 children that were the issue of such liaisons (known in France as *les enfants Boches*) were often treated badly by their neighbors. If, however, someone trades a piece of critical information to the occupier in return for food or lingerie, this constitutes active collaboration.

the conditions affecting the rate of collaboration are national in scope, whereas others are more purely local.

An Example: Palestinian Collaboration with Israel in the Occupied Territories

From 1987 to 1993 Israeli security forces recruited tens of thousands of Palestinians from the occupied territories of the West Bank and Gaza as collaborators.[19] The Israeli Human Rights Group B'Tselem produced a detailed report on collaboration in 1994.[20] The primary reason the government employed collaborators was to gather intelligence information about resistance activity.[21]

The first thing to note is that the definition of collaboration is very much in the eyes of the beholder. Whereas Israel limits the definition of Palestinian collaborators to those who work for the various security agencies operating in the territories, Palestinians employ a much broader definition – including those whose actions are perceived to have a pernicious effect on Palestinian society (including criminals, prostitutes, and women engaging in extramarital sex). For the Palestinian resistance the most egregious form of collaboration is land dealing.

In occupation, basic social conventions are often turned upside down. Because the Israeli occupation of the territories is largely viewed as illegitimate by Palestinians, social order came to be perceived as being in Israel's interest, and the judicial system as a tool to impose Israel's will. Law violation and disrespect for authority thus acquire an aura of patriotism. To combat this resistance, Israeli authorities set up a network of agents among the Palestinian population. What motivated Palestinians to collaborate with these authorities?

The collective goods, or services, that the occupation authorities are required to supply to subjects are generally not provided as *entitlements*, but instead are awarded in a *discretionary* manner such that they can be revoked. In this way, access to goods and services is often granted as a favor in exchange for information.[22] For instance, during this period the Israeli authorities required permits for family reunification, to have one's relatives from abroad enter the area, or to travel abroad. Likewise, permits were also necessary to work in Israel, to obtain a driver's license, and to build a house. In addition, the regime also promised individuals accused of criminal offenses lighter sentences or better

---

[19] For an analysis of the Israeli occupation and how its goals have changed over time, see Gordon (2008).

[20] I am grateful to Yoav Peled for supplying me with a copy of this report.

[21] This implies that the Israelis never took seriously the notion that Palestinian collaborators could ever help legitimate their occupation.

[22] In 1967, Moshe Dayan, then Israel's minister of defense, said "Let the individual know that he has something to lose. His home can be blown up, his bus license can be taken away, he can be deported from the region; or the contrary: he can exist with dignity, make money, exploit other Arabs, and travel in [his] bus" (B'Tselem 1994: 12).

1. A member of the Belgian resistance paints a swastika on the forehead of a woman who collaborated with the Germans during the occupation of Belgium. The resistance shaved her head and the heads of four other women in Lanaken as part of their public humiliation.

conditions for their collaboration (B'Tselem 1994: 12–16). Sexual blackmail is another strategy that can motivate collaboration, although there was little evidence of its use among the Palestinians.

For their part, the authorities seek out individuals who have economic, social, family, mental, or other problems, offering them assistance in return for their collaboration. A former general security services (GSS, or Shin Bet) agent discussed recruitment methods:

You don't just take people off the street. The first thing is that you look for people from inside the [Palestinian] organizations. You try to recruit people who are involved in activity. Let's say there is a group of twenty people. From them we look for the people who have a good motive for enlisting. For example, a bad economic situation, family reunification, need for help, for assistance, cutting a prison term ... the need for medical treatment is a good motive. You have to understand that today it is extremely difficult to recruit agents, and the [GSS] invests tremendous resources in this. (B'Tselem 1994: 16–17)[23]

---

[23] There is something general in this account; it would not be terribly out of place in Caro's (2003) analysis of the means by which Lyndon Johnson attained power in the U.S. Senate.

11. A member of the French resistance publicly shears the hair of a woman who consorted with the Germans during the occupation.

The occupying authorities often turned a blind eye to the human rights violations committed by collaborators against their co-nationals. Israelis often gave weapons to some of these collaborators (ostensibly for their own protection), but frequently the collaborators used the weapons to enrich themselves by offering to act as intermediaries with the authorities. For example, residents who needed permits from the authorities paid large amounts of money to collaborators to act on their behalf as lobbyists with the occupation authorities.[24] These intermediaries thus compensated for the occupying power's poor provision of collective goods by engaging in corruption. Most were open about their collaboration. The authorities allowed the intermediaries to profit from these transactions as a reward for their collaboration. Because most collaborators

[24] Thus a collaborator in Jaffa explained why he became an informer for the Israelis: "I was young. I was attracted by the idea of having power and status and earning fast, easy money. I liked walking around with a concealed weapon, getting through [Israel Defence Forces, or IDF] roadblocks with no problems, dispensing favors, especially permits to whoever I wanted" (B'Tselem 1994: 13).

III. Civilians and members of the French resistance lead a female collaborator through the streets of Rennes after her head was shaven and covered with iodine.

were not salaried, the occupying power was provided information at minimal expense.[25] The more the authorities placed obstacles to the granting of permits and services, the greater the demand for intermediaries.

Some Palestinians also collaborate willingly, out of a desire to contribute to their community. A thirty-eight-year-old collaborator explains how he was recruited at the age of sixteen:

One day, on my way back from work in Netanyah, I found two rifle magazines and a helmet that had apparently fallen from a military vehicle. The following day I brought the objects to the police. The police officer thanked me and said that if I ever needed help, I shouldn't hesitate to call on them. Until then I hadn't known anything about spying, the GSS, *Mossad*. A few months later the village *mukhtar*, from my *hamulah*

---

[25] This also holds for the treatment of collaborators who have been settled in Israel. Rather than being rewarded amply for their service to the state, most of these collaborators are treated poorly (B'Tselem 1994: 133). This is reminiscent of the American government's relatively poor treatment of translators during the recent occupation of Iraq; perhaps there is something universal in this reluctance to adequately acknowledge individuals who occupy a dishonorable role, even if they are allies.

iv. Belgian women who had collaborated with the Germans are shaved, tarred, and feathered and forced to give a Nazi salute.

(clan), passed away. People from the *humulah* turned to me because they saw that a relationship had developed between me and the authorities. They asked that I try to pressure the authorities. I did, and they told me not to worry, and that everything would be alright. One day I saw a police vehicle parked by the house of the new *mukhtar*. I entered the house and met two Israelis inside. They explained to me that although they had a police patrol car, they were not from the police but from the GSS. After we spoke a bit, they told me that I looked like a good guy, and that if I needed any help, I should go to them. But already by the next day two GSS agents showed up at my place and spoke with me about collaboration. After a few more meetings I began to work.... Sometimes recruitment is arranged through means that [the recruiters promise] serve the interests of the Palestinian people. They say to them: "We have a budget of one million dollars," and offer that the person "help" them to "distribute the money." In this manner they lead them to believe that they are operating for the good of the Palestinian people. (B'Tselem 1994: 16)

The Palestinian nationalist movement targets individuals it deems to be collaborators, frequently executing them. Often this results in killing individuals as a result of grudges or other private motives unrelated to their actual anti-nationalist activity. For instance, many women are targeted and killed on account of ostensibly immoral behavior and purported assaults on family honor. Thus, the nature of the occupation regime provides great latitude for corruption and disorder among the occupied population.

v. Women accused of collaborating with the Nazis are publicly humiliated by having their heads forcibly shaved after the war in either France or Belgium.

Societal Characteristics

The first impression one has of military occupation is that it pits the alien ruler against the native society *tout court*. A native society will unite into a solidary brotherhood dedicated to resistance when a foreign ruler comes on the scene. Although this kind of scenario indeed may occur, it is far from universal. It depends, in good part, on a variety of characteristics of the native society.

To the degree that the native society is rent with social divisions – by class, ethnicity, nationality, religion, and language among others – this will blunt its capacity to engage in any kind of collective action, let alone resistance.[26] On the one hand, bureaucrats may reckon (with some justification) that their patriotic duty lies with continuing to supply electricity, water, education, mass transit, sanitation, public health, dispute resolution, and other collective goods to

---

[26] During the Napoleonic occupation of Western Europe, indirect rule was only successful in larger territories if there was a correct balance between social cohesion and social disorganization. "Too much social cohesion – the Tyrol springs to mind – might encourage a generally hostile environment in which no potential conciliators or collaborators might come forward. A lack of social cohesion – Spain is an obvious example – in contrast might result in the absence of patron-client relationships; in such an environment, the French might attract local collaborators, only to find they were not attached to anything. In parts of Italy, in contrast, a degree of social disharmony – for example, urban-rural conflict in Tuscany – ensured that an important constituency backed Napoleonic rule" (Rowe 2003: 13).

their compatriots. On the other, the occupier may provide some groups with a counterbalance to an even more hateful internal enemy. Thus Protestants welcomed the Dutch *stadtholder* William of Orange to the English throne in 1688 to thwart the political ambitions of their Catholic rivals for power. This illustrates that the occupier-collaborator relationship may be between two principals (rather than between a principal and an agent), each having their own agendas (Kalyvas 2008b). Moreover, collaborators are not necessarily unpatriotic nor do they necessarily support the occupier's agenda. Thus occupiers and, at least some natives, have certain common interests that make collaboration mutually beneficial. When one of the parties in this relationship ceases to benefit from it, collaboration will likely cease.[27]

An occupier who is aware of preexisting ideological, political, social, or ethnic cleavages in native territory and takes advantage of them will be more likely to succeed. In Arab Palestine under the British Mandate, two leading camps had formed whose rivalry was rooted in social and political structures dating from Ottoman period (Cohen 2008: 7). Whereas the Palestinian nationalists (the Husseini camp) hoped to liberate the country from the British and Zionists, the Arab opposition (including the Nashashibi and the Abu-Gosh families) allied themselves with both of these alien forces. Needless to say, the Zionists took full advantage of this cleavage within Palestinian society.[28] Nazi Germany also profited from the social divisions of many of the countries it invaded (Mazower 2008: 8). Many of the countries in Central and Eastern Europe were newly established and characterized by deep social cleavages that inspired internecine clashes once war broke out. As the French case indicates, however, even relatively nationally integrated societies can be torn asunder in the face of occupation.[29]

---

[27] Other collaboration examples are more difficult to consider as a principal-principal relationship. General Nedić's collaborationist administration in Serbia (May 1941 – October 1944) pursued its own goals: to have Serbia "become an equal member of the 'New European Order' dominated by the Nazis" (Ristović 2008: 186), and to more precisely reorganize Serbian society "on the basis of the long tradition of rural extended family communities, traditional values of rural life and preserved traditional morals." But Nedić so openly and thoroughly embraced Nazi principles and policies that he can perfectly be said to have been a Nazi agent in Serbia – Ristović (2008: 188) characterizes Nedić's administration as the German occupier's "product and instrument." Baranova (2008: 123) argues that both "collaboration and resistance are occupier-driven phenomena: the population of [Nazi-]occupied countries did not formulate its attitude and behaviour towards the Germans spontaneously but, rather, reacted to the comportment of the occupation authorities." This does not contradict Kalyvas's argument about the possibility of principal-principal relationships. That many occupied populations decided to collaborate reactively (as a response to a particular occupation) does not make them agents of the occupier; they can still have their own agenda.

[28] Fast-forwarding to the present day, the Israeli intelligence service, Shin Bet, is engaged in a comprehensive strategy to develop Palestinian collaborators within the Gaza Strip who will provide information about Hamas' military capacities (Barthe 2009).

[29] "Had the country not been so bitterly divided when it was invaded, the occupation would probably have taken a very different course.... In fact, many French welcomed the collapse of

Collaboration can also emanate from more idiosyncratic roots. At the ground level the alien ruler tends to be seen as one of the actors in a microcosm rather than as a key player in the national struggle (Kalyvas 2008a: 111). Most individuals live the conflict (and help produce its outcomes) only from a local perspective, primarily taking into account survival considerations and opportunities for private benefit that mostly determine whether collaboration takes place (Kalyvas 2006: 12; Cohen 2008: 236).[30] Thus, many Chinese collaborators with the Japanese administration in Shanghai saw their recruitment by the new occupation administration as "getting their job back" (Brook 7: 170), whereas other examples – such as Belorussian collaboration with the Nazis to obtain confiscated Jewish property (Baranova 2008: 120) – are easier to classify as the consequence of economic opportunism. One of the leading collaborators in Japanese-occupied Nanjing, "Jimmy" Wang, is reported to have said that the Japanese occupation was "such a good opportunity to make a fortune" (Brook 7: 155). Likewise, after World War II, Eastern Germans enjoyed the opportunity to materially advance in the Soviet-occupied area: the Soviets staffed the zonal administration with German communists, but for less ideologically committed Germans "loyalty could be ensured by material inducements or by blackmail" (Seton-Watson 1984: 10).

Another example is provided by Palestinian collaboration with Zionism before the establishment of the Israeli state. In this period Arabs had ample opportunity to reap private benefits by selling their lands to Jewish settlers. These purely material considerations often trumped ideology: the willingness of Arabs to sell land and arms to Jews increased in tandem with Jewish immigration to Palestine. This occurred despite the nationalist movement's strictures against such trafficking. In 1929, the Arab Executive Committee called on Arabs to boycott Jewish stores and products, but this prohibition was increasingly ignored by the Arab merchants, who needed Jewish-produced merchandise and who therefore violated the ban (Cohen 2008: 40–41).

When the local population must decide whether to collaborate with the occupier, another factor that trumps ideology is actual control on the ground – that is, the degree to which a given group is able to establish exclusive rule on

---

parliamentary democracy and saw occupation as the chance to settle scores with the left that went back decades" (Mazower 2008: 417); they saw German domination as the price that had to be paid for restoring France to greatness (see also Ermakoff 2008).

[30] One must "go below the superstructure of ideology by which every state justifies its existence and look instead at what went on down at the most local level of the occupation state. It is plausible that collaboration there, in country towns on the Yangtze Delta, involved the considerations of national honor and personal integrity that haunted politicians of the new regime; but most of the time ... collaboration dealt with more mundane problems – supplying food, organizing transportation, arranging security – the sorts of matters that local elites and local officials have to solve under any political dispensation to ensure social reproduction and to maintain themselves in power" (Brook 2007: 12).

a territory (Kalyvas 2000: 152–153; 2006: 111). Thus, the higher its control, the greater the extent of native collaboration. For instance, Brook (2007: 7–8) found that as the Japanese army consolidated its control across the Chinese Yangtze Delta in the spring of 1938, the incentives to cooperate with the new rulers increased.

One of the few quantitative analyses of collaboration concerns Greece in the later stages of World War II when Germany was already losing the war; 20,000 to 30,000 men are estimated to have fought on the German side against fellow Greeks (Kalyvas 2008b). In the southern territory of the Argolid, standard economic, social, and political variables had no capacity to predict levels of collaboration. Instead, the key determinants were violence that was perpetrated by the Communist-led National Liberation Front (EAM) in the period preceding recruitment of armed collaborators[31] and the degree of German control over particular regions. These findings suggest that the principal motives for collaboration in the Argolid were the desire to wreak revenge for previous victimization at the hands of the resistance movement and the opportunity to take advantage of incentives that the Germans could mete out in the territories in which they exercised full control.

As discussed, native elites play a vital role in the reaction to occupation. Those who confer their allegiance on the occupiers can help legitimate the regime, whereas rebellious elites are likely to mobilize popular resistance. This is revealed by a comparison of popular reactions to the Japanese occupation of Taiwan and Korea. Hell hath no fury like a native authority scorned by an occupying regime (Petersen 2002; see also Ricks 2006 on the Sunni reaction to the American occupation of Iraq).

Exogenous Factors

The preceding analysis concentrated on determinants located within the boundaries of native society. However, two exogenous factors, in particular, also contribute to the likelihood of resistance. The first has to do with the occupiers' wartime prospects. The idea here is simple. As an occupying power finds itself losing the war, it is compelled to extract more resources – including manpower – from the native society. When the Nazis' resources began to be sapped by their losses in a two-front war, they instituted forced labor even in the most favored occupied lands, such as the Channel Islands (Bunting 1995). This increases the burden of the occupation and, therefore, the prospects for resistance. Losses in war not only affect resources but also attitudes. Postwar expectations regarding who will ultimately win and the political scenarios that this will bring are also important determinants of collaboration. After all, the Germans took control of Europe so swiftly and ruthlessly that it was easy for

---

[31] Presumably this violence stimulated resentment against the resistance. For similar conclusions about the sources of Palestinian collaboration with Zionists, see Cohen (2008: 151–152).

both sides to imagine that Nazi rule was there to stay. That sense of inevitability disappeared once the tides of war turned (Liberman 1996: 24).[32]

During the Arab Rebellion in Palestine of 1936–1939, expectations of a final Jewish victory affected the willingness to collaborate: "[S]ome of [the collaborators] assumed that the Jews, with British assistance, would be able to subdue the [Arab Palestinian] rebellion and that it would be best to support the winning side from the start" (Cohen 2008: 115). Similarly, one of the main goals of the Japanese "pacification teams" when they were sent to newly conquered locations in the Yangtze Delta (China) in 1937 was to "convince collaborators and noncollaborators alike that Japan would succeed in its project to control China, and that this control was in China's long-term interests" (Brook 2007: 62). They expected to reassure those who had already been collaborating with the Japanese army during the armed conflict and hopefully to convert some non-collaborators as well.

The second exogenous determinant is external support for the resistance. To the degree that the resistance is afforded territory for sanctuary, or more directly funds and arms, its prospects improve. Successful insurgent movements tend to have access to such external support.[33] One of the most impressive examples was the U.S. Central Intelligence Agency's covert support to the Islamic resistance against the Soviet-imposed government of Afghanistan in the 1980s. The CIA poured over $1 billion to fund the *mujahedeen* – the largest covert action ever undertaken (Crile 2007). External support is often a critical factor in all types of insurgency. Most recently, a prominent New York hedge fund billionaire, Raj Rajaratnam, founder of Galleon Group, has been accused of being one of a number of wealthy Sri Lankans in the United States whose donations to a Maryland-based charity were channeled instead to the Liberation Tigers of Tamil Eelam, the Tamil nationalist insurgency (Perez and

---

[32] During the Franco-Belgian occupation of Germany's industrial Ruhr Valley after World War I, France denied any intentions of annexing the region. Hence, the local population knew that eventually sovereignty would be returned to Germany. "Potential collaborators … had more to fear from German prisons than French ones, and therefore German collaboration with the Franco-Belgian occupiers was low – at least until starvation became an issue in fall 1923" (Liberman 1996: 96). Likewise, "The wave of resistance that swept Nazi-occupied Europe on the eve of the Allied landings reflected the fact that the odds-on, imminent Allied campaign diminished the likelihood of German reprisals and increased the chances that resistance might have an impact" (Liberman 1996; 149). The perception that the Nazis were losing ground in Belarus offers another example from World War II: "During the spring and summer of 1942, the German advance came to a standstill and the Red Army managed to regain the initiative and returned to the attack. The population feared allying with the losing side and often sought to join the stronger one. German victory was no longer sure and previous experiences of Soviet rule suggested that there would be retributions for collaborating with the invaders. Therefore, by the end of 1942, to be seen as not compliant with the Germans became increasingly important for many civilians" (Baranova 2008: 124).

[33] See, for instance, the secret agent's pocket manual that the Allies provided to members of the European resistance movements during the Nazi occupation (Bull 2009).

Bellman 2009). Eight people pleaded guilty to attempting to provide material support to the organization, which was designated as terrorist by the United States. Ostensibly collecting money for the victims of the tsunami, the charity instead funneled support to the Tamil Tigers. Groups from the Irish Republican Army to Al Qaeda and the Taliban likewise have profited handsomely from external funding sources.

Conclusion

Resistance to failed occupations and collaboration in military occupations are social phenomena that are intrinsically difficult to study. Nationalist historians and journalists are apt to exaggerate the prevalence of the former and under-state that of the latter. For this reason, if no other, evidence about resistance and collaboration is elusive. In spite of this, there is an impressive consistency of findings from a variety of historical case studies conducted in widely vary-ing societies. This enables us to provide two tentative models, one of resis-tance and one of collaboration. The first concentrates on the macroscopic level (Figure 5.1) and proposes that resistance is a function of the characteristics of the regime, the native society, the mediating factor of legitimacy, and exoge-nous factors (namely, the occupiers' wartime prospects and external support for the resistance). Since no quantitative studies exist to provide indicators of all of these kinds of elements, the relative importance of these causes of resis-tance to occupation cannot be estimated at this time.

The second model concentrates on the microscopic level and suggests that the rate of collaboration is a function of the natives' dependence on the occu-pier for access to private goods, relative to the native community (Figure 5.2). The greater the net benefits provided by the occupier to the native commu-nity, the greater the probability of collaboration.[34] Conversely, the greater the net benefits provided by native organizations, the less the probability of collaboration.

Some of the determinants of the occupier's capacity to provide private ben-efits include their understanding of the relationship of effective and fair gov-ernance to the attainment of legitimacy,[35] their fortunes in war, and the degree of their internal political support (this hampered the American occupation of

---

[34] Louis Malle's superb movie *Lacombe, Lucien* (1974) provides a graphic illustration of this point. Lucien Lacombe, a bored teenager living in a rural village in unoccupied France, attempts to join the resistance to provide some spice to his life, but they rebuff him. He then turns right around and approaches the Vichy authorities, who welcome him with open arms.

[35] The American experience in Iraq is especially instructive. After the invasion the United States pursued a counterterrorism strategy aimed to defeat the resistance. Although this strategy was a spectacular failure, it was maintained for years. The relatively successful surge strategy was based on a different theory – namely, counterinsurgency theory – which aimed to protect native society against the insurgents and to provide them with collective goods (Ricks 2009).

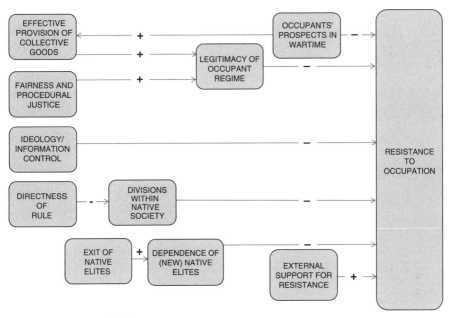

FIGURE 5.1 A model of resistance to occupation.

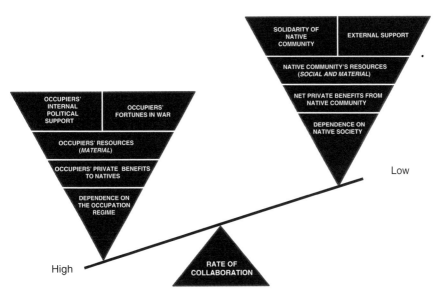

FIGURE 5.2 A microlevel model of collaboration.

Vietnam). The determinants of dependence on the native community include its degree of solidarity (Hechter 1987) and the aforementioned external support.

These models are clearly incomplete and should be amended in subsequent research. Nevertheless they offer a starting point for more systematic analyses of military occupation to be carried out in the future.

6

Academic Receivership as Alien Rule

By Gail Dubrow and Debra Friedman

> *Self-government is better than good government.*
> — *Sir Henry Campbell-Bannerman*

Academic receivership – a relatively rare event in which a departmental chair is imposed from the outside by a dean or provost when the department is judged unable to govern itself effectively – is an instance of alien rule within the academy. In one of the few articles on the subject, Charlotte Allen (1998) wrote, "Receivership may be academe's dirtiest word ... receivership is a shameful secret, a dark blot on academic reputation and institutional self-image" – strong words indeed to describe instances in which an anthropology department is chaired by a historian and a literature department chaired by a linguist. This chapter explores what makes an academic leader alien, the conditions that may increase the probability that outsiders are chosen to lead academic departments, why disciplinary affinity might matter, the possible reasons for faculty preferences for leaders of "one's own kind," and what motivates alien rulers to accept the mantle of leadership.

As with nationalism, in which grievances are given voice in nationalist terms principally under conditions of alien rule (Hechter 2000), academic receivership may turn the universal language of academic grievances into something with a distinctly disciplinary tone. Yet as with nationalism, the veneer may also represent something with deep meaning, and it is that which the analysis seeks to understand.

It is important to note that there are no systematic data on receivership and few analytic treatments. Tammy Stone's article on academic receivership, which arises out of a broader interest in factionalism and alliance formation in small-scale societies, provides some evidence from assistant and associate deans in U.S. colleges of arts and sciences (Stone 2009). Here, evidence has been drawn from journalistic accounts, mostly in local (campus) sources, and some, in places such as the now defunct magazine, *Lingua Franca*. Using the power of Internet search engines, scores of internal university documents have been identified from faculty senate and academic council meeting minutes to personal faculty blogs. These scattered reports have been augmented with in-depth interviews with three colleagues who have served as chairs of departments other than their own – namely, who have served as alien rulers. Anecdotes have also been gathered, but not in any systematic fashion.

The Risk of Receivership

What marks an academic department as ripe for receivership? In casual, journalistic accounts, the story line follows a certain progression: first, the department is marked by strife that permeates faculty relationships,[1] and second, the faculty can no longer agree on whom to hire, tenure, or select as chair. This infighting leads to poorly managed tenure and promotion cases and squandered opportunities. Soon, the faculty collectively find themselves unable to come to consensus on any matters at all, including programs beneficial to students. The fights become increasingly bitter and divisive and, perhaps more importantly, publicly visible. In response, the dean or provost becomes fed up and appoints a leader whom he or she trusts from outside the unit. With the appointment of an alien chair, the relative balance of power and authority shifts with respect to key decisions and control over resources, including faculty positions.

The first chapters of this story, however, should seem quite familiar to faculty in any academic department: strife among faculty and disputes about the value of different kinds of work are quite common. Yet receivership is rare. Therefore there must be distinctive characteristics of a department or unusual precipitating conditions that propel a department from merely difficult and ineffective – as well as a thorn in the side of the dean – to a candidate for receivership.[2]

---

[1] Not all examples of alien rule are marked by strife. In occasional instances, a department with a largely junior faculty may intentionally seek an outside chair, a kind of alien rule without receivership.

[2] Although the threat usually remains latent, some programs slated for receivership have come perilously close to being targeted for elimination. Receivership is intended by administrators as a final opportunity for the faculty to get its act together or risk more serious consequences of merger or program closure. At the University of Tennessee, lessons learned from the School of Planning's close call with elimination read like an advice manual for avoiding receivership: "don't let internal tensions affect the efficacy of the degree program, student recruitment or other key matters.... If the program is under threat, try to work out your differences within the institution" (Gale 2001: 6). Work hard to foster a constructive dialogue with administration, rather than relying on confrontation and political end runs that undermine good faith efforts to solve problems. In his study of threats to planning programs' existence, Dennis Gale (2001: 10) concluded that the most important strategy for preventing program elimination "is through communicating, on an ongoing basis, the program's contributions and value to its various constituencies."

Departmental Characteristics

Although the information about receivership is spotty, one differentiating condition between those departments that have been marked for receivership and those that have not is type of field. There is no comprehensive list of instances of receivership, but some kinds of departments repeatedly appear, such as English and political science, whereas others, such as chemistry or physics, appear rarely.[3] Hints about what puts a department at risk of receivership are in this observation.[4]

The first characteristic is that departments vulnerable to receivership are marked by contested disciplinary identities or transcend customary divisional structures (e.g., humanities or social sciences). In some cases, they are – as in the case of American ethnic studies or women studies – departments that are not rooted in a single discipline at all. In other cases, the departments embody disciplines that are undergoing dramatic changes in definition, as in anthropology or English. In these fields, the scope of study and intellectual paradigms are hotly contested. The boundaries of departmental identity are set by neither internal norms nor external ones.

Consider the case of the anthropology department at Columbia University. Their departmental strife mirrored a shift in the field from a classic conception of the ideal anthropologist, a generalist knowledgeable about multiple subfields, to a modernist conception in which the ideal anthropologist was one who specialized (Allen 1998). Disciplinary redefinition can also lead departments to incorporate an expansive array of subfields, such as large English departments with "folklore, ESL, composition and rhetoric, cinema studies, traditional literary criticism, creative writing, theory, and so on" (Edwards 1999: 19). Given the uncertainty that accompanies this level of diversity in intellectual interests, decisions that are routinely made by departmental faculties – the requirements for degrees, promotion criteria, and hiring priorities principal among them – become problematic in these unwieldy, heterodox entities and can lead to ideologically charged debates and unpredictable outcomes.

The second characteristic of departments at risk for receivership is that they have become misaligned with university priorities. Almost any change in

[3] We know, for example, that the Indiana State University's Department of Physics was put into receivership during the 2001–2002 academic year and filed a grievance through the Faculty Senate, and the receivership was rescinded. See the ISU Faculty Senate's December 13, 2001, minutes: http://www.indstate.edu/facsenate/d/fs/minaby2001dec_13.htm.

[4] It appears that reconfiguration and merger in the sciences may be more common than receivership, although this is difficult to substantiate. In the biological sciences, for instance, there are two contrasting cases. At the University of Washington, botany, zoology, and the undergraduate program in biology merged voluntarily, and a chair was selected from the former zoology department. At Berkeley, however, the chancellor, "on the recommendation of the University's leading biologists, put all of the biology departments at Berkeley into a kind of receivership under the authority of the Advisory Council – a condition in which the departments no longer have the ordinary degree of control" (Trow 1999: 10).

university-level strategic priorities, whether it is in research or education, can unleash confusion or backlash at the departmental level. A department that is clear about its direction, however, typically can find a way to articulate its contribution to the broader institutional agenda. Not so for a department lacking leadership and a clear intellectual or professional identity. For example, if a university declares that undergraduate education must become more responsive to students and more efficient, departments have multiple ways to respond. They might develop new, innovative programs to attract top students, streamline major requirements to shorten time to degree, or mount large classes to increase access. These require some degree of faculty collective action and, possibly, individual sacrifice to benefit the common good, which, in turn, requires some degree of group solidarity. Other departments might argue effectively that they should be treated as an exception (e.g., music performance should not be held to general efficiency standards) or that they have a paradigm that is an effective and innovative alternative to whatever is being proposed institutionally (e.g., architectural design education as a model of student-centered inquiry). A department that cannot pull itself together to respond to new challenges not only may bear the consequences internally, but its inability to respond also may come to the attention of the next level of administration as an unwelcome instance of failure to respond. Those units that appear to resist institutional mandates lose standing in the resource allocation process and increase their vulnerability to receivership.

A third characteristic is connected to academic quality. Departments with long histories of excellence, faced with new disciplinary and/or institutional requirements, seem particularly challenged in responding. They may be loath to change what has been an instrumental ingredient in their past recipe for excellence, fearing that to do so would undermine the basis of their reputation. Or the new demands may upset a delicate political balance that was critical to harmonious relations, hence to collective decision making. Other members of such departments, sensitive to external shifts, convinced of the inevitability of change, and able to see an alternative future of excellence, may challenge the more conservative views of their colleagues, leading to an internal battle. This faction might well (secretly) welcome alien rule, having been a latent and silenced minority group prior to the imposition of alien rule and the entry of the department into receivership. An administrative decision to empower a new faction within a department, intended to bring the unit into alignment with strategic objectives at the institutional level, typically exacerbates internal tensions on the way to transformation.

Another variation on the relationship between quality and vulnerability to receivership results from a weak department faced with a new set of disciplinary and/or institutional requirements. These departments, although weak, are often marked by a relatively high degree of internal consensus. This consensus is akin to that of workers who agree on a slower rate of work than management desires of them. When pressures from the outside threaten to disrupt internal norms, for example, around issues of teaching loads or research productivity, collegiality may break down for the same kinds of reasons as in a top department. Whereas some members of the department certainly will defend local customs, other faculty are likely to recognize that the status quo will not do and move for change, and in so doing, end up in an alliance with higher administration. In fact, some are likely to recognize that their own personal productivity will be rewarded by the administration and resent that their colleagues' lower standards are undermining the status of the department and are obstructing its access to institutional resources. These differences often lead to a split among faculty in their alignment with and resistance to externally imposed leadership.

A fourth characteristic arises from isolation of a department, either from other units in the same university, or its own discipline. Isolation creates insularity; insularity separates units from the sorts of evolutionary changes that are typically absorbed in a more gradual fashion by better-connected departments. When a new subfield arises, faculties connected to a larger disciplinary world match existing strengths to external opportunities. They can also quickly mobilize to recruit faculty trained in emerging areas. Or when a university administration calls for proposals for innovation in curriculum or other areas, connected departments are usually at the ready to compete for resources, often in partnership with other units. This is not so with isolated departments or those suffering from paralyzing factionalism.

These are some of the necessary but insufficient conditions that mark departments as candidates for receivership. These characteristics are not wholly independent of one another, and of course, departments that display more of these traits probably are at greater risk of having leadership imposed on them by administration. However, any observer of higher education will note that these characteristics are not unusual even in academically successful departments. As has been noted, receivership is rare. What, then, separates the departments that invite alien rule from those that do not?

Precipitating Conditions

Departments at risk of receivership greatly increase that risk by capturing the attention of higher administration. They do so when the characteristics noted morph from being private matters to public ones. In actual instances of receivership, there is almost always a precipitating condition, or several. For instance, a poorly managed tenure or promotion case often reveals to deans and provosts that the department is unable to do right by its members, particularly if it becomes clear that the fight over such a case owes more to internal departmental divisions than it does to the record of the professor under consideration.[5]

---

[5] Can alien rule of departments under receivership increase the legal vulnerability of institutions of higher education in negative tenure decisions? During Yale University Department of Philosophy's

This has a direct cause in the greater confusion over identity and separation from institutional norms characteristic of departments ripe for receivership that, in turn, increase the likelihood that the faculty will simply be unable to come to a consensus about the merits of an individual's case.

A similar logic applies with respect to hiring, and especially at the senior level. It is exceedingly difficult to recruit stars to a department known for its internal strife. Senior-level professors will have better alternatives. Should candidates choose to go through the search process, they are often in a position to share with deans their perspectives on a department, and why they choose not to accept an offer. This contributes to public awareness and administrative knowledge of issues formerly contained within the department. Departments at risk, therefore, typically are unable to hire their first or second choices at any level, but especially the senior level.

To illustrate, Columbia University's Department of English reportedly was one of the bloodiest battlegrounds in the annals of departmental dysfunction.[6] So polarized were faculty searches at ground zero in the culture wars that in 2002 only thirty-seven of forty-six tenure line faculty positions were filled. To break the ideological logjam, responsibility for faculty searches was turned over to five professors of English from peer institutions – an unusual approach to bridging the gap between native and alien rule in a department that effectively had been placed into receivership for the most significant decisions about its intellectual future.

Likewise, junior faculty with choices hesitate to accept appointments at a place where their colleagues simply cannot agree on what is important. Paired with evidence that existing junior faculty are poorly treated, the administration may consider themselves provoked into a stance, as at Notre Dame. After a series of searches for new junior faculty at Notre Dame were derailed by factional conflict between adherents of mainstream and alternative approaches to economics, the future of the Department of Economics became the focus of the university's academic council meetings.[7] Regime change – whether in the form of splitting the department into two separate units or placing the existing one into receivership – was regarded as the surest way to send a strong signal to the outside world that the institution would take appropriate measures to protect

period of receivership, junior faculty member Susan Neiman was denied tenure. She brought a lawsuit for breach of contract against Yale University based on the theory of unqualified evaluators. Under conditions of receivership, she argued, her case for promotion was entrusted to "a group of scholars who were not trained in her field and did not understand her work" (Allen 1998: n.p.). For more on this subject, see Allen's 1998 *Lingua Franca* article and Ann H. Franke and Lawrence White's paper, "Responsibilities of Department Chairs: Legal Issues" (2002: 11).

[6] See former University of Pennsylvania English department faculty member Erin O'Connor's March 17, 2002, *Critical Mass* blog post at http://www.erinoconnor.org/archives/2002/03/hot_off_the_pre.html. Accessed May 10, 2013.

[7] See Peter Monaghan's January 24, 2003, account of the conflict in the *Chronicle of Higher Education*, http://chronicle.com/article/Taking-On-Rational-Man/24901/

the careers of junior faculty, thus increasing the likelihood of recruiting the best and brightest in the field.

Failure to recruit over several seasons not only leads to squandered opportunities for new resources, but certainly captures the attention of a competent dean. A sure sign of a departmental power struggle is when multiple factions protest to the dean about procedural irregularities that undermine the legitimacy of the search process. Healthy units can usually agree on terms that allow them to hire, even if they do not always have consensus about who is the best candidate.

There are other precipitating conditions that attract negative attention to the internal workings of a department. Plummeting national ratings are a sure red flag. Consider the condition that brought the decade-long internal dissent in Yale's philosophy department to a head. A damning report released in September 1995 by the National Research Council "showed that Yale's doctoral program in philosophy had plummeted from eighteenth place in 1982 to fifty-ninth (tied with Michigan State) in 1992" (Zonderman 1995: n.p.). Efforts to reverse this decline and "put the department back together" were launched in earnest after several years of receivership, beginning with the appointment of a distinguished philosopher and capable administrator from the University of California, Los Angeles. Yet these efforts clearly were complicated by uncertainties of disciplinary definition, as the boundaries of philosophy reached beyond the canon to touch on a wide range of fields, from "psychoanalytic theory and medical ethics to computer science and international affairs," while tactical uncertainties remained about how best to rebuild the faculty, according to a report in the *Yale Alumni Magazine* (Zonderman 1995: n.p.).

Yet another precipitating condition can be an escalating conflict between a chair and a dean. Partisans of quantitative and qualitative approaches to political science at New York University, who had coexisted but "had never gotten along well" as a result of the differing value each camp assigned to the other's work, ended up in conflict with their dean over a proposed senior hire whose qualitative approach ended the era of departmental détente (Blecher 2002: n.p.). When a senior faculty member from the quantitative faction expressed concern to the dean, with whom he reportedly was close, and the dean intervened to show his displeasure with the proposed hire, relations with the sitting department chair deteriorated rapidly. Escalating conflict between the chair and dean led the department directly into receivership, which allowed the dean to rebuild the department in accordance with his preferences – namely, along quantitative lines.

Scandal – unaddressed sexual harassment, excessive or improper consulting, or textbook-kickback schemes – that engages numerous offices of the university in investigative activity also can bring a department into the limelight. Another is an ongoing financial deficit, a sign that the unit leader is unable to control spending and may be trying to buy peace from a restive faculty. All of these conditions raise the visibility of the department in negative ways and increase its vulnerability to receivership, particularly if the department chair is implicated in the problems directly or regarded as an ineffective manager.

One less obvious precipitating condition is student activism. When students are affected by internal strife, they are sometimes able to express their displeasure collectively. In itself, student activism around academic issues is quite rare and inspires scrutiny. Students are far more unfettered by fear of their individual fate should they protest than are faculty, which makes student collective action considerably more threatening to a department. Students – for whom the complicated academic hierarchy and university organization chart can be impenetrable – often choose to go directly to the president, and sometimes the governing board, bypassing chairs, deans, and provosts. At the University of Washington, for instance, students in the American ethnic studies department became deeply involved in the divisive battles of the faculty around core academic and governance issues. They engaged in protest focused, at least initially, on a disputed tenure case. By all accounts, their vocal and persistent activism, directed at the president of the university, is widely regarded as the key precipitating condition for the department's eventual receivership.

Instant public exposure ensues from this sort of student activism, and a president's inquiry to the relevant dean can inspire new plans for action or departmental leadership in the future. The demand for a plan of action can bring tensions to a head. What constitutes a plan of action? The president might want to know how the students' concerns will be met, which almost certainly ensures external scrutiny. The dean will want to know how a unit in the college has come to such a point and how it intends to right itself. Yet the very conditions that brought forth the student activism are those that make the likelihood of a measured and workable departmental response highly unlikely. Instead, the demand by a central administrator is more likely to lead to a highly defensive response than a proactive one. Isolated and contentious departments can become more entrenched in their battles – and now have a new battle to wage, as well – rather than provoked into positive change.

In this kind of situation, the departmental leader's capacity and suitability for leadership is called into question. What is the chair to say to the dean who asks why the department is unable to hire or promote, to spend resources appropriately, or to respond to student demands? The kind of implicit agreement that exists between a dean and departmental chair in which departments should be permitted, on the whole, to manage their own affairs according to the standards set by their faculty is called into question. Indeed, the strongly held norm of self-governance may be revealed to be entirely dependent on a minimum level of accommodation to central directives as well as basic leadership competence. As will be discussed, the standard methods for selecting departmental leadership, which rely on a high degree of consensus between academic administration and department faculty, essentially conspire against choosing strong leaders. For departments in distress, this increases the probability of alien rule under conditions of receivership.

Departmental Reactions

Just as the imposition of alien rule can coalesce nationalist sentiment, even among political actors with diverse allegiances and previously untapped bases for group solidarity, the imposition of alien rule in the context of academic receivership has its parallels institutionally. Faculty generally are opposed to and offended by the appointment of an outsider to head their unit, leading to a suppression of internal disagreements in response to an external threat to their autonomy. The news of such an appointment is rightly regarded as a signal of upper administrators' dissatisfaction with unit performance or operations. Alien rulers are generally regarded as more accountable to the administrators who chose them than to the faculty they serve. Furthermore, as outsiders their ability to understand local norms is suspect from the outset, not being "native speakers" of the language of the discipline.

Interviews conducted for this chapter suggest that even when there are many bases for mutual understanding, faculties under receivership actively participate in constructing imposed leaders as aliens by minimizing similarities and exaggerating perceived differences along disciplinary, ideological, methodological, or other lines. No basis for identification between the alien ruler and the faculty is so solid that it cannot be deconstructed to constitute a meaningful difference, under conditions of imposed governance. Although the alien rulers may have taken up the leadership challenge out of an intellectual affinity for, or long-standing political loyalty to, the unit in receivership – having previously served as adjunct faculty, worked closely with core faculty, or served on relevant committees – they typically receive a chilly greeting or worse, find themselves the objects of abject hostility. How they manage that response is one of the most significant tests of their actual leadership abilities. Even the most competent leaders pay a high emotional price as their efforts to "save" the unit are continually interpreted through the lenses of personal ambition, incompatible values, or mistrusted motives.

For their part, faculties under receivership are legitimately distressed by the vote of no confidence in their internal capacity to generate leadership or guide their own affairs, because under ordinary conditions of shared governance, units are encouraged to identify leaders from among their own ranks and to manage a variety of decisions, large and small. Serious conflict between the unit and the administration raises genuine threats to autonomy and access to resources. For under these circumstances, departments can win the battle by securing an internal administrator but lose the war by lacking sufficient administrative confidence to secure future resources. Or they may sacrifice autonomy by accepting an alien ruler in whom the administration has high confidence, winning resources for the unit but potentially sacrificing control over locally held values that diverge from the institutional agenda. In either case, the move into receivership is fraught with tension because it violates normative expectations within institutions of higher education of shared governance, disciplinary leadership, and departmental autonomy.

The Importance of Disciplinarity

Disciplinary credentials are universally regarded as a key qualification for leadership of academic departments. In some cases, outstanding scholars of the discipline are chosen as highly visible leaders, particularly when there is a drive to raise the department's profile and reputation nationally. In other cases, the position of department chair is a low-status service obligation, rotated among senior members of the faculty, requiring no special scholarly or leadership credentials other than disciplinary affiliation and widespread acceptability. A 1975 survey of department chairs at Miami University revealed one nearly universal quality of leadership: "Chairmen overwhelmingly (83 percent) view themselves as faculty members, not as administrators. They are discipline-oriented scholar-teachers whose interests and loyalties lie with their fields, faculty colleagues, and students" (Waltzer 1975: 11). Of course, chairs' sense of identity may vary at different types of higher education institutions. Nevertheless, a central aspect of this inquiry concerns the actual skills that disciplinary experience and identity bring to the work of leading academic departments.

So ubiquitous is the expectation of disciplinary credentials for departmental leadership that little critical thought has been given to what they actually bring to the task at hand. However, if the concept of alien rule is to have any meaning, surely it is defined in contrast to accepted notions of "native rule" exercised by widely acceptable departmental insiders. Resistance to alien rule is at least in part based on the notion that chairs drawn from other disciplines are not intellectually or culturally competent to lead units outside of their discipline. This conventional wisdom, examined critically, raises the broader questions of which powers and responsibilities of department chairs depend on disciplinary expertise and what constitutes the universal competencies of departmental administration and leadership. Or, put another way, why is there such a limited market for academic administration at the departmental level and why is it so clearly segmented by disciplinary expertise?

Richard Edwards (1999: 18) has argued that "the department, and in particular its leader, the department chair, gets assigned very demanding and complicated organizational responsibilities, most of which are completely independent of the department's disciplinary basis." Similarly, Gmelch and Miskin (1993: n.p.) have written that "the time of 'amateur administration' where professors temporarily step into the administrative role of department chair has lost its effectiveness." To assess their claims, it is worth reviewing the major responsibilities and prerogatives of department chairs.[8] Perhaps the best point of reference on this topic is the American Council on Education's Online Center, which hosts the most comprehensive collection of resources about the roles and responsibilities of department chairs.[9] Surveys of department chairs have identified

---

[8] Gmelch and Miskin (1993) provide a systematic review of the literature on the duties of departmental chairs.

[9] See the ACE's Department Chair Online Resource Center at http://www2.acenet.edu/resources/chairs/index.cfm.

several distinctive but common roles including administrative, leadership, interpersonal, and resource development (Graham and Benoit 2004). Only a few of these roles – specifically related to faculty recruitment, mentoring, and evaluation – might legitimately be regarded as dependent on disciplinary knowledge. The vast majority of chair roles, including fiscal oversight, scheduling coordination, staff supervision, mediation, advocacy, and warrior-entrepreneur in the battle for resources, require more general administrative capabilities.

Some would argue further that recent developments within higher education have reduced the ceremonial value of "prestigious scholars within the discipline" as department chairs and placed new emphasis on the administrative skills needed to effectively manage the consequences of "budget cuts, declining enrollments, productivity reports, accountability measures, fund raising, or changing technology" (Hecht et al. 1999: ch. 2, p. 1).[10] If disciplinary expertise constitutes a declining proportion of department chairs' actual responsibilities, it nevertheless assumes enormous symbolic importance to faculty who count on their chair to represent their interests and values to central administration. There can be little doubt that department chairs are the quintessential middle managers who have dual responsibilities to present administrative mandates and priorities to faculty, while serving as the faculty's "primary spokesperson and advocate." Yet as Hecht et al. (1999: ch. 2, p. 4) aptly noted, "Some faculty may even be outraged to think of their chair as an agent of the administration." Nowhere is this faculty perception more acute or their outrage more vocal than in cases when academic administrators appoint outside chairs to head departments in receivership.

Based on the evidence, one must conclude that disciplinary expertise on the part of their leadership matters more to departmental faculty than it actually should when the requisite skills are considered objectively. This disjuncture hints at the symbolic value of disciplinary credentials for departmental leadership within higher educational institutions, because they appear to trump actual leadership ability in chair appointments. This raises the deeper question of how and why disciplinary expertise matters to faculty. Or, framed in terms of classic relations between empires and their colonies, why is native leadership preferred over alien rule even when actual benefits do not seem to follow?

The Selection of Department Chairs

The process of choosing a department chair varies by institution.[11] In some places, particularly where a rotational model exists, there may be a shared understanding of whose turn is next, or the new chair may be selected by a vote

---

[10] The rising demands for administrative and managerial skill in the office of the department chair, particularly as a result of a decentralization of functions, is also addressed by Robert Kelly in his 2004 *Academic Leader* article, "Dealing with Administrative Mandates."

[11] Means of chair selection are outlined by Irene W. D. Hecht (2002) in "Appointment and Compensation: A Theme with Variations," an unpublished manuscript available through the

of the faculty. In other places, chair search committees accept nominations and screen prospective candidates for a provost or dean, who has exclusive responsibility for final selection. Certainly there are many variations on these themes. Whatever the approach, however, few would argue that the ideal outcome occurs when a reasonable degree of consensus has been achieved between faculty and administration about the preferred leader.

Outside of schools of medicine where chair appointments are indefinite, a general observation is that academic departments tend to select relatively weak leaders. Why should this be the case? One possibility is that weak chairs provide a higher level of comfort and certainty. Individual members of the department may believe that, if need be, they can assert their superior academic qualifications to overcome any possible initiative by a chair who does not serve their interests. Another possibility is that weak chairs appear to ensure collective governance. If an individual is not strong enough to lead, their next best option is to promote collective leadership; these two are often posed in opposition. Thus, the appointment of an alien chair not only contravenes the practice of choosing a member of the tribe but also goes against the grain of choosing weak leadership.

There are two parts to the role of most department chairs from the point of view of departmental faculty. The first is to compete favorably for institutional resources. The second is to mete out individual rewards. The first favors stronger leadership and advantages alien rulers; the second favors weaker leadership and advantages the selection of native rulers. In institutions where there are few resources to go after – or where there is the perception of few additional resources up for grabs – there is no particular call to select a strong chair who can align the priorities of the institution with the values of the department. Given that almost all faculty members have a continuous preoccupation with their own salaries, teaching loads, and other characteristics of their own

American Council on Education's Department Chair Online Resource Center. For a thorough discussion of considerations that should go into the choice of a department chair, see William J. Ehmann (n.d.), "Advice on Anointing: Some Faculty Considerations on Choosing a New Chair," an unpublished manuscript also available through the ACE Department Chair Online Resource Center. "Is your department truly ready for change?" Ehmann inquires provocatively (p. 2). He is remarkably enthusiastic about the potential benefits of faculty selecting "a colleague from a closely related department or even an outside chair" (p. 2). His list of signs that faculty should consider an outside chair closely corresponds to our own list of departmental receivership characteristics. "Some indications of your collective readiness might be found in how your department reacted to the most recent external review, whether there is any history of failed searches despite adequate applicant pools, or how willing the group would be to giving second chances to faculty who have been less involved in the department (should the new chair reach out to them). Candid discussions with the dean also may indicate how your department is perceived beyond your building, and what he or she may be looking for in a new chair" (p. 2). Unfortunately, nowhere else in the literature have we seen any indication that faculty share Ehmann's fondness for alien rulers, and it probably would be safe to conclude that they are usually selected by administrative fiat rather than through faculty deliberations about their leadership preference.

employment situations and that in most academic workplaces faculty negotiate individually rather than collectively over their specific working conditions, there tend to be more immediate reasons and personal benefits that attend faculty preferences for weak leaders.

A more analytic view of the role of chairs suggests that there are two major responsibilities: governance and administration. The special nature of governance in the academy means that chairs are responsible for ensuring that collective governance is preserved on all important matters. Yet there are also a set of skills in administration for which there is precious little preparation in institutions of higher education. It is largely presumed that achievements and developmental abilities acquired coming up through the ranks as faculty members or personal traits constitute adequate preparation for leadership at the departmental level. What are the matches and mismatches in skill, personal characteristics requisite for success, and perspective in these transitions from faculty to chair, chair to dean, and so forth? How might formal training enhance skills and reshape perspective(s) to meet the predictable demands of these positions? What are the generic competencies of these positions that require training over and above disciplinary and faculty skills? From many corners of academe, there are growing calls for leadership training to prepare department chairs for the myriad demands of the position.[12]

Preference for Native Rule

Thus, a preference for native rule might reflect more than concerns with comfort or familiarity, but might also speak to a preference for weaker leaders within the context of faculty participation in shared governance. The preferred unit leaders are more beholden to their faculty because there are many more opportunities for self-policing within the context of common disciplinary membership. The tendency of disciplinary leaders to maintain local customs contributes greatly to explaining the difficulty of aligning academic departments with wider institutional priorities. Thus disciplinary leadership fosters departmental autonomy, even at some expense to a department's access to institutional resources.

If these comprise some of the costs and benefits of disciplinary leadership at the departmental level, they pose some interesting problems as academic institutions have attempted, in recent years, to reposition themselves to foster interdisciplinary connections in the interest of liberating intellectual energy to solve problems that cross the disciplines. Departments and their preferred leaders may be among the most significant sources of resistance to the kinds of intellectual mobility that lies at the core of interdisciplinary initiatives. Inversely, the appointment of alien leaders may be one of the neglected hinge pins of

---

[12] See, for example, Bridget Murray's 1999 *APA Monitor* article, "Department Chairs Call for Leadership Training: Universities Should Bolster Their Guidance of Chairs, Faculty Say."

institutional transformation, not only for troubled departments but also for those that have successfully policed their boundaries by virtue of disciplinary vigor, effective functioning, perceived health, and academic quality. Alien rule appears to have greater power than disciplinary leadership to bring critical questioning to local norms and increased potential to align departments with the objectives of the wider institution.

Leaders who can reach beyond a narrow departmental and disciplinary focus can foster interdisciplinary collaboration. In many ways, alien rulers embody the news that "insularity is no longer acceptable" collective behavior at the departmental level (Hecht et al. 1999: ch. 14: 7). Their placement in units isolated by destructive territorial behavior models the idea that intellectual vigor and productivity depend on achieving higher levels of institutional connectivity. The question remains whether alien rule ought to be limited to units that blatantly exhibit signs of dysfunction or whether it might be adopted as a proactive strategy for institutional transformation.

In a 1999 article in the higher education journal *Change*, Richard Edwards (1999: 18) raised the broader question of how the academic department fits into the university reform agenda. Edwards astutely observed the disjuncture between institutional reform and unchanged departmental culture.

No plans, no hopes, no change agenda for departments has emerged out of the larger reform movement. Yet the department is arguably the definitive locus of faculty culture, especially departments that gain their definition by being their campus's embodiment of distinguished and hallowed disciplines. We can note the repeated calls for universities to place more weight on teaching performance in their promotion and tenure decisions; yet the crucial locus of such decisions lies within the department, and the crucial variable is departmental culture. Is it desirable, or even possible, for reform to be successful if it operates at the institutional and individual levels but leaves the intervening levels unchanged?

Douglas J. Murray (2000: n.p.) has argued that department chairs have a critical place in the process of institutional transformation. In his view, the time has come to redefine their roles, to make department chairs "as responsible for the college or university as they are for their departments." Furthermore, "they must lead the effort to change the existing mindset that focuses inward rather than outward."

Selection of Alien Rulers

The qualities that make a person a promising candidate for an alien ruler are closely related to the conditions that precipitate departmental receivership. Deans and provosts who are concerned with the lack of internal leadership or a mismatch between unit values and academic standards held at higher levels, or who seek more effective conflict management often recruit alien rulers with demonstrated leadership experience or recognizable signs of leadership potential and high scholarly credentials, normed to college/university promotion and tenure standards. To gain some measure of acceptance, it is often helpful if the person has some connection with the department going into receivership (e.g., appointment as an adjunct member of the faculty) and previous participation in unit planning or governance, although some distance is needed from the problems that led the unit into receivership. In some cases, this administrative appointment may also resolve, at least temporarily, a problematic misfit between a valued individual (with leadership potential) and his or her disciplinary home. Thus a "foreign assignment" might be a good idea until conditions become more hospitable in the person's actual home department.

Willingness to Serve

There can be a number of compelling reasons why a department is ripe for receivership from the dean's or provost's point of view, but how do they ever get anyone to take the job? The norms about self-governance in the academy are well known, and so, by taking such a position, the occupant is nearly guaranteed some degree of ostracism from the faculty the occupant governs.

Although it is possible to find some writing on the conditions that drive departments into receivership, almost nothing has been written about what would motivate a senior faculty member with high scholarly credentials to accept the obviously difficult assignment of leading a department in receivership. Our interviews with those who had accepted these appointments hinted at some possible reasons, including frustrated leadership potential, a sense of unhappiness or marginalization within their departmental home, and sense of "otherness" along multiple dimensions that contributes to a sense of alienation within the institution.

The frequency with which we encountered alien rulers with marginal social identities (e.g., gay and lesbian people, women of color, or some combination) led us to speculate that those who know they will encounter discrimination in their quest for more desirable leadership positions may be more open to difficult assignments for several reasons: people with marginal social identities are required to (repeatedly) demonstrate their leadership competencies on the way to higher positions, they are likely to have developed a fortitude that serves them in hostile environments, and sometimes, ironically, they experience greater freedom to "be themselves" at some distance from "home."

In fact, the very same characteristics that make some individuals attractive to a dean as alien rulers are also those that increase the probability that they will accept such positions. Marginal social identities at the personal and professional levels mean that there are few, if any, places in the academy where these individuals are members of a normative status quo or experience a complete sense of belonging. One implication of this is that there are fewer leadership opportunities for this pool than for others with similar (or fewer) talents, even as those very same characteristics may lead to a set of skills and predispositions *especially* conducive to excellent leadership (e.g., creative problem solving, fortitude). If these individuals with a set of leadership skills and blocked opportunities are to advance, their pathways will not be ordinary ones.

Still, to accept a position as an alien ruler has considerable risk associated with it – the risk of adding an unpopular portfolio to an already marginalized set of personal and professional characteristics. Why then do they do it? Individual rewards and altruistic motives come into play. To compensate individuals for the well-known risks involved, deans are likely to offer salary and perquisites well beyond the average for departmental chairs, being willing to contort the salary scale to do so. Still, this might not be sufficient if there were a more conventional alternative opportunity. However, as we have argued, there usually is not. When comfortable desk jobs are filled by more privileged individuals, advancement through the ranks requires a willingness to accept combat assignments.[13]

Deans may also play hardball. Knowing that people with leadership talent may be particularly interested in chairing the department of their own discipline, the dean may use the receivership position as a prerequisite for that plum job. One of our interviewees confirmed this conjecture: although generally perceived to be in line for the chair of the disciplinary department, the dean explicitly stated that he would not consider her unless she took on the receivership chair. In another case, despite clear leadership potential, the departmental chair position was not a likely option because an increasing gulf between the department's and the person's work. Thus the alien chair presented the only immediate option for earning the necessary stripes and experience for advancement. The fact that this small study encountered three out of three individuals with marginal social identities may suggest that alien rulers accept such assignments to overcome discrimination against women, gay and lesbian people, and people of color in administrative advancement within the university.

Although they may play hardball in securing the leadership needed to turn around dysfunctional departments, deans are also motivated to help their preferred chair succeed. Remember that the motivation for receivership is to get the department back into a quiescent and functioning phase. In this way, the candidate is also in a position to argue for resources that would be much less

---

[13] Women faculty in the STEM disciplines such as engineering, for example, report interest in leadership positions such as department chairs, but "felt that nobody was thinking of them in that way" (Tresa Pollock, cited in Mathias-Riegel 2004: n.p.). According to Judy Vance, a participant in the year 2000 National Science Foundation-sponsored Women Engineering Leadership Conference, women entering academic administration "are more likely to jump from full professor to assistant or associate dean without ever being a chair, thus missing a crucial step and 'knocking down' chances for further job opportunities or promotion to dean" (Mathias-Riegel 2004: n.p.) These observations lend credence to our observation that untapped leadership potential among women, racial, and sexual minorities, and discrimination against them in selection for leadership positions within their home departments, may explain their overrepresentation in less desirable, but considerably more challenging, administrative assignments as alien rulers.

likely to be forthcoming in a chair negotiation, such as multiple positions and the power to fill them. Indeed, the alien rulers who were interviewed made it clear that their decision to take the position was contingent on a negotiation with the appointing dean that brought new resources into the department, often in the form of authorization for a series of critical hires, discretionary funds, assistance in resolving difficult personnel problems, or access to other resources necessary for success. These sorts of dowries make alien rulers significantly more powerful than the preferred internal candidates of units at odds with upper administration and set the stage for the internal politics of alien rule, which trade departmental autonomy for access to institutional resources and which condition opportunities for development on greater conformity to wider institutional norms related to academic quality, productivity, or civility.

There are altruistic motivations for accepting the leadership of a department in receivership, as well. Alien chairs usually have a history with the department they come to lead, care about its health and future, and may see themselves as the only hope for that department. They believe that they can do the job, which means ultimately returning the department to leadership by one of its own. They may also believe that they can win the hearts and minds of those they serve – that is, move from alien to native status.

Finally, as one of our interviewees noted: "The department was far enough from my field that no matter how badly it went, it wouldn't damage me professionally." In this sense, the course of alien rule is a relatively safe testing ground for leadership because it lies at some professional distance from the chair's disciplinary home and comes with built-in explanations for failure should the experience prove to be unsuccessful.

Ironically, the improved prospects for mobility that attend successful runs as alien rulers tend to reinforce the judgments of the most skeptical faculty in units that have experienced receivership. The departure of the alien ruler for a new and higher administrative position only confirms what faculty suspected all along: that the individual took the position as a launching pad for personal ambitions, with no long-term commitment to the unit the alien ruler led. That the alien ruler improved the department is of little consequence when the master narrative is about the return of the department to rightful self-governance.

Of course, from the point of view of the alien ruler, the level of hostility encountered daily from the faculty of a department in receivership may serve to reinforce the perception that the grass is greener at the helm of one's own discipline, where at least there is some basis for social acceptance and group solidarity. Alternatively, the experience of sharp separation between faculty and administrative perceptions – that characterizes alien rule to a greater extent than native rule – may constitute significant preparation for an upper administrative position, where loyalty to a particular discipline has a diminished place in decision making, and faculty interests are only one of many considerations.

Conclusion

There are intriguing parallels between the pride of place given to disciplinary expertise and its contribution to a rich and diverse intellectual environment in universities, on the one hand, and the celebration of strong ethnic and national identities in nation-states on the other. Their respective contributions to institutional and social order – and the instances in which order breaks down – also make for compelling comparisons. In particular, when those identities threaten the larger goals of the organization, institution, or nation, deeply embedded institutional or governance norms can be more fully appreciated. Additionally, although academic receivership may be seen as a specific case of the breakdown of social control, it is little different than similar instances that compromise any social order.

The normative practice of selecting chairs from among disciplinary disciples appears to be as firmly embedded as ever. There is no inkling of an emerging market for chairs independent of discipline. Still, there is some reason to believe that there might be a slow erosion of the one-to-one correspondence between discipline of chair and department owing to two forces. The first is the growing importance of interdisciplinarity in most major universities. The second is the growing demand for accountability for universities in general, which places more administrative, compared to governance, responsibility on chairs.

The academic and organizational complexity of universities leads to multiple sources of domination of the collective over the individual. It is clear that alien chairs are considered akin to colonial rulers. Yet, as we have indicated, democratic governance in departments can also lead to something akin to tyranny of the majority, even when the majority does not represent the highest ideals of academic freedom and quality. Disputes over theoretical and methodological principles and approaches can turn from rich intellectual fare to incivility, poor treatment of junior faculty and graduate students, and ineffective decision making. In those instances, academic receivership may serve as protection for academic ideals and those who practice them.

That there are individuals in the academy with scholarly credentials and administrative ambitions ready to take on alien rule results, at least in part, from continuing, subtle discrimination against those who are socially and professionally marginalized. This serves as a subtle counterpoint to the apparent inclusiveness of "choosing one's own." One's own turns out to be a constricted set, not entirely defined by discipline.

Finally, it may be instructive to note that the alien chairs who were interviewed were able to claim some measure of success. Turning points in climate, tenure cases, hiring and curricular development in each case brought hard-won respect to the chair. Incremental progress toward a healthier departmental climate typically was reinforced by the release of new resources, approval of new degree programs, or an improved relationship with university administration.[14] Although these alien rulers never gained acceptance as natives, they often secured a reasonable level of trust and respect from a significant portion of the faculty, even those who had initially made their lives a living hell. Sources of satisfaction included these small personal victories, marked progress in terms of the substantial issues within the department, and a well-deserved reputation for leadership under difficult conditions. Improved social capital within the university and improved prospects for obtaining plum leadership positions within the wider institution rarely were mentioned directly by alien rulers, but our observations about their career trajectories suggest that substantial professional rewards can accrue to them after a successful term of office.

The implications of this work for the transformation of the academy are particularly interesting. This chapter comprises part of a critique of existing structures in universities that have – among other things – excluded from leadership individuals with social characteristics and intellectual predilections who joined the academy after the rules and norms of governance were established. This chapter attempts to reveal not only the formal politics of governance in the everyday life of an institution of higher education, and to chronicle the protestations of those who perceive that they are governed without consent, but also the motivation to rule and the standards by which leadership is judged. Alien rule in the academy lays bare latent criteria for leadership, and so opens the possibility for fresh analysis.

[14] Columbia University has begun to trumpet the turn-around story of the Department of English and Comparative Literature. See Margaret Hunt Gram's May 9, 2005, article, "After Civil War, New Life for English Dept." in the *Columbia Spectator*, available at http://www.columbiaspectator.com/2005/03/10/after-civil-war-new-life-english-dept.

7

Conclusion

All great truths begin as blasphemies.

– George Bernard Shaw

As a form of governance, alien rule is at least as old as the longest-lived empire, in ancient Egypt. Beginning in the seventeenth century, classical liberalism's emphasis on the sovereignty of the individual – and the right of individuals to self-determination – began to subvert the legitimacy of alien rule. At least since the American and French revolutions, the scope of this right has been expanded to apply to entire societies: the norm of national self-determination has flourished across the globe.

The track record of alien rulers often has been lamentable. Too frequently, the motives behind its imposition are exploitative. Colonialism developed not to bring civilization to the benighted populations of the Third World but rather largely because metropoles sought markets, labor, and primary products for their own domestic ends. Likewise, dominant powers typically occupy the territory of defeated enemies solely for their own strategic and economic benefit. Because these powers are not in it for the long haul – apart from seeking a certain modicum of social order that is required to efficiently exploit the territory – there is little point in investing in the kind of governance that might curry favor with the populace.[1] To the degree that rule is instituted for exploitative ends, alien rulers and their regimes will *not* attain legitimacy. Rather, at some point they will suffer anti-regime, often nationalist, resistance. Likewise, when alien rule following military conquest damages or destroys a country's infrastructure, as occurred during the American invasion of Iraq, the probability of resistance and civil war increases (Peic and Reiter 2011). For these

---

[1] In a classically sour grapes type of rationalization, after the victory of the African nationalists, the colonial powers attempted to portray decolonization as an inevitable consequence of their plans (Shepard 2006; Young 1994: 208).

reasons, alien rule has come to be regarded as a blasphemy that is a relic of the past.

This blanket condemnation of alien rule fails to accord with all the facts, however. Even if it is generally unacknowledged, alien rule persists in many different guises in the modern world. As an essential component of state building, it exists whenever culturally distinctive nations are ruled by those of a different culture. Whereas such situations often are the crucible for the development of nationalist movements, by no means do they foreordain them. Not all instances of alien rule lead to the demand for nationalism (Hechter 2000: ch. 7). Some national groups that lack their own states, such as the Swedes in Finland, express no demand for sovereignty.

Evidently the demand for national sovereignty can be trumped by other factors. The survival and even the proliferation of alien rule may not necessarily be a cause for concern. Despite the taken-for-grantedness of the norm of self-determination, alien rulers can be legitimated in the modern world if they govern effectively and fairly.[2]

In some ways, however, this conclusion offers cold comfort because the requirements for effective and fair governance are difficult to come by. Perhaps this is what Campbell-Bannerman meant by his statement that self-rule is better than good government.[3] Government effectiveness is to a great extent determined by sustained economic growth. However well intentioned governments may be, their attempts to stimulate the economy often appear to be feckless. The multiple veto points in democratic regimes (Tsebelis 1990) have recently presaged gridlock rather than decisive action in many countries. Issues of gridlock aside, governments in advanced countries seem to be at a loss to understand the kinds of measures that are necessary to promote economic growth. There is broad, if not universal, consensus that stable property rights and the rule of law are key foundations of economic development (Acemoglu, Johnson, and Robinson 2005), but much less is known about the determinants of these institutions (North 2006). Beyond these nostrums there is little agreement about how to spur economic growth. In the wake of the current worldwide recession, it is far from clear whether the discipline of macroeconomics offers any surefire recipes for economic growth (Elster 2007; Lo forthcoming). Perhaps the fault lies not with macroeconomic theory but instead with failures of political will and implementation.

---

[2] Further supportive evidence for the present theory comes from a recent study of violent insurgency in the Caucasus. Whereas violence in the Caucasus has often been attributed to the presence of alien fighters (jihadists), it turns out that aliens are welcome – and influential – only in those villages that have previously been subject to repression by the central government. In villages lacking such grievances against the central government, however, alien fighters are given the cold shoulder (Toft and Zhukov 2012).

[3] He was far from alone in this respect. According to Emerson (1960: 43), "The simple truth is that, once a certain stage of development is passed, colonial peoples will not accept good government as a substitute for self-government."

Attaining government fairness is also far more chimerical than one might imagine. A particular key indicator of this is found on statistics on corruption. By definition, a corrupt government is one in which policy and distribution is skewed toward the powerful and wealthy. In less developed countries corruption is rampant and well appreciated, but it is also found in spades in advanced societies, not least in the United States and the European Union (Rothstein 2011; Warner 2007). Nonetheless, good governance is not an all or nothing affair. Noticeable improvements in effectiveness and fairness are likely to be rewarded by increased consent – and legitimacy – on the part of citizens and subjects.

To be perfectly clear, this book does *not* attempt to make the case that alien rule is superior to native rule. Nonetheless the preceding chapters do show that alien rule can be legitimated under certain specific conditions. What are these conditions? The first is the incompetence or breakdown of native rule. Incompetent native rulers sometimes make alien rulers look good. Thus intractable interclan conflict in the Republic of Genoa led to the institution of the podesteria, which provided a century of peace to this formerly turbulent city-state. The Qing Dynasty's inability to regulate foreign trade and provide social order enabled the Chinese Maritime Customs Service to step in, produce a panoply of collective goods, and attain at least some measure of legitimacy. Likewise, university administrators resort to academic receivership when departments are unable to govern themselves. Yet the incompetence of native rulers alone does not guarantee the success of alien rulers. Poor alien rulers are no more likely to be acceptable than poor native ones.

The second condition is the establishment of equal treatment, a key component of the fairness of rule. Following its postwar constitutional assembly in 1946, during which the French decided how they would administer their empire, some colonies were granted political equality, whereas others were not. None of the six French colonies that were granted political equality developed nationalist movements, whereas nationalist movements arose in all of the twenty-three colonies that were denied political equality. This relationship also holds at the subnational level. After it abolished slavery in 1848, France granted citizenship to the residents of only four Senegalese communes: Dakar, Rufisque, Gorée, and St. Louis. The remaining residents of Senegal were treated as colonial subjects, not citizens. The Senegalese who had French citizenship rights made no nationalist demands, but instead mobilized for further inclusion (Lawrence 2013). By contrast, the residents of modern Iraq, who have been ill served by rulers both alien and native for more than a century, remain restive to this day.

The third condition is the adoption of some form of indirect rule, which can allow collaborators to mediate between alien rulers and native subjects. Even though military occupations offer the least favorable conditions for the attainment of legitimacy, collaborators can play a key role in dampening resistance. Japan's greater success in Taiwan than Korea owes, in part, to Taiwanese collaborators who were appointed to administrative positions in the wake of the departure of Chinese incumbents. Because they owed their increased status to their Japanese rulers, these collaborators had reason to be grateful to their Japanese masters. Whereas a good proportion of the Chinese elite fled from Taiwan after Japan's occupation, no comparable exodus occurred for Korea's elite. Once the Japanese began to strip away their traditional powers, the yangban took the lead in fomenting nationalist resistance to alien rule. The advocates of regime change in international politics must recognize that if they want to legitimate a new government in addition to investing ample resources in ruling effectively and fairly, they also must provide rewards to the new regime's collaborators. None of these steps were taken during the American occupation of Iraq; this surely contributes to the country's unstable aftermath.

The last condition concerns incentives. Alien rule typically is disastrous because the aliens have few, if any, incentives to govern well. The role that individual incentives play in generating social outcomes can hardly be overstated.[4] What then might be the incentives for alien rulers to engage and invest in good governance? Here again, the chapters in this book offer some answers. The Genoese podestá was provided with ample financial rewards for the difficult job of creating order out of chaos. The Chinese Maritime Customs Service helped govern well because it was anxious to prop up a shaky central government that had granted valuable trading privileges to Western powers. Both the collaborators in military occupations and academic receivers were compensated personal privileges and monetary rewards for undertaking highly unpopular roles. Palestinian collaborators with the Israeli occupation authorities are granted vital privileges that are withheld from their fellows. University administrators reward academic receivers with substantially increased salary and perquisites. Moreover, these individuals frequently are promised plum administrative positions in return for accepting this hard duty. Finally, to sweeten the deal, new chairs are likely to be granted exceptional resources to turn the department's fortunes around. To the degree that these academic receivers succeed, they are likely to earn grudging respect and legitimacy, even from those departmental members who had initially made their lives a living hell.

Although the bulk of attention in this book has been devoted to the legitimation of political regimes and states, the validity of these principles can be demonstrated by looking at smaller-scale social organizations as well. Similar to a traditional empire, the modern research university is a highly multicultural

---

[4] For a compelling recent discussion of the efficacy of individual incentives in economic development, see Acemoglu and Robinson (2012). Financial incentives played a critical role in defanging and integrating the newly superfluous, but extremely dangerous, caste of samurai warriors into the Meiji regime in Japan (Jha 2012). Yet the mere existence of incentives is no guarantee of favorable outcomes. As a recent study of community-driven development projects in Kenya reveals, the incentives behind such development programs often are not properly aligned to achieve the desired results (Ensminger 2012).

entity that is governed by a central administration.[5] Instead of having cultural divisions that are defined by ethnicity or religion, the university is made up of subunits – that is, departments – each of which is characterized by distinct intellectual histories, languages, and disciplinary norms. Most sociologists would be at sea if they suddenly found themselves in a department of physics, and vice versa. Moreover because of the high cost of acquiring disciplinary expertise, there is far less multilingualism in the academic world than in most multicultural states. The organizational structure of the university also resembles an empire far more than it does a modern unitary state. Since the *raison d'être* of the research university is to produce new knowledge, which is a highly uncertain enterprise, central administrators lack the technical expertise that would enable them to make profitable investments in the vastly different programs and personnel that comprise the university. This means that, as in empires, the central administrators of the university fundamentally must rely on a strategy of indirect rather than direct rule. As a result of this organizational imperative, the norm mandating departmental self-determination is exceptionally strong.

Just as the Holy Roman Empire imposed a podestá on the Republic of Genoa, however, the central administration of the university occasionally imposes an alien ruler – an academic receiver – on a department. Receivership is so counter-normative that universities are loath to reveal its very existence, and for this reason there is hardly any systematic evidence about it. Whereas receivership is most likely to occur when a department is rent by conflict, it may also occur when a highly solidary department is so set in its ways that it cannot adapt to new disciplinary or institutional requirements. After a time, these failings come to the attention of the center, and it responds by placing the unit under the control of an alien ruler. In effect, the new leader collaborates with the center in an attempt to make the wayward unit comply with central directives. Whereas some faculty may welcome a new chair from another discipline because they feel their views may be taken more seriously, most react with outright hostility, exaggerating the new chair's differences along disciplinary, ideological, or methodological lines. They claim that chairs from other departments are not intellectually or culturally competent to lead units outside of their discipline.

In principle, the present theory should also apply to other smaller social organizations, such as corporations and families.

Legitimating Corporate Mergers and Acquisitions

Just as countries can be taken over by alien rulers as a result of imperial expansion or military conquest, many different kinds of organizations smaller

---

[5] Universities sometimes have been considered to be similar to nonpolitical institutions, as well. For example, in a typically insightful analysis, Stinchcombe (1990: ch. 9) discusses them as analogous to fiduciary institutions such as banks.

than the state can suffer a similar fate. Legitimacy is problematic in all hierarchical organizations because authorities cannot monitor and sanction every
move of their subordinates. Because of this incapacity, compliance must be
generated by additional means. Legitimacy is a crucial resource for the attainment of compliance in firms (Williamson 1975; Ouchi 1981; Tyler 2001).
One prime example of alien rule occurs as a function of corporate mergers and acquisitions, which are sometimes referred to as *combinations*. The
acquisition of one firm by another is in a number of respects similar to a
military or colonial occupation. As in these other examples of regime change,
the employees of the acquired firm are initially likely to fear for their future
welfare. Questions such as these come to the forefront: Will they be subject to
layoffs down the road? How will their status within the firm be affected by the
new regime? Indeed, the machinations behind some mergers and acquisitions
resemble campaigns for military occupation. Consider the language used by
one prospective acquirer:

The diversification drive had taken on the air of a military invasion with its atmosphere
of haste and secrecy. In board discussions acquisition targets were labeled with cryptic
combinations of letters and numbers, such as S-8, B-9, G-6 ... Or, swept away by the
slick presentations of the MBA-trained "song and dance team," as Polk's venture team
became known to some, a bemused director might turn to one of his fellows after a vote
and ask, equally *sotto voce*, what company he had just voted to let General Mills buy.
(Wojahn 1988: 42–43)

Similar to other examples of alien rule, combinations often generate resistance
among those who are subject to them. For instance, when the merger is multinational, each firm's managers typically have deep sentimental ties to their
national culture and a strong desire not to dilute it (Olie 1990: 149). Similar
in-group loyalties also frequently crop up, however, in combinations occurring
between firms in one country:

DC was an independent firm; GrandCo was a multibillion dollar U.S. conglomerate.
DC's president was "very committed to participative management," while GrandCo had
"an organizational culture dominated by the power of the aristocrats." Early in 1978
DC was acquired by GrandCo, and the two cultures came into contact. DC found that
participative management was Greek to GrandCo. "They never heard of that ... it's like
going to another planet." (Sales and Mervis 1984: 107)

As a result of a merger or acquisition, employees – such as one Mr. Barton, the
chief executive officer (CEO) of an acquired firm – may find their position and
status threatened:

After years of loose-reigned management and mutual respect ... Barton now found
himself under the whip of a man who had recently been his professional equal. To
Barton, Loomis and his newly established toy group office in New York City represented a new and unwelcome level of governance within the conglomerate. ... [Loomis]
had elbowed Parker Brothers into ever closer product-development cooperation with
Kenner and its trendy toys. It seemed both Barton and Parker Brothers had lost rights

to self-determination that might never be regained.... By 1980 the seeds of a managerial mutiny were sprouting in the toy group. (Wojahn 1988: 94–95, 106)

Although much research has been devoted to mergers and acquisitions, most of it concerns their effects on the newly organized firm's share price and profitability. Less attention has been paid to the problem of legitimation. Perhaps this is because, unlike many citizens, the employees who retain their jobs can either elect to stay with the firm or move on to greener pastures. Traditionally, corporations have been regarded as quintessential *gesellschaften* (Tönnies 1988) comprised of largely purposive and instrumental actors. From this point of view, the stuff of culture – norms, values, identity, and affect – is usually not considered to be crucial in profit-making firms. The glue that binds managers to their work is termed the employment relation (March, Simon and Guetzkow 1993). As Adam Smith ([1776] 1961: 18) famously put it with respect to a somewhat different context, "It is not from the benevolence of the butcher, the brewer, or the baker, that we can expect our dinner, but from their regard to their own interest." Employees need not identify with their firms, need not believe in them, or need not feel any particular loyalty to them. It is not that these sentiments are held to be unimportant or missing in social life, but they are supposed to surface mostly in *gemeinschaften* – families and small communities made up of like-minded members of long acquaintance, who are often tied to the land or other forms of property.

Yet despite their common legal standing, employees consider corporate governing regimes to be more or less legitimate. After a takeover the new management may find itself regarded as illegitimate and may face resistance to its rule as a result (see Hirsch 1986 among many other studies). Forms of this resistance vary in seriousness from negative attitudes to distrust, job dissatisfaction, labor turnover, and even sabotage (Sales and Mirvis 1984). Indeed, nearly two-thirds of corporate combinations fail to live up to financial or strategic expectations.

Thus when corporations execute a combination, employees often regard their new managers as alien rulers. Yet some combinations breed employee resentment more than others. What determines the legitimacy of these new resultant firms?

Organizational sociologists think they have the answer. Indeed, legitimacy is the central concept in what has come to be known as "the new sociological institutionalism" (Haveman and David 2008). According to these writers, organizations are legitimate when they justify themselves in ways that make them subjectively plausible (Berger, Berger, and Kellner 1973). More specifically, they hold that an organization's legitimacy depends on the cultural support it obtains from its environment (Meyer and Rowan 1977; Meyer and Scott 1983). To the degree that this cultural support is incoherent or divided – say, if the state promotes one set of cultural values, and the church another – then the resulting legitimacy of any organization within the society (for instance, a school) diminishes. Therefore its legitimacy will be determined not by its performance, but by the amount of normative consensus in its specific environment.

Sociological institutionalism is principally concerned with external sources of legitimacy. Organizations are conceived to exist within a field of similarly designated entities, and a given organization must mimic its competitors if it desires to be a recognizable member of a particular field. Moreover, the criteria responsible for its recognition are principally normative. For example, to be considered a valid member of the field of corporations, every firm must have an organizational chart, a human relations department, a customer service department, and so forth. Firms that lack these requisite divisions fail to be readily countenanced by investors, customers, and competitors. They are simply not recognized as members of the field. On this account, their very survival is threatened. The upshot of this view is that people regard organizational directives as legitimate largely because they are taken for granted. For example, because you expect to take a test when applying for a driver's license, to have your blood pressure measured in the doctor's office, and to put on your seatbelt when you board an airplane, you do not really engage in benefit/cost calculations about doing any of these things. After all, most of us do not wonder if the sun will rise tomorrow. One of the implications of this view is that firms compete for social fitness rather than economic efficiency (Greenwood et al. 2008: 31; Powell 1991).

The novelty of this new sociological institutionalism[6] therefore resides in its analysis of firms and other kinds of bureaucratic organizations as if they were communities.[7] These institutionalist theories explicitly draw on constructivist premises:

> To illustrate, consider the verbs typically used in the literatures we highlight. With interactionist arguments, scholars commonly use the terms *saving face* or *affirming*. In ethnomethodology, *negotiate* and *improvise* have primacy. With sensemaking, *enact* is the standard bearer. Research on legitimation processes finds *associated with, orient towards, comply with,* and *accept.* Note that we rarely find words like *choose, plan,* or *determine.* These verbs are more constructivist, constitutive and interpretive than calculative or purposive. The individuals in these theories *behave,* but they seldom *choose.* (Powell and Colyvas 2008: 278)

The key to the new institutionalism is the primacy that it gives to cultural factors – norms, values, beliefs, and myths – in the process of legitimation. This

---

[6] To complicate matters further, there is also a new institutionalism in economics that takes issue with many of these sociological assumptions (North 1990; Ostrom 1990).

[7] This conception built on the earlier work of Barnard (1938), which emphasized the importance of norms in generating the firm's productive output. Even so, Meyer and Rowan (1977) argue that normative considerations should be greatest in nonmarket organizations – such as nongovernmental organizations and nonprofits. Because survival is less driven by market selection, the rules for organizational success are far more ambiguous in these settings. As a result, myths are likely to have greater purchase in nonmarket organizations.

view is in line with findings that cultural and identity concerns are crucial to employees' reactions to their new authorities after a merger has taken place (Hirsch 1986 provides one example among many). The idea that has gained the greatest currency in the literature is that culture – which ultimately is derived from shared norms and values – provides the glue that holds these firms together. A firm's culture is denoted by things such as its name, organizational structure, management processes, and reward systems. Firms have corporate cultures that organize the activities of employees and help them work together as a team. These cultures are akin to national cultures where employees come to believe that they share distinctive way of behaving. Mixing two disparate cultures together, on this view, is asking for trouble: it is an invitation to a culture clash in which the employees of each firm regard the others as illegitimate intruders.

It can readily be appreciated that the sociological institutionalists principally subscribe to a normative view of legitimation.[8] These considerations lead to the expectation that employee resistance should increase with the cultural dissimilarity of combining firms. By the same token, resistance should decrease when the new managers enact measures to diminish cultural differences (such as cultural learning exercises, socialization processes, and prohibitions against denigrating original group identities) in the combined workforce.

Although new institutionalism has generated many empirical studies (Powell and DiMaggio 1991), some sociologists have complained about its theoretical capaciousness (Kraatz and Zajac 1996, among others).[9] Most individuals in modern societies typically belong to multiple groups and, by this account, have many different social identities in their quiver (Simmel [1922] 1955). If people can successfully navigate the disparate cultures of their workplaces, families, churches, voluntary associations, it is difficult to understand why the cultural changes resulting from a corporate merger ought to inspire so much angst. On this view, it is intuitive that when a merger results in the imposition of managers from another country, employees are most likely to resist. Mergers may pose identity threats to workers by dissolving firm boundaries (Hirsch and Andrews 1983; Hirsch 1986).

---

[8] See Chapter 1 for the distinction between normative and instrumental views of legitimation.

[9] "If institution and institutionalization mean everything and explain everything – change and stability; routines, values and norms; intra-organizational and interorganizational structures and behaviours; cognitive, regulative and normative processes – then they mean nothing and explain nothing. The institutional 'tent' houses a loose collection of propositions, of varying degrees of formality, some seemingly incompatible and others only tenuously connected.... This lack of the accumulation of knowledge happened because institutionalists eschewed 'theories of the mid-range' – logically interconnected sets of propositions, derived from assumptions about essential facts (axioms) and causal mechanisms (unobservables), that yield empirically testable hypotheses and deal with delimited aspects of social phenomena" (Haveman and David 2008: 583). Because the new institutionalist economists do not share many of the core assumptions of their sociological counterparts, they naturally disagree with many of the latters' conclusions.

By contrast, the view of firms taken in this book is aligned with the much older tradition of institutional economics. According to this tradition, people run institutions by organizing activities on their behalf. Organizations thus are created by instrumentally oriented people seeking specific collective outcomes (Stinchcombe 1997). The argument in this book suggests that legitimation rests on straightforward instrumental bases. It follows from this view that combinations are legitimated not by resolving cultural conflicts but by governing effectively and fairly.

Consider effectiveness first. Because mergers sometimes result in job losses, there are many reasons to expect that some combinations might raise employees' concerns about their welfare. From the workers' standpoint, a firm's management is effective to the degree that it contributes to the employees' welfare. Factors such as the security of future employment, the promise of higher compensation, promotion opportunities, and the existence of a persuasive economic rationale for the combination should allay employees' fears about the effect of a merger on their welfare. Finally, for reasons discussed previously, evidence that the new regime intends to treat all its employees fairly will also allay instrumental concerns. Thus, resistance will be greater where employers fail to adopt the principles of procedural justice.

Which of these views – normative or instrumental – is superior for understanding legitimation in organizations? To a remarkable degree, these two literatures have seldom confronted one another empirically.[10] This very issue has recently been addressed by one of my graduate students, Allison Demeritt, in a study of mergers and acquisitions in capitalist firms (2012).

The fine-grained evidence required to assess the relative merits of these two theoretical expectations can only be found in individual case studies. Assembling a sample of case studies used for teaching in a prominent business school, Demeritt employed cross-case analysis spanning multiple observations to yield generalizations related to these two theoretical expectations. Cross-case analysis takes advantage of the strengths of each method by capturing the details of case studies without sacrificing the benefit of cross-sectional analysis. Relevant studies were identified by making key word searches of academic journals, library holdings, and case studies used for teaching. To be included, a case study had to describe a specific merger or acquisition involving an attempt to integrate the firms' respective work forces, contain at least two pages of

[10] Sociological institutionalists have carried out an impressive amount of empirical research, and some of this research has claimed that a variety of organizational forms are better conceived as socially legitimate (that is, culturally appropriate) rather than economically efficient (that is, instrumentally rational). This is not the same thing as conducting a contest between the two kinds of views, however. Likewise, an integration of instrumental and cultural organizational theories requires "an agnostic blending of a respect for social structural constraints on action with the notion that organizational actors strive to be, and indeed can be quite purposeful at times. In this respect, institutional theorists are too often skeptical of research that adopts the latter orientation" (Roberts 2008: 568).

information on organizational and human resource management issues related to the relevant causal variables, and cover at least one year of the post-combination time period. All told, the selection process yielded ten cases.[11]

The analysis set out to determine whether cultural or instrumental factors provide superior explanations of the legitimation of newly combined firms in this sample. As in most of the chapters in this book, it used resistance – the active and passive opposition by employees to the acquisition and integration process – as an indicator of illegitimacy. Whereas the concept of culture clash is widely invoked to account for the poor performance of a combination, Demeritt found that instrumental variables provided a superior explanation of the legitimacy of mergers and combinations than did cultural ones. Perhaps most significantly, the use of procedural justice to attain post-merger legitimacy received the greatest empirical support. Although concerns for employee welfare clearly outweigh those of identity, cultural issues also crop up in this realm. As in the case of occupation regimes discussed in Chapter 5, during the initial period of a combination uncertainties about individuals' future prospects as a result of their identity with the firm that has been taken over are likely to be in full flower. Once the new authorities take control, however, the stage is set for resistance, legitimation, or some intermediate outcome.

All told, this study revealed that instrumental concerns trump cultural ones with respect to the legitimation of corporate mergers and acquisitions. Based as it is on an unrepresentative sample of combinations, the generalizability of these findings is questionable. Given the absence of studies based on more adequate samples, they are nonetheless suggestive. The conclusions of this study are broadly consistent with the present theory, for they suggest that the managers of combinations who govern both effectively and fairly are likely to gain legitimacy, whereas those who fail to do so will tend to face resistance. In this situation, as elsewhere in this book, cultural differences can be overcome by incentives designed to realign identity and to promote intergroup cooperation.

In one sense, this conclusion is hardly surprising: it is quite in line with the expectations of classical sociologists and institutional economists. Given the recent current cultural turn in the social sciences, however, it may count as something of a revelation.

Legitimating Stepparents

Now consider a much smaller organization, the family, or the household more generally. In *The Politics*, Aristotle regarded the family as the first political society:

---

[11] A principal reason why so few cases qualified for inclusion was the lack of evidence regarding the consequences of human resource integration in the new firms. As mentioned, most analyses focus primarily on strategic or financial aspects of mergers and acquisitions rather than on personnel issues.

One ought to rule a wife and children as free persons, though it is not the same mode of rule in each case. The wife being ruled in political, the children in kingly fashion.... Rule over the children is kingly. For the one who generates is ruler on the basis of both affection and age, which is the very mark of kingly rule. (Aristotle 1984: 52; Book I, ch. 12)

Likewise, Max Weber (1978: 231) defines patriarchalism as "the situation where, within a group (household) ... a particular individual governs who is designated by a definite rule of inheritance." If, following these sages and others, families can be considered to be sites of rule, then stepfamilies can count as examples of alien rule.

Although stepfamilies were hardly unknown in premodern societies, they arose for quite different reasons than those in modern times. In modern times, most stepfamilies result from divorce, whereas previously they resulted from the death of a parent (Phillips 1997).[12] Increasing rates of divorce have led to the proliferation of stepfamilies in most advanced societies (Sweeney 2010). Indeed,

The stepfamily is a family form well matched to post-industrial society. This kind of society is typified by an emphasis on personal freedom and emotional fulfillment, sexual experimentation and egalitarianism, a reduced importance of kinship and consequent salience of nonfamily agencies that care for and educate the young, nurture the elderly, and carry on almost all economic activity. (Beer 1989: 7)

Whether or not they are well adapted to the rhythms of postindustrial society, this factor alone is not likely to affect stepfamily outcomes.

There is pervasive evidence – across cultures and historical eras – that children who are genetically related to their parents are happier and better cared for than those who are raised in a stepfamily.

In the sixteenth century one Norwich (England) widow, Katherine Andrews, informed her widower suitor that she could not marry him because doing so would form a stepfamily: "I will never be a stepmother, for I understand ye have children, and that should cause us never to agree." In the early nineteenth century a French legislator had this to say about stepfamilies: "Experience proves only too clearly that second marriages are generally disastrous for the children of the first marriage. The law does not suppose that a father has the same tenderness, the same care, for his children by his first marriage." (Phillips 1997: 11)

Most empirical research on stepfamilies confirms the truth of this anti-stepfamily norm (Ihinger-Tallman and Pasley 1997). In this way, stepparents can be likened to alien rulers.[13] Various forms of child abuse are correlated with stepfamilies

---

[12] Despite this, divorce was legalized in most of Protestant Europe in the sixteenth century. In France, it was legalized in 1792, and in the following decade there were around 20,000 divorces there (Phillips 1997: 10).

[13] Not all stepparents exercise equal rule, and a dauntingly large number of causes other than parental governance affect the integration of children in their families. Outcomes are affected by factors such as if the absence of a parent is a result of divorce or death, the gender of the absent

compared to natural families (Daly and Wilson 1991). In addition, household expenditure on food is negatively affected by the presence of step and foster parents in a household (Case, I-Fen, and McLanahan 1999). Parents report a lower obligation to provide financial assistance to stepchildren, and provide less actual assistance, than to biological or adoptive children (Sweeney 2010: 677). The most recent scholarship finds that youth living with a stepparent tend not to fare as well as those with two married biological parents with respect to a wide array of educational, cognitive, emotional, and behavioral outcomes assessed from early childhood through the transition to adulthood (Sweeney 2010: 673). Finally, children leave home sooner when they live in stepfamily households as those in single-parent or first-family households (Ihinger-Tallman and Pasley 1997: 23).

Much attention has been devoted to explaining these findings. A common view among sociologists is that the cause is fundamentally normative. Compared to natural families, stepfamilies have (at least until recently) been incompletely institutionalized (Cherlin 1978). Presumably, untoward things are more likely to occur in the home given the absence of clear norms regulating the behavior of the members of stepfamilies. Whereas there is a bright line against parental incest (indeed, it is illegal in many jurisdictions), the issue is obscure when it comes to stepfamilies. In Finland, which does not criminalize sexual steprelations, the incidence of stepfather-stepdaughter incest was found to be sixteen times greater than father-daughter incest (Sariola and Uutela 1996). Although Woody Allen received a great deal of opprobrium when he married his wife's adopted daughter, Soon-Yi Previn, he was not prosecuted. Despite this, his son Ronan disowned his dad and remarked, "He's my father married to my sister. That makes me his son and his brother-in-law. That is such a moral transgression" (Clarke 2011).

Another explanation for these welfare differentials is evolutionary. On this view, stepparents have less parental solicitude than genetic parents. This is because parental solicitude is a way of aiding the survival of one's genes in future generations; therefore it is an evolutionarily adaptive strategy (Daly and Wilson 1999; Hofferth and Anderson 2003).

Of course, variations in parental solicitude may have quite a different root. As parents age, their concern for elder care increases. They are likely to wonder if they will be given adequate emotional and material support in their

---

parent, the age and gender of the children after the absence of the parent, the willingness of the natural parent to countenance the parental role of the stepparent and to establish a united front regarding childrearing, the presence of siblings, half-siblings, and step-siblings, the availability of grandparents and other kin, household wealth, and last but not least parental behavior toward the children – especially with respect to communication and affection (Barnes 1998; Cath and Shopper 2001; Hetherington and Jodl 1994). The complexity of stepfamily settings makes it difficult to draw firm conclusions about the general effects of parental governance on children's acceptance of their stepparents (Shopper 2001: 15–16).

declining years. Given the relative paucity of adequate market or government solutions for elder care in the United States and many other countries today, parents often look to their children for future support. To increase the probability of receiving this support, they are likely to differentially invest in their children – or, better yet, their children's children – if they have more than one (Friedman, Hechter, and Kreager 2008; Geurts, Poortman, and van Tilburg 2012). It stands to reason that they are more likely to place their bets for future emotional and financial support on their natural children rather than stepchildren. However, this investment strategy violates the fair treatment required for the legitimation of stepparents.

Whereas these arguments provide plausible accounts of the difficulties with stepfamilies, none of them speak to the conditions under which some stepparents might become accepted by stepchildren – and therefore legitimated – rather than resisted. About this issue, which is critical for the theory advanced in the present book, there is very little systematic evidence (Sweeney 2010: 677). Some relevant clues derived from in-depth interview data, however, suggest that

Even though gaining a "new" parent was not always a smooth process, in these cases, it ultimately enlarged a child's emotional and practical support, expanded their notion of kinship, and provided a more uplifting vision of what a family could be. These marriages show how the "case for marriage" ... really depends on which marriage. Like families, *we need to look beyond the fact of a remarriage to its quality*. For children who benefited from remarriages, the breakup of an unhappy, destructive relationship provided an opportunity for parents to create a new, more cooperative and cohesive one. (Gerson 2010: 64; my emphasis)

Closeness is a particularly salient dimension of the stepfather-child relationship that is associated with better outcomes for children (King 2006: 911).

Stepmothers are "doubly challenged by their perceived need to disprove their 'wickedness' and to love and be loved by their partners' children while simultaneously remaining 'good' mothers to their own children. Meeting such high expectations is difficult, if not impossible, and may set these women up for considerable stress of failure" (Weaver and Coleman 2010: 307). Despite this,

Findings from stepfamily research on mothers seem to support the assumption that good mothering in stepfamilies is similar to good mothering in nuclear families. That is, children perform better in school and have fewer internalizing and externalizing behavior problems when mothers engage in *authoritative parenting*. Authoritative parenting is engaging in supportive and warm behaviors along with providing structure and assertive control of children's behaviors. Greater warmth and involvement, better communication, and more maternal assertiveness are related to better parent-child relationships regardless of family structure. (Ganong and Coleman 2004: 110)

As for stepfathers, the most successful model of parenting is friendship:

Developing a friendship is less likely to elicit opposition from anyone who otherwise might feel threatened (e.g. nonresidential parents, grandparents, stepsiblings). Several researchers have found that stepparents who initially engage in supportive relation-ships, rather than disciplinary relationships, have more positive bonds with stepchil-dren. (Ganong and Coleman 2004: 131)

According to the present theory, close bonds with stepchildren – and hence stepparental legitimacy – should be associated with, if not caused by, fairness in the allocation of emotional, temporal, and material resources between multiple children and familial effectiveness, entailing low levels of parental conflict, high stability, and sufficient prosperity to keep the wolf from the door.[14] Note that this proposition leaves ample room for the potential effects of a wide variety of other factors – biological, psychological, and social – on the children's accep-tance of their stepparents.

When do stepparents engage in fair and effective parenting? Although sys-tematic evidence is difficult to find, the theory suggests that we consider the following conditions. The first condition has to do with the competence and quality of natural parents. Stepparents are likely to gain favor with stepchil-dren to the degree that natural parents are incompetent to provide a safe and stable home environment, or are abusive.

The second condition concerns the degree to which step- and natural chil-dren are treated equally. Consider the Grimms' famous rendering of the tale of Cinderella. One short year after the girl's mother gets ill and dies, her rich father marries a woman with two grown daughters. These selfish stepsisters demand the lion's share of the resources – fancy clothes and jewelry among them – showered on the children, and their mother willingly accedes to their wishes at Cinderella's expense. Worse, the poor girl is compelled to act as her stepsisters' servant. At some point in the tale the king proclaims that there will be a festival to enable his son to meet all the eligible young women in the territory.

When the two step-sisters heard that they too were to appear among the number, they were delighted, called Cinderella and said, "Comb our hair for us, brush our shoes and fasten our buckles, for we are going to the festival at the King's palace." Cinderella obeyed, but wept, because she too would have liked to go with them to the dance, and begged her step-mother to allow her to do so. "Thou go, Cinderella!" said she; "Thou art dusty and dirty and wouldst go to the festival? Thou hast no clothes and shoes, and yet wouldst dance!" As, however, Cinderella went on asking, the step-mother at last said, "I have emptied a dish of lentils into the ashes for thee, if thou hast picked them out again in two hours, thou shalt go with us (http://classiclit.about.com/library/bl-etexts/grimm/bl-grimm-cinderella.htm).

Cinderella overcomes a series of her stepmother's increasingly formida-ble tests with magical assistance and ultimately wins the hand of the prince.

---

[14] There is a wealth of research on attachment processes in adults, and it is reasonable to suspect that similar mechanisms are responsible for close relationships in stepfamilies. One of the con-clusions of this research accords with the present theory – namely, that attachment to a given person varies with the degree to which that person is relied on for comfort and security (Doherty and Feeney 2004).

Meantime, her stepsisters are punished by being blinded. Curiously, nothing untoward befalls the stepmother in the tale. The egregiously unfair treatment meted out by Cinderella's evil stepmother is replicated in over 300 versions of the story from all over the world (Smith 1953). Indeed, the French word for stepmother – *maratre* – means both stepmother and a cruel or harsh mother. Unsurprisingly, the reputation of stepfamilies was extremely negative in pre-industrial Europe.

The last condition deals with the stepparents' incentives to provide good parenting. On the one hand, stepparents may be rewarded by their spouses for being warm and supportive to their stepchildren. On the other, they may hope to get something out of their investments in stepchildren, such as support in their old age.[15]

The Future of Alien Rule

I am unaware of any country that considers aliens to be eligible to become head of state. Even the World Bank – committed as it is to expanding the domain of free trade – explicitly disavows any interest in a free market in governance services. Yet the only hope we have of addressing many global social problems, such as climate change, piracy, and political instability, that cannot be resolved by individual states lies in our acceptance of some form of alien, in this case international, rule. Apart from this, because native rule does not necessarily lead to good governance, alien rule is likely to be with us in the indefinite future.[16] If so, all of us better learn how to live with it.

The growth of international trade and immigration has already helped diminish some important shibboleths in this respect. One example comes from the corporate world, another from the world of sports. As one of the most culturally exclusive of all advanced societies, Japan places great emphasis on ancestral purity (Lipset 1993), and legal immigration is nearly impossible. Antipathy to aliens is taken for granted: the notion that key Japanese institutions might be led by *gaijin* contravenes deeply held nations of Japanese exceptionalism. For this reason, the news that leading Japanese corporations such as Nissan Motors and Sony appointed aliens, Carlos Ghosn (Lebanese and French) and Howard Stringer (Welsh), to be their chief executive officers was little short of astonishing. Japanese exceptionalism has been eroding in other realms, as well. For example, in 2011 Japan loosened the law concerning corporate mergers by promoting greater openness to foreign markets (Marquis and Kameoka 2012).

[15] Note that collaboration, which plays such a prominent role in other instances of alien rule, has no obvious analogue in nonhierarchical modern families.
[16] As an alternative to alien rule, states can be more receptive to adopting alien models of organization, as Japan, China, and the Ottoman Empire did during the nineteenth century (Westney 1982). For a plea that the United States ought to consider adopting some of the governance practices currently existing in China, such as demanding performance qualifications for prospective political leaders, see Lee (2012).

No doubt these developments are a harbinger of things to come in what once had been the paragon of culturally exclusive societies. In another surprising departure from convention, in November 2012 the British government selected Mark J. Carney, a Canadian, to become the first foreigner to lead the Bank of England. In this position, he will take responsibility for the health of the British financial system.[17]

Increasing multinational corporate mergers are another case in point. The Swedish industry minister explained his support for a Swedish-Swiss merger by arguing that it "would lead to a greater internationalization of Swedish industry, and that this was desirable for the survival of Swedish companies. He said that, if Sweden wanted to be part of the international economy, it would have to give and take even if people were unhappy that the HQ would not be in Sweden" (Barham and Heimer 1998: 50). Indeed as Warren Bennis, a prominent management consultant, observed:

The ability to align, create and empower will characterize successful [corporate] leaders well into the twenty-first century.... The emergence of federation is the structure uniquely suited to balancing the seemingly incompatible drives toward global cooperation and the putting-down of deep local roots. This paradox is evident in world politics, where intense ethnic and national identities co-exist with the widespread recognition that new economic and political alliances must be forged outside one's borders. (quoted in Barham and Heimer 1998: xii)

The World Cup, the single most nationalistic sporting event on earth, offers an illuminating example of the growth of alien rule. This competition is open to football (soccer) teams from every country in the world, and unlike professional soccer, the members of each team are limited to the citizens of that country. Not so for their coaches, however. Whereas one might expect nationalistic sentiments to mandate a similar rule for the coaches, fully 38 percent of the 2010 World Cup teams were coached by aliens. In both of these examples, increased competition between firms and states has led to a new climate in which expertise has trumped national identity as the principal criterion for office holding. As a result of increasing interdependence in the world system in one form or another, alien rule is likely to be on the rise.

Less invasive forms of alien rule occur whenever a state is compelled to adopt new policies as a condition for foreign aid, membership in an international institution such as the World Trade Organization, or inclusion in the European Union. The international war crime tribunals offer a case in point. To carry out their mandate, these tribunals must elicit the cooperation of the governing regimes in lands that experienced violations of human rights. The tribunals demand that nationals who have been accused of war crimes be apprehended, but because they have no enforcement capacity, this is impossible in the absence

---

[17] Seeking to allay concerns about an alien taking over responsibility for governing such a hallowed national institution, the bank hastened to explain that Carney was a subject of the queen.

of the regimes' cooperation. For their part, many such regimes are inclined to stonewall the tribunals by claiming that they represent victor's justice – and on this account are illegitimate. In Serbia, it was made clear that membership in the European Union would not be a possibility unless the regime cooperated with the tribunal (Goodliffe et al. 2012; Peskin 2008). After time, the requisite cooperation was forthcoming. The growing concern with human rights therefore has ushered in a new kind of alien rule.

A similar conclusion can be drawn from the recent fiscal difficulties in the Euro zone. In January 2012, a German proposal for a European Union budget commissioner came to light. Under this proposal, the budget commissioner would be able to veto any expenditures that were not in line with targets set by international lenders. Greece would also legally commit itself to servicing its debt, before spending any money in any other way. According to the proposal, surrender of a portion of Greek financial sovereignty was the price that had to be paid to qualify for an external bailout.

In reality, Greece's finances are largely controlled by alien powers. The enormous bailouts that Greece subsequently received from the European Union and the International Monetary Fund were conditional on deep cuts and fiscal reforms drawn up largely by officials in Brussels. It should be no surprise that Greeks reacted to the austerity plan adopted by the Parliament by rioting in their major cities. "Anti-German sentiment is also on the rise in Greece, where memories of the Nazi occupation during World War II are still vivid. 'This is worse than the '40s,' said Stella Papafagou, 82, who wore a surgical mask at the demonstration to fend off the tear gas. 'This time the government is following the Germans' orders. I would prefer to die with dignity than with my head bent down'" (Kitsantonis and Donadio 2012).[18] The election of June 17, 2012, pitted a new party (Syrzia) that was explicitly opposed to the austerity policies demanded by the European Union against a conservative party (New Democracy) that vowed to enact the austerity measures required for external financial support. New Democracy – the party that promised to accede to alien (fiscal) rule – won a narrow victory over its left nationalist opposition, but at this writing its ability to govern remains in doubt.

An International Market in Governance Services?

The reaction to alien intervention need not produce such nationalist resistance, however. For example, an experimental field study carried out in Liberia suggests that, contrary to much speculation in the literature, foreign aid – which is usually contingent on reciprocation with donor countries and therefore constitutes a veiled form of alien influence – can promote social order following civil war (Fearon, Humphreys, and Weinstein 2009). Indeed, the incidence of alien

---

[18] A similar loss of fiscal sovereignty could also befall Portugal. At the time of this writing, the fiscal fate of Spain and Italy remains uncertain.

rule is growing at the international level. Many global governance organizations (Koppell 2010) have arisen to regulate activity in specific policy spheres ranging from trade (World Trade Organization), to health (the World Health Organization), to the use of the Internet (Internet Corporation for Assigned Names and Numbers). True, these organizations regulate activities in relatively narrow substantive arenas, and this is a far cry from what might be considered the pure form of alien rule.

Yet the European Union provides an important example of the development of alien rule; it is moving toward something similar to a supranational state, albeit gradually and haltingly. It already regulates a host of economic and social activities among its member states. Whereas many of its policies do not violate sovereignty because they require the agreements between member states, the European Union also has exclusive authority to make directives and conclude international agreements with respect to its customs union, the establishment of competition rules for the functioning of its internal market, the monetary policy for all members of the Euro zone, the conservation of marine biological resources, and common commercial policy. In all of these policy arenas, member states have already surrendered their sovereignty to an entity that is alien to all of them.

Moreover, proposals are currently afoot that would increase the incidence of alien rule. One idea to foster economic development among the poorest countries essentially relies on alien rule. The Charter Cities initiative aims to encourage the adoption of new rules that are known to work better than the ones poor countries already have (Romer 2010). Because these rules constitute a sharp break with the traditional rules that are held to be responsible for suboptimal development, they have to be implemented by aliens who are not beholden to indigenous social forces. The initiative cites the highly productive governance rules adopted in British Hong Kong that subsequently were applied in China's Special Economic Zones, where new cities such as Shenzhen developed. These zones in effect created small laboratories through which Hong Kong governance rules spread to the mainland, helping unleash the most rapid economic growth in history. The Charter Cities initiative seeks to voluntarily charter new cities for the purpose of changing rules, using a range of new legal and political structures analogous to the ones that made possible the rapid economic development of Hong Kong and Shenzhen.

If the blind commitment to the norm of national self-determination is weakened, this may ultimately have implications for the development of an international market in governance services. Some national markets for governance services already exist. For example, as noted in Chapter 2, American and European city managers are usually alien to the communities they administer. Much the same is true for the superintendents of American school systems. In both of these cases, it is thought that aliens can govern more objectively – and with less corruption – than natives, who are considered more likely to be compromised by their ties to local, often competing, interest groups.

Difficult as it may be to imagine, at some point in the future individuals of any nationality might be able to stand for election as president or prime minister in some states. This could come about in a variety of ways depending on the nature of a country's political system. In the United States, for example, the constitutional provision that election to the presidency (and vice presidency) is limited to natural-born citizens, intended to protect the nation from foreign influence, would have to be repealed. Were it repealed, however, then these high offices would be opened to a global pool of candidates. Just as businesses, professional sports teams, and research universities increasingly comb the world for the most talented executives, players, and scientists, countries could scour the world for the most accomplished political leaders. As in these other realms, individuals' track records would be critical for assessing their talent. Granted, leaders who have met great success in one country may not function all that well in quite a different political context. Despite this context-dependence of administrative performance, it is likely that, all else equal, some individuals have greater ability to lead than others and that this ability could be discerned by the members of political parties, the media, and electorates. At the same time, current legal restrictions on the financing of political campaigns by foreign individuals, corporations, and governments could, at least in principle, continue to ensure the country against the risk of selecting Manchurian candidates. In this fanciful future, Genoa's long experience with the podesteria might well be a model to be studied for hints about the design of a contract that provides alien rulers with appropriate incentives to govern fairly and effectively.

The bottom line is that all rulers – both native and alien – must struggle to attain the consent of the governed. It is seldom appreciated how challenging it is to produce good governance – and especially so when the state's access to resources is highly constrained. Whereas native rulers have clear initial advantages over their alien counterparts in this respect, the historical record is replete with examples of their incompetent and illegitimate rule. In the final analysis, both native and alien rulers must enact effective and fair governance if they hope to legitimate their regimes over the long run. Although this is no easy task, it is by no means an impossible one.

Bibliography

Abizadeh, Arash. 2012. "On the Demos and Its Kin: Nationalism, Democracy, and the Boundary Problem." *American Political Science Review* **106**(4):867–882.

Acemoglu, Daron, Simon Johnson, and James Robinson. 2005. "The Rise of Europe: Atlantic Trade, Institutional Change, and Economic Growth." *American Economic Review* **95**(3):546–579.

Acemoglu, Daron, and James Robinson. 2012. *Why Nations Fail: The Origins of Power, Prosperity and Poverty*. New York: Crown Publishers.

Achen, Christopher, and Larry M. Bartels. 2012. "Blind Retrospection: Why Shark Attacks Are Bad for Democracy." Unpublished paper.

Acton, Lord (John Dalberg-Acton). [1862]1907. *The History of Freedom and Other Essays*. Freeport, NY: Books for Libraries Press.

Ahmadi, Nader. 2003. "Migration Challenges Views on Sexuality." *Ethnic and Racial Studies* **26**(July):684–706.

Alberts, Bruce, Alexander Johnson, Julian Lewis, Martin Raff, Keith Roberts, and Peter Walter. 2002. *Molecular Biology of the Cell*. New York: Garland Science.

Alesina, Alberto, Reza Baqir, and William Easterly. 1999. "Collective Goods and Ethnic Divisions." *Quarterly Journal of Economics* **114**:1243–1284.

Al-Eyd, Kadhim A. 1979. *Oil Revenues and Accelerated Growth: Absorptive Capacity in Iraq*. New York: Praeger.

Allen, Charlotte. 1998. "As Bad as It Gets: Three Dark Tales from the Annals of Academic Receivership." *Lingua Franca* **8**(2):52–59.

Alnasrawi, Abbas. 2002. *Iraq's Burdens: Oil, Sanctions, and Underdevelopment*. London: Greenwood Press.

Althusius, Johannes. [1614] 1964. *Politics*. Boston, MA: Beacon Press.

Anderson, Christopher, Andre Blais, Shaun Bowler, Todd Donovan, and Ola Listhaug. 2005. *Losers' Consent: Elections and Democratic Legitimacy*. Oxford and New York: Oxford University Press.

Anderson, Perry. 1998. "A Belated Encounter: Perry Anderson Retraces his Father's Career in the Chinese Customs Service." *London Review of Books* **30**(July):3–10; 30–34.

Andrews, Lori. 2012. "Facebook Is Using You." *New York Times*, February 4.

Annual Report on the Island of Formosa. 1997. *Taiwan: Political and Economic Reports, 1861–1960.* Vol. 7: 1924–1941, edited by Robert L. Jarman. Slough: Archive Editions.

Aristotle. 1984. *The Politics.* Chicago: University of Chicago Press.

Atiyyah, Ghassan R. 1973. *Iraq, 1908–1921: A Socio-Political Study.* Beirut: Arab Institute for Research and Publication.

Axelrod, Robert. 1984. *The Evolution of Cooperation.* New York: Basic Books.

Aziz, M. A. 1955. *Japan's Colonialism and Indonesia.* The Hague: Martinus Nijhoff.

Bachrach, Michael, and Diego Gambetta. 2001. "Trust in Signs." In *Trust in Society,* edited by Karen S. Cook, 148–184. New York: Russell Sage Foundation.

Balandier, Georges. 1966. "The Colonial Situation: A Theoretical Approach." In *Social Change: The Colonial Situation,* edited by Immanuel Wallerstein, 34–61. New York: John Wiley & Sons.

Baldassarri, Delia, and Guy Grossman. 2011. "Centralized Sanctioning and Legitimate Authority Promote Cooperation in Humans." *Proceedings of the National Academy of Sciences of the United States of America* 108(27):11023–11027.

Baranova, Olga. 2008. "Nationalism, Anti-Bolshevism or the Will to Survive? Collaboration in Belarus under the Nazi Occupation of 1941–1944." *European Review of History* 15:113–128.

Barham, Kevin, and Claudia Heimer. 1998. *ABB: The Dancing Giant.* London and San Francisco: Financial Times Pitman Publishing.

Barnard, Chester Irving. 1938. *The Functions of the Executive.* Cambridge, MA: Harvard University Press.

Barnes, Gill Gorell. 1998. *Growing Up in Stepfamilies.* Oxford and New York: Clarendon Press.

Barron, Stephanie, and Peter W. Guenther. 1991. *Degenerate Art: The Fate of the Avant-Garde in Nazi Germany.* Los Angeles and New York: Los Angeles County Museum of Art and H.N. Abrams.

Barth, Fredrik (Ed.). 1969. *Ethnic Groups and Boundaries.* London: Allen and Unwin.

Barthe, Benjamin. 2009. "Á Gaza, les 'Collaborateurs,' Enjeu d'une Guerre Secrète entre Israël et le Hamas." *Le Monde* 12(November):6.

Batatu, Hanna. 1978. *The Old Social Classes and the Revolutionary Movements of Iraq.* Princeton: Princeton University Press.

Baum, Joel A. C., and Walter W. Powell. 1995. "Cultivating an Institutional Ecology of Organizations – Comment." *American Sociological Review* 60(4):529–538.

Baum, S. D., J. D. Haqq-Misra, and S. D. Domagal-Goldman. 2011. "Would Contact with Extraterrestrials Benefit or Harm Humanity? A Scenario Analysis." *Acta Astronautica* 68(11–12):2114–2129.

BBC News. 2011. "Jamaicans Would Have Been Better Off British – Poll." June 28, http://www.bbc.co.uk/news/world-latin-america-13952592, accessed May 9, 2013.

Beer, William R. 1989. *Strangers in the House: The World of Stepsiblings and Half-siblings.* New Brunswick, NJ: Transaction Publishers.

Beetham, David. 1991. *The Legitimation of Power.* Basingstoke, Hampshire: Macmillan Education.

Bendix, Reinhard. 1964. *Nation-Building and Citizenship: Studies of our Changing Social Order.* New York: Wiley.

Beissinger, Mark R. 2002. *Nationalist Mobilization and the Collapse of the Soviet State.* Cambridge: Cambridge University Press.

Beissinger, Mark R., and Crawford Young. 2002. *Beyond State Crisis?: Postcolonial Africa and Post-Soviet Eurasia in Comparative Perspective*. Washington, DC: Woodrow Wilson Center Press.

Bengio, Ofra. 2003. "Pitfalls of Instant Democracy." In *U.S. Policy in Post- Saddam Iraq*, edited by Michael Eisenstadt and Eric Mathewson, 15–26. Washington, DC: Washington Institute for Near East Policy.

Berger, Joseph, Cecilia L. Ridgeway, M. Hamit Fisek, and Robert Z. Norman. 1998. "The Legitimation and Delegitimation of Power and Prestige Orders." *American Sociological Review* 63(3):379–405.

Berger, Peter L., Brigitte Berger, and Hansfried Kellner. 1973. *The Homeless Mind: Modernization and Consciousness*. New York: Random House.

Binder, Leonard. 1955. "Al-Ghazali's Theory of Islamic Government." *The Muslim World* 45(3):229–241.

Blaisdell, Donald C. 1929. *European Financial Control in the Ottoman Empire: A Study of the Establishment, Activities, and Significance of the Administration of the Ottoman Public Debt*. New York: Columbia University Press.

Blau, Peter Michael, and Joseph E. Schwartz. 1984. *Crosscutting Social Circles: Testing a Macrostructural Theory of Intergroup Relations*. Orlando: Academic Press.

Blecher, Ian. 2002. "How Cult Internet Character Mr. Perestroika Divided NYU's Political Science Department." *New York Observer*, January 7, http://www.observer.com/2002/01/how-cult-internet-character-mr-perestroika-divided-nyus-political-science-department/. Accessed May 9, 2013.

Boldizzoni, Francesco. 2011. *The Poverty of Clio: Resurrecting Economic History*. Princeton, NJ: Princeton University Press.

Boone, Catherine. 2003. *Political Topographies of the African State: Territorial Authority and Institutional Choice*. Cambridge and New York: Cambridge University Press.

Bosniak, Linda. 2006. *The Citizen and the Alien: Dilemmas of Contemporary Membership*. Princeton: Princeton University Press.

Braw, Monica. 1991. *The Atomic Bomb Suppressed: American Censorship in Occupied Japan*. Amonk, NY: East Gate.

Breen, Michael. 1998. *The Koreans: Who They Are, What They Want, Where Their Future Lies*. London: Orion Business Books.

Bremer, Paul. 2006. *My Year in Iraq*. New York: Simon & Schuster.

Bridges, Emma, Edith Hall, and P. J. Rhodes. 2007. "Introduction." In *Cultural Responses to the Persian Wars*, edited by Emma Bridges, Edith Hall, and P. J. Rhodes, 15–26. Oxford: Oxford University Press.

Broers, Michael. 2003. "Centre and Periphery in Napoleonic Italy: The Nature of French Rule in the *Departments Réunis, 1800–1814*." In *Collaboration and Resistance in Napoleonic Europe. State-Formation in an Age of Upheaval, c. 1800–1815*, edited by Michael Rowe, 55–73. New York: Palgrave Macmillan.

Brook, Timothy. 2007. *Collaboration: Japanese Agents and Local Elites in Wartime China*. Cambridge, MA: Harvard University Press.

Brosnan, Sarah F., and Frans B. M. de Waal. 2003. "Monkeys Reject Unequal Pay." *Nature* 425(6955):297–299.

Brown, Horatio F. 1895. *Venice: An Historical Sketch of the Republic*. London: Rivington, Percival.

Brown, Shannon. 1978. "The Partially Opened Door: Limitations on Economic Change in China in the 1860s." *Modern Asian Studies* 12:177–192.

Browning, Christopher R. 1992. *Ordinary Men. Reserve Battalion 101 and the Final Solution in Poland.* New York: HarperCollins.

Brubaker, R., M. Loveman, and P. Stamatov. 2004. "Ethnicity as Cognition." *Theory and Society* 33:31–64.

Brubaker, Rogers. 2002. "Ethnicity without Groups." *European Journal of Sociology* 43(August):163–189.

Brudnoy, David. 1970. "Japan's Experiment in Korea." *Monumenta Nipponica* 25(1/2):155–195.

Brunero, Donna. 2006. *Britain's Imperial Cornerstone in China: The Chinese Maritime Customs Service, 1854–1949.* London and New York: Routledge.

B'Tselem. 1994. *Collaborators in the Occupied Territories: Human Rights Abuses and Violations.* Jerusalem: B'Tselem – The Israeli Information Center for Human Rights in the Occupied Territories.

Buchanan, Allen E. 2004. *Justice, Legitimacy, and Self-determination: Moral Foundations for International Law.* Oxford and New York: Oxford University Press.

Buchanan, Allen E., and Dan W. Brock. 1989. *Deciding for Others: The Ethics of Surrogate Decision Making.* Cambridge, England, and New York: Cambridge University Press.

Buchanan, James M., and Gordon Tullock. 1965. *The Calculus of Consent. Logical Foundations of Constitutional Democracy.* Ann Arbor: University of Michigan Press.

Bull, Timothy. 2009. *The Secret Agent's Pocket Manual, 1939–1945.* London: Conway.

Bunce, Valerie. 1999. *Subversive Institutions: The Design and the Destruction of Socialism and the State.* New York: Cambridge University Press.

Bunting, Madeleine. 1995. *The Model Occupation: The Channel Islands under German Rule, 1940–1945.* London: HarperCollins.

Burke, Edmund. [1774] 1887. "Speech to the Electors of Bristol, on Being Declared by the Sheriffs Duly Elected One of the Representatives in Parliament for that City," Pp. 90–98 in *The Works of the Right Honorable Edmund Burke*, Volume II. London: John C. Nimmo.

Burt, Ronald S. 1992. *Structural Holes: The Social Structure of Competition.* Cambridge, MA: Harvard University Press.

2004. "Structural Holes and Good Ideas." *American Journal of Sociology* 110(2):349–399.

Buzo, Adrian. 2002. *The Making of Modern Korea.* London and New York: Routledge.

Calhoun, Craig J., Frederick Cooper, Kevin W. Moore, and Social Science Research Council (U.S.). 2006. *Lessons of Empire: Imperial Histories and American Power.* New York: New Press: Distributed by W.W. Norton.

Caprio, Mark. 2009. *Japanese Assimilation Policies in Colonial Korea, 1910–1945.* Seattle: University of Washington Press.

Carlton, Eric. 1992. *Occupation. The Policies and Practices of Military Conquerors.* New York: Routledge.

Caro, Robert A. 2003. *Master of the Senate: The Years of Lyndon Johnson.* New York: Vintage.

Case, Anne, Lin I-Fen, and Sara McLanahan. 1999. "Household Resource Allocation in Stepfamilies: Darwin Reflects on the Plight of Cinderella." *American Economic Review* 89(2):234–238.

Cashdan, Elizabeth. 2001. "Ethnocentrism and Xenophobia: A Cross-Cultural Study." *Current Anthropology* 42(5):760–765.

Cath, Stanley H., and Moisy Shopper. 2001. *Stepparenting: Creating and Recreating Families in America Today*. Hillsdale, NJ: Analytic Press.

Cederman, Lars-Erik. 1995. "Competing Identities: An Ecological Model of Nationality Formation." *European Journal of International Relations* 1:331–365.

Chai, Sun-Ki. 1996. "A Theory of Ethnic Group Boundaries." *Nations and Nationalism* 2(2):281–307.

Chancer, Lynn S. 1992. *Sadomasochism in Everyday Life: The Dynamics of Power and Powerlessness*. New Brunswick, NJ: Rutgers University Press.

Chao, Linda, and Ramon H. Myers. 1998. *The First Chinese Democracy: Political Life in the Republic of China of Taiwan*. Baltimore and London: The Johns Hopkins University Press.

Chatterjee, Partha. 1993. *The Nation and Its Fragments: Colonial and Postcolonial Histories*. Princeton, NJ: Princeton University Press.

Chehabi, H.E., and Juan J. Linz. 1998. *Sultanistic Regimes*. Baltimore: Johns Hopkins University Press.

Chen, Ching-Chih. 1975. "The Japanese Adaptation of the *Pao-Chia* System in Taiwan, 1895–1945." *Journal of Asian Studies* 34:391–416.

Chen, Edward I-te. 1968. *Japanese Colonialism in Korea and Formosa: A Comparison of Its Effects upon the Development of Nationalism*. Philadelphia: University of Pennsylvania, PhD, International Relations.

——— 1970. "Japanese Colonization in Korea and Formosa: A Comparison of the Systems of Political Control." *Harvard Journal of Asiatic Studies* 30:126–158.

——— 1972. "Formosan Political Movements Under Japanese Colonial Rule, 1914–1937." *Journal of Asiatic Studies* 31(3):477–497.

Cheng, Tun-Jen. 2001. "Transforming Taiwan's Economic Structure in the 20th Century." *China Quarterly* 165(March) 19–36.

Chesneaux, Jean, Marianne Bastid, and Marie-Claire Bergère. 1976. *China from the Opium Wars to the 1911 Revolution*. New York: Pantheon Books.

Chittolini, Giorgio. 1989. "Cities, 'City-States,' and Regional States in North-Central Italy." *Theory and Society* 18:689–706.

Chou, Wan-Yao. 1996. "The Kominka Movement in Taiwan and Korea: Comparisons and Interpretations." Pp. 40–70 in *The Japanese Wartime Empire: 1931–1945*, edited by Peter Duus, Ramon H. Myers, and Mark R. Peattie. Princeton: Princeton University Press.

Chou, Whei-ming. 1989. *Taiwan unter Japanisher Herrschaft 1895–1945*. Bochum: Univ.-Verl. Brockmeyer.

Chu, Yun-han, and Jih-wen Lin. 2001. "Political Development in 20th-Century Taiwan: State-Building, Regime Transformation and the Construction of National Identity." *China Quarterly* 165(March):102–129.

Chung, Chin Sung. 1995. "Korean Women Drafted for Military Sexual Slavery By Japan." In *True Stories of the Korean Comfort Women*, edited by Keith Howard Pp. 11–30. London: Cassell.

Chwe, Michael Suk-Young. 2001. *Rational Ritual: Culture, Coordination, and Common Knowledge*. Princeton, NJ: Princeton University Press.

Clark, Gregory. 2007. "A Review of Avner Greif's *Institutions and the Path to the Modern Economy: Lessons from Medieval Trade*." *Journal of Economic Literature* 45:727–743.

Clay, Christopher. 2000. *Gold for the Sultan: Western Bankers and Ottoman Finance 1856–1881: A Contribution to Ottoman and to International Financial History.* London and New York: I.B. Tauris.

Clarke, Donald. 2011. "Neurotic? Who, Me?" in *The Irish Times.* March 19th, P. D12. Dublin, Ireland.

Clifford, Nicholas R. 1965. "Sir Frederic Maze and the Chinese Maritime Customs, 1937–1941." *Journal of Modern History* 37:18–34.

Cockburn, Andrew, and Patrick Cockburn. 2002. "Saddam at the Abyss." In *Inside Iraq,* edited by John Miller and Aaron Kennedy, 167–207. New York: Marlowe & Company.

Cohen, Hillel. 2008. *Army of Shadows. Palestinian Collaboration with Zionism, 1917–1948,* Berkeley and Los Angeles: University of California Press.

Cole, Juan. 2004. "The Three-State Solution?" *Nation* 278(March): 27–30.

Coleman, James S. 1986. *Individual Interests and Collective Action. Selected Essays.* New York: Cambridge University Press.

    1990. *Foundations of Social Theory.* Cambridge, MA: The Belknap Press of Harvard University Press.

Cooley, Alexander. 2005. *Logics of Hierarchy: The Organization of Empires, States, and Military Occupations.* Ithaca, NY: Cornell University Press.

Coontz, Stephanie. 2005. *Marriage, A History: From Obedience to Intimacy or How Love Conquered Marriage.* New York: Viking.

Cooper, Frederick. 2002. *Africa Since 1940: The Past of the Present.* Cambridge, UK, and New York: Cambridge University Press.

    2005. *Colonialism in Question: Theory, Knowledge, History.* Berkeley: University of California Press.

    2005. "Postcolonial Studies and the Study of History." In *Postcolonial Studies and Beyond,* edited by Ania Loomba, Suvir Kaul, Matti Bunzl, Antoinette Burton, and Jed Esty, 400–422. Durham, NC: Duke University Press.

Cooper, Frederick, and Ann Laura Stoler. 1997. *Tensions of Empire: Colonial Cultures in a Bourgeois World.* Berkeley: University of California Press.

Copper, John F. 1996. *Taiwan: Nation-State or Province?* Boulder, CO: Westview Press.

Coser, Lewis. 1956. *The Functions of Social Conflict.* New York: Free Press.

    1974. *Greedy Institutions; Patterns of Undivided Commitment.* New York: Free Press.

Costin, W. C. 1968. *Great Britain and China, 1833–1860.* Oxford: Clarendon Press.

Crile, George. 2003. *Charlie Wilson's War: The Extraordinary Story of the Largest Covert Operation in History.* New York: Atlantic Monthly Press.

Cumings, Bruce. 2002. *Parallax Visions: Making Sense of American-East Asian Relations.* Durham: Duke University Press.

    2005. *Korea's Place in the Sun: A Modern History.* New York and London: W. W. Norton.

Dahl, Robert Alan. 1963. *A Preface to Democratic Theory.* Chicago: University of Chicago Press.

Daly, Martin, and Margo I. Wilson. 1985. "Child Abuse and Other Risks of Not Living with Older Parents." *Ethology and Sociobiology* 6:197–210.

    1991. "A Reply to Gelles: Stepchildren *Are* Disproportionally Abused, and Diverse Forms of Violence *Can* Share Causal Factors." *Human Nature* 2(4):419–426.

1996. "Violence against Stepchildren." *Current Directions in Psychological Science* 5:77–81.

1999. *The Truth About Cinderella: A Darwinian View of Parental Love*. New Haven, CT: Yale University Press.

Daniels, Gordon 1984. "The American Occupation of Japan, 1945–52." In *Armies of Occupation*, edited by Roy A. Prete and A. Hamish Ion, 157–176. Waterloo, Ontario: Wilfrid Laurier University Press.

Dann, Uriel. 1969. *Iraq under Qassem*. Jerusalem: Israel University Press.

Deák, István. 1990. *Beyond Nationalism: A Social and Political History of the Habsburg Officer Corps, 1848–1918*. New York: Oxford University Press.

Demeritt, Allison. 2012. "Legitimate Authority after Regime Change: The Case of Mergers and Acquisitions." Unpublished paper. Department of Sociology, University of Washington.

Diamond, Larry. 2004. "Testimony to the Senate Foreign Relations Committee." http://www.stanford.edu/~ldiamond/iraq/Senate_testimony_051904.htm (accessed on October 7, 2006).

2005. *Squandered Victory*. New York: Henry Holt and Company.

Dilworth, Richardson. 2005. *The Urban Origins of Suburban Autonomy*. Cambridge, MA: Harvard University Press.

Dimaggio, Paul J., and Walter W. Powell. 1983. "The Iron Cage Revisited: Institutional Isomorphism and Collective Rationality in Organizational Fields." *American Sociological Review* 48(2):147–160.

Dirks, Nicholas B. 2001. *Castes of Mind: Colonialism and the Making of Modern India*. Princeton, NJ: Princeton University Press.

Dobbins, James. 2003. *America's Role in Nation-building: From Germany to Iraq*. Santa Monica, CA: RAND.

Dodge, Toby. 2003. *Inventing Iraq*. New York: Columbia University Press.

Doherty, N. A., and J. Feeney. 2004. "The Composition of Attachment Networks throughout the Adult Years." *Personal Relationships* 11:469–88.

Donadio, Rachel, and Elisabetta Povoledo. 2011. "How to Trim a Public Debt? Italy Tries Raising the Social Stigma on Tax Evaders." *New York Times*. December 25.

Dong, Wonmo. 1965. "Japanese Colonial Policy and Practice in Korea, 1905–1945: A Study in Assimilation." Dissertation. Washington, DC: Georgetown University.

Dowe, Dieter, Heinz-Gerhard Haupt, Dieter Langewiesche, and Jonathan Sperber, eds. 2001. *Europe in 1848: Revolution and Reform*. Translated by David Higgins. New York: Berghan Books.

Doyle, Michael W., and Nicholas Sambanis. 2006. *Making War and Building Peace: United Nations Peace Operations*. Princeton: Princeton University Press.

Durkheim, Emile. [1897] 1951. *Suicide*. New York: Free Press.

Durkheim, Emile. [1893] 1933. *The Division of Labor in Society*. Glencoe, IL: Free Press.

Duus, Peter, Ramon Hawley Myers, Mark R. Peattie, and Wanyao Zhou. 1996. *The Japanese Wartime Empire, 1931–1945*. Princeton: Princeton University Press.

Eckert, Carter J. 1991. *Offspring of Empire: The Koch'ang Kims and the Colonial Origins of Korean Capitalism, 1876–1945*. Seattle and London: University of Washington Press.

1996. "Total War, Industrialization, and Social Change in Late Colonial Korea." In *The Japanese Wartime Empire: 1931–1945*, edited by Peter Duus, Ramon H. Myers, and Mark R. Peattíe. Princeton: Princeton University Press, 3–39.

Edelstein, David. 2004. "Occupational Hazards: Why Military Occupations Succeed or Fail." *International Security* 29:49–91.

Edwards, Richard. 1999. "The Academic Department: How Does It Fit into the University Reform Agenda?" *Change* 31(5): 16–27

Ehmann, William J. (N.d.)"Advice on Anointing: Some Faculty Considerations on Choosing a New Chair." Unpublished manuscript available through the American Council on Education's Department Chair Online Resource Center. http://www2. acenet.edu/resources/chairs/docs/ehmann.pdf (accessed May 9, 2013).

Elias, Norbert. 1983. *The Court Society*. Oxford: Blackwell.

1993. *The Civilizing Process*. Cambridge, MA: Blackwell.

Elster, Jon. 2007. *Explaining Social Behavior: More Nuts and Bolts for the Social Sciences*. New York: Cambridge University Press.

Emerson, Rupert. 1960. *From Empire to Nation: The Rise to Self-assertion of Asian and African Peoples*. Cambridge, MA: Harvard University Press.

Ensminger, Jean. 2012. "Inside Corruption Networks: Community Driven Development in the Village." Division of Social Science, California Institute of Technology.

Ermakoff, Ivan. 2008. *Ruling Oneself Out: A Theory of Collective Abdications*. Durham: Duke University Press.

Ertman, Thomas. 1997. *Birth of the Leviathan: Building States and Regimes in Medieval and Early Modern Europe*. Cambridge: Cambridge University Press.

Esdaile, Charles. 2001. "Popular Mobilisation in Spain, 1808–1810: A Reassessment." Pp. 90–106 in *Collaboration and Resistance in Napoleonic Europe: State Formation in an Age of Upheaval, c. 1800–1815*, edited by Michael Rowe. London: Palgrave Macmillan.

Evans-Pritchard, E. E. 1944. *The Nuer*. Oxford: Oxford University Press.

Fackler, Martin. 2012. "Where the Songs Linger, but the Tune is Different." *New York Times*. February 21.

Fairbank, John King. 1953. *Trade and Diplomacy on the China Coast; The Opening of the Treaty Ports, 1842–1854*. Cambridge, MA: Harvard University Press.

1986. *The Great Chinese Revolution, 1800–1985*. New York: Harper & Row.

Fairbanks Jr., Charles H. 2002. "Weak States and Private Armies." In *Beyond State Crisis?: Post-Colonial Africa and Post-Soviet Eurasia in Comparative Perspective*, edited by Mark R. Beissinger and Crawford Young, 129–160. Washington, DC: Woodrow Wilson Center Press.

Fanon, Frantz. 1968. *The Wretched of the Earth*. New York: Grove Press.

Fearon, James D., and David D. Laitin. 1996. "Explaining Interethnic Cooperation." *American Political Science Review* 90(December):715–735.

2003. "Ethnicity, Insurgency, and Civil War." *American Political Science Review* 97(1):75–90.

2004. "Neotrusteeship and the Problem of Weak States." *International Security* 28:5–43.

Fearon, James D., Macartan Humphreys, and Jeremy M. Weinstein. 2009. "Can Development Aid Contribute to Social Cohesion after Civil War? Evidence from a Field Experiment in Post-Conflict Liberia." *The American Economic Review* 99(2):287–291.

Ferguson, N., and M. Schularick. 2006. "The Empire Effect: The Determinants of Country Risk in the First Age of Globalization, 1880–1913." *Journal of Economic History* 66:283–312.

Finer, S. E. 1997. *The History of Government from the Earliest Times*. Oxford and New York: Oxford University Press.

Fiorina, Morris P. 1981. *Retrospective Voting in American National Elections*. New Haven, CT: Yale University Press.

Foner, Eric. 1988. *Reconstruction: America's Unfinished Revolution, 1863–1877*. New York: Harper & Row.

Fortna, Virginia Page. 2008. *Does Peacekeeping Work?: Shaping Belligerents' Choices After Civil War*. Princeton, NJ: Princeton University Press.

Fox, Grace Estelle. 1940. *British Admirals and Chinese Pirates, 1832–1869*. London: K. Paul Trench Trubner & Co. Ltd.

Franck, Rafael, and Ilia Rainer. 2012. "Does the Leader's Ethnicity Matter? Ethnic Favoritism, Education, and Health in Sub-Saharan Africa." *American Political Science Review* 106(2):294–325.

Franke, Ann H., and Lawrence White. 2002. "Responsibilities of Department Chairs: Legal Issues." Paper prepared for Collaboration Toward the Common Good: Faculty and Administrators Working Together, a conference sponsored by the American Association of University Professors and the American Conference of Academic Deans, Washington, DC, October 26–28, 2000. Revised by the authors in July 2002. Available at the American Council on Education's Department Chair Online Resource Center. http://www2.acenet.edu/resources/chairs/docs/franke_white.pdf (accessed May 9, 2013).

Franke, Wolfgang. 1967. *China and the West*. Columbia: University of South Carolina Press.

Freud, Sigmund. 1961. *Civilization and its Discontents*. New York: Norton & Company.

Friedman, Debra, Michael Hechter, and Derek Kreager. 2008. "A Theory of the Value of Grandchildren." *Rationality and Society* 20(1):31–63.

Fromm, Erich. 1941. *Escape From Freedom*. New York: Rinehart.

Fujii, Shozo. 2006. "The Formation of Taiwanese Identity and the Cultural Policy of Various Outside Regimes." In Liao, Ping-Hui and David Der-Wei Wang, eds., *Taiwan Under Japanese Colonial Rule 1895–1945: History, Culture, Memory*. New York: Columbia University Press, 62–77.

Fulda, Andreas Martin. 2002. 'Reevaluating the Taiwanese Democracy Movement: A Comparative Analysis of Opposition Organizations under Japanese and KMT Rule.' *Critical Asian Studies*. 34(3): 357–394.

Fry, Suzanne E. 2005. *When States Kill Their Own: The Legitimating Rhetoric and Institutional Remedies of Authority Crises*. Unpublished PhD Dissertation, Department of Politics, New York University. Ann Arbor, MI: University Microfilms.

Galbraith, Peter W. 2006. *The End of Iraq: How American Incompetence Created a War Without End*. New York: Simon & Schuster.

Gale, Dennis E. 2001. "Threatened Planning Schools: Lessons from Experience." Paper commissioned by the Association of Collegiate Schools of Planning's Standing Committee on Strategic Communications for Planning Programs. http://www.acsp.org/sites/default/files/_doc/reports/ACSP%20SCC%20ThreatenedSchools.pdf (accessed May 9, 2013).

Gamson, William A., Bruce Fireman, and Steven Rytina. 1982. *Encounters with Unjust Authority*. Homewood, IL: Dorsey Press.

Ganong, Lawrence H., and Marilyn Coleman. 2004. *Stepfamily Relationships: Development, Dynamics, and Interventions*. New York: Kluwer Academic/Plenum Publishers.

Gavrilis, James. 2005. "The Mayor of Ar Rutbah." *Foreign Policy* 151:28–35.

Gellner, Ernest. 1983. *Nations and Nationalism*. Ithaca, NY and London: Cornell University Press.

2009. "Trust, Cohesion and the Social Order." In *Theories of Social Order: A Reader*, edited by Michael Hechter and Christine Horne, 300–305. Stanford, CA: Stanford University Press.

Gerlach, Michael L. 1992. *Alliance Capitalism: The Social Organization of Japanese Business*. Berkeley: University of California Press.

Gerring, John, Daniel Ziblatt, Johan Van Gorp, and Julián Arévalo. 2011. "An Institutional Theory of Direct and Indirect Rule." *World Politics* 63(3):377–433.

Gerson, Kathleen. 2010. *The Unfinished Revolution: How a New Generation Is Reshaping Family, Work, and Gender in America*. New York: Oxford University Press.

Geurts, T., A. R. Poortman, and T. G. van Tilburg. 2012. "Older Parents Providing Child Care for Adult Children: Does It Pay Off?" *Journal of Marriage and Family* 74(2):239–250.

Ghazi, Yasir, and Christine Hauser. 2013. "Violence in Iraq Swells at Year's End, Leaving at least 3 Dozen Dead." *New York Times*, January 1.

Giddens, Anthony. 2000. *Runaway World: How Globalization Is Reshaping Our Lives*. New York: Routledge.

Gide, André. 2000. *Journals. Volume 4: 1939–1949*. Edited by Justin O'Brien. Champaign-Urbana: University of Illinois Press.

Gilley, Bruce. 2006a. "The Determinants of State Legitimacy: Results for 72 Countries." *International Political Science Review* 27(1):47–71.

2006b. "The Meaning and Measure of State Legitimacy: Results for 72 Countries." *European Journal of Political Research* 45:499–525.

Gillingham, John. 1987. "Images of Ireland, 1170–1600: The Origins of English Imperialism." *History Today* 37:16–22.

Ginsborg, Paul. 2003. *Italy and its Discontents: Family, Civil Society, State, 1980–2001*. London: Penguin.

Gluckman, Max. 1955. "Peace in the Feud." *Past & Present* 8(1):1–14.

Gmelch, Walter H., and Val D. Miskin. 1993. *Leadership Skills for Departmental Chairs*. Boston: Anker Publishing.

Goldstein, Cora Sol. 2008. "A Strategic Failure. American Information Control Policy in Occupied Iraq." *Military Review* 88(March–April):58–65.

2009. *Capturing the German Eye: American Visual Propaganda in Occupied Germany*. Chicago: University of Chicago Press.

Goodliffe, J., D. Hawkins, C. Horne, and D. L. Nielson. 2012. "Dependence Networks and the International Criminal Court." *International Studies Quarterly* 56(1):131–147.

Gordon, Neve. 2008. *Israel's Occupation*. Berkeley: University of California Press.

Gorski, Phillip S. 2000. "The Mosaic Moment: An Early Modernist Critique of Modernist Theories of Nationalism." *American Journal of Sociology* 105(5):1428–1468.

2003. *The Disciplinary Revolution*. Chicago: University of Chicago Press.

Gould, Roger V. 2003. *Collision of Wills: How Ambiguity about Social Rank Breeds Conflict*. Chicago: University of Chicago Press.

1996. "Patron-Client Ties, State Centralization, and the Whiskey Rebellion." *American Journal of Sociology* 102(2):400–429.

Grafstein, Robert. 1981. "The Failure of Weber's Conception of Legitimacy – Its Causes and Implications." *Journal of Politics* 43(2):456–472.

Graham, Steven, and Pam Benoit. 2004. "Constructing the Role of Department Chair." Paper written for the American Council on Education's Department Chair Online Resource Center. http://www2.acenet.edu/resources/chairs/docs/Graham_Constructing.pdf (accessed May 9, 2013).

Granovetter, Mark. 1973. "The Strength of Weak Ties." *American Journal of Sociology* 78:1360–1380.

Greif, Avner. 1998. "Self-Enforcing Political Systems and Economic Growth: Late Medieval Genoa." In *Analytic Narratives*, edited by Robert Bates, Avner Greif, Margaret Levi, Jean-Laurent Rosenthal, and Barry R. Weingast, 23–63. Princeton: Princeton University Press.

2005. *Institutions and the Path to the Modern Economy: Lessons from Medieval Trade*. Cambridge and New York: Cambridge University Press.

Greenwood, Royston, Christine Oliver, Kerstin Sahlin, and Roy Suddaby. 2008. "Introduction." In *The SAGE Handbook of Organizational Institutionalism*, edited by Royston Greenwood, Christine Oliver, Kerstin Sahlin, and Roy Suddaby, 1–46. Los Angeles and London: SAGE.

Grimm, Jacob and Wilhelm Grimm. 1884. *Cinderella*. Translated by Margaret Taylor. http://classiclit.about.com/library/bl-etexts/grimm/bl-grimm-cinderella.htm

Haddad, Fanar. 2011. *Sectarianism in Iraq: Antagonistic Visions of Unity*. New York: Columbia University Press.

Haggard, Stephan, David Kang and Ching-in Moon. 1997. Japanese Colonialism and Korean Development: A Critique. *World Development*, 25 (6): 867–881.

Hale, Henry E. 2004. "Explaining Ethnicity." *Comparative Political Studies* 37:458–485.

Hamilton, Alexander, James Madison, John Jay [1788] 1961. *The Federalist Papers*. New York: Penguin.

Hamilton, William D. 1964. "The Genetical Evolution of Social Behaviour." *Journal of Theoretical Biology* 7:1–52.

Han-Yu Chang and Ramon H. Myers, 1963. "Japanese Colonial Development Policy in Taiwan, 1895–1906: A Case of Bureaucratic Entrepreneurship." *The Journal of Asian Studies* 22(4): 433–449.

Hannan, Michael T. 1979. "The Dynamics of Ethnic Boundaries in Modern States." In *National Development and the World System*, edited by John W. Meyer and Michael T. Hannan, 253–275. Chicago: University of Chicago Press.

Hardin, Russell. 1993. "The Street-Level Epistemology of Trust." *Politics & Society* 21(4):505–529.

Hart, Robert, Katherine Frost Bruner, John King Fairbank, and Richard J. Smith. 1986. *Entering China's Service : Robert Hart's Journals, 1854–1863*. Cambridge, MA: Council on East Asian Studies Distributed by the Harvard University Press.

Hart, Robert, Richard J. Smith, John King Fairbank, and Katherine Frost Bruner. 1991. *Robert Hart and China's Early Modernization: His Journals, 1863–1866*. Cambridge, MA: Council on East Asian Studies Harvard University: Distributed by the Harvard University Press.

Haveman, Heather, and Robert J. David. 2008. "Ecologists and Institutionalists: Friends or Foes?" In *The SAGE Handbook of Organizational Institutionalism*, edited by Royston Greenwood, Christine Oliver, Kerstin Sahlin, and Roy Suddaby, 572–595. Los Angeles; London: SAGE.

Hayek, Friedrich A. 1973. *Law, Legislation and Liberty. Volume 1: Rules and Order.* Chicago: University of Chicago Press.

Hecht, Irene W. D. 2002. "Appointment and Compensation: A Theme with Variations." Unpublished manuscript written for the American Council on Education's Department Chair Resource Center.http://www2.acenet.edu/resources/chairs/docs/Hecht_appointments.pdf (accessed May 9, 2013).

Hecht, Irene W. D., Mary Lou Higgerson, Walter H. Gmelch, and Allan Tucker. 1999. *The Department Chair as Academic Leader.* Phoenix, AZ: The Oryx Press. Chapter 2 available from http://www.uky.edu/Provost/APFA/Department_Chairs/HECHT_roles_respon.pdf.Chapter 14 available from http://www.provost.buffalo.edu/facultyaffairs/pdf_external_audiences.pdf (accessed May 9, 2013).

Hechter, Michael. 1975. *Internal Colonialism: The Celtic Fringe in British National Development, 1536–1966.* Berkeley: University of California Press.

    1978. "Group Formation and the Cultural Division of Labor." *American Journal of Sociology* 84(2):293–318.

    1987. *Principles of Group Solidarity.* Berkeley: University of California Press.

    1998. *Internal Colonialism: The Celtic Fringe in British National Development.* New Brunswick, NJ: Transaction Publishers.

    2000. *Containing Nationalism.* Oxford and New York: Oxford University Press.

    2004. "From Class to Culture." *American Journal of Sociology* 110(September):400–445.

Hechter, Michael, ed. 2009. "Special Issue: Legitimacy in the Modern World." *American Behavioral Scientist* 53(3).

Hechter, Michael, and Elizabeth Borland. 2001. "National Self-Determination: The Emergence of an International Norm." In *Social Norms*, edited by Michael Hechter and Karl-Dieter Opp, 186–233. New York: Russell Sage Foundation.

Hechter, Michael, and Christine Horne. 2009. *Theories of Social Order: A Reader.* Second Edition. Stanford, CA: Stanford University Press.

Hechter, Michael, Debra Friedman, and Satoshi Kanazawa. 1992. "The Attainment of Global Order in Heterogeneous Societies." In *Rational Choice Theory: Advocacy and Critique*, edited by James S. Coleman and Thomas J. Fararo, 329–344. Newbury Park, CA: Sage Publications.

Hechter, Michael, Hyojoung Kim, and Justin Baer. 2005. "Prediction Versus Explanation in the Measurement of Values." *European Sociological Review* 21(2):91–108.

Hechter, Michael, James Ranger-Moore Guillermina Jasso, and Christine Horne. 1999. "Do Values Matter? An Analysis of Advance Directives for Medical Treatment." *European Sociological Review* 15(4):405–430.

Henderson, Gregory. 1968. *Korea: The Politics of the Vortex.* Cambridge, MA: Harvard University Press.

Herzog, Don. 1989. *Happy Slaves: A Critique of Consent Theory.* Chicago: University of Chicago Press.

Hetherington, E. Mavis, and Kathleen M. Jodl. 1994. "Stepfamilies as Settings for Child Development." In *Stepfamilies: Who Benefits? Who Does Not?*, edited by Alan Booth and Judy Dunn, 55–79. Hillsdale, NJ: Lawrence Erlbaum Associates.

Hewstone, M., M. Rubin, and H. Willis. 2002. "Intergroup Bias." *Annual Review of Psychology* 53:575–604.

Hicks, George. 1994. *The Comfort Women: Japan's Brutal Regime of Enforced Prostitution in the Second World War.* New York: W.W. Norton and Company.

Hirsch, Paul M. 1986. "From Ambushes to Golden Parachutes: Corporate Takeovers as an Instance of Cultural Framing and Institutional Integration." *American Journal of Sociology* 91 (4): 800–837.

Hirsch, Paul M. and John A. Y. Andrews. 1983. "Ambushes, Shootouts, and Knights of the Roundtable: The Language of Corporate Takeovers." In *Organizational Symbolism*, edited by L. Frost, G. Morgan and T. Dandridge, 145–157. Greenwich, CT: JAI.

Ho, Samuel P. S. 1975. "The Economic Development of Colonial Taiwan: Evidence and Interpretation." *Journal of Asian Studies* 34 (2): 417–439.

    1984. "Colonialism and Development: Korea, Taiwan, and Kwatung." In *The Japanese Colonial Empire, 1895–1945*, edited by Ramon H. Myers and Mark R. Peattie, 347–398. Princeton, NJ: Princeton University Press.

Hobbes, Thomas. [1651] 1996. *Leviathan.* Oxford: Oxford University Press.

Hochschild, Adam. 1998. *King Leopold's Ghost: A Story of Greed, Terror, and Heroism in Colonial Africa.* Boston: Houghton Mifflin.

Hodge, Nathan. 2011. *Armed Humanitarians: The Rise of the Nation Builders.* New York: Bloomsbury.

Hofferth, S. L., and K. G. Anderson. 2003. "Are All Dads Equal? Biology versus Marriage as a Basis for Paternal Investment." *Journal of Marriage and Family* 65(1):213–232.

Hoffmann, Stanley. 1968. "Collaborationism in France during World War II." *Journal of Modern History* 40:375–395.

Hollingsworth, Cristopher. 2001. *Poetics of the Hive: The Insect Metaphor in Literature.* Iowa City: University of Iowa Press.

Honan, William H. 1999. "Roman L. Hruska Dies at 94: Leading Senate Conservative." *New York Times*, April 27.

Honig, Bonnie. 2001. *Democracy and the Foreigner.* Princeton, NJ: Princeton University Press.

Hörnqvist, Mikael. 2004. *Machiavelli and Empire.* Cambridge and New York: Cambridge University Press.

Horowitz, Richard S. 2004. "International Law and State Transformation in China, Siam, and the Ottoman Empire during the Nineteenth Century." *Journal of World History* 15(4): 445–486.

Hourani, Albert Habib. 1991. *A History of the Arab Peoples.* Cambridge, MA: Belknap Press of Harvard University Press.

Hroch, Miroslav. 1985. *Social Preconditions of National Revival in Europe: A Comparative Analysis of the Social Composition of Patriotic Groups Among the Smaller European Nations.* Cambridge: Cambridge University Press.

Hu, Sheng. 1955. *Imperialism and Chinese Politics.* Peking: Foreign Languages Press.

Hudson, Michael C. 1977. *Arab Politics: The Search for Legitimacy.* New Haven, CT: Yale University Press.

Human Rights Watch/Middle East. 1995. *Iraq's Crime of Genocide: The Anfal Campaign Against the Kurds.* New Haven, CT: Yale University Press.

Huntington, Samuel P. 1968. *Political Order in Changing Societies.* New Haven, CT: Yale University Press.

1991. *The Third Wave: Democratization in the Late Twentieth Century.* Norman: University of Oklahoma Press.

Hurd, Ian. 1999. "Legitimacy and Authority in International Politics." *International Organization* 53:379–408.

2007. *After Anarchy: Legitimacy and Power in the United Nations Security Council.* Princeton, NJ: Princeton University Press.

Huxley, Aldous. 1946. *Brave New World: A Novel.* New York: Harper and Row.

Ihinger-Tallman, M., and K. Pasley. 1997. "Stepfamilies in 1984 and Today – A Scholarly Perspective." *Marriage and Family Review* 26(1–2):19–40.

International Crisis Group. 2006. "The Next Iraqi War? Sectarianism and Civil Conflict." *Middle East Report* (February).

Jabar, Faleh A. 2003. "Sheikhs and Ideologues: Deconstruction and Reconstruction of Tribes under Patrimonial Totalitarianism in Iraq, 1968–1998." In *Tribes and Power: Nationalism and Ethnicity in the Middle East*, edited by Faleh Abdul-Jabar and Hosham Dawod, 69–109. London: Saqi.

Jackson, Robert H. 1990. *Quasi-states: Sovereignty, International Relations, and the Third World.* Cambridge: Cambridge University Press.

Jennings, M. Kent, and Jan W. Van Deth (Eds.). 1990. *Continuities in Political Action.* Berlin: Walter de Gruyter.

Jensen, Michael C., and William H. Meckling. 1976. "Theory of the Firm: Managerial Behavior, Agency Costs and Ownership Structure." *Journal of Financial Economics* 3(4):305–360.

Jha, Saumitra. 2012. "Sharing the Future: Financial Innovation and Innovators in Solving the Political Economy Challenges of Development." In *Research Paper Series, Stanford Graduate School of Business*, 1–24. Stanford, CA: Stanford Graduate School of Business.

Jones, Charles Brewer. 1999. *Buddhism in Taiwan: Religion and the State, 1660–1990.* Honolulu: University of Hawai'i Press.

Jones, P. J. 1997. *The Italian City-State: From Commune to Signoria.* Oxford: Clarendon Press.

Jost, John T., and Brenda Major. 2001. *The Psychology of Legitimacy: Emerging Perspectives on Ideology, Justice, and Intergroup Relations.* Cambridge and New York: Cambridge University Press.

Ka, Chih-ming. 1995. *Japanese Colonialism in Taiwan: Land Tenure, Development, and Dependency, 1895–1945.* Boulder, CO: Harper Collins Publishers.

Kahneman, Daniel, and Amos Tversky. 1979. "Prospect Theory: An Analysis of Decision Under Risk." *Econometrica* 47:263–291.

Kalyvas, Stathis N. 2000. "Red Terror: Leftist Violence During the Occupation." In *After the War Was Over: Reconstructing Family, State, and Nation in Greece, 1944–1960*, edited by Mark Mazower, 142–183. Princeton, NJ: Princeton University Press.

2006. *The Logic of Violence in Civil War.* New York: Cambridge University Press.

2008a. "Collaboration in Comparative Perspective." *European Review of History* 15:109–111.

2008b. "Armed Collaboration in Greece, 1941–1944." *European Review of History* 15:129–142.

2008c. "Ethnic Defection in Civil War." *Comparative Political Studies* 41:1043–1068.

Kang, Hildi. 2001. *Under the Black Umbrella: Voices from Colonial Korea, 1910–1945.* Ithaca and London: Cornell University Press.

Kang, Man-Gil. 1994. *A History of Contemporary Korea.* Korea: Changbi Publishers. English translation in Kent: Global Oriental, 2005.

Katz, Paul R. 2005. *When Valleys Turned Blood Red: The Ta-pa-ni Incident in Colonial Taiwan.* Honolulu: University of Haiwaii Press.

Kedourie, Elie. 1960. *Nationalism.* London: Praeger.

Kedward, H. R. 1993. *In Search of the Maquis: Rural Resistance in Southern France, 1942–1944.* Oxford: Oxford University Press.

Kelidar, Abbas. 2003. "Iraqi National Integration under the British." In *U.S. Policy in Post-Saddam Iraq*, edited by Michael Eisenstadt and Eric Mathewson, 27–37. Washington, DC: Washington Institute for Near East Policy.

Kelly, Robert. 2004. "Dealing with Administrative Mandates." *Academic Leader* 20(12) December 1–2.

Kerr, George H. 1974. *Formosa: Licensed Revolution and the Home Rule Movement: 1895–1945.* Honolulu: The University Press of Honolulu

Khadduri, Majih. 1970. *Socialist Iraq: A Study in Iraqi Politics Since 1968.* Washington, DC: The Middle East Institute.

Khan, M. Masud R. 1979. *Alienation in Perversions.* New York: International Universities Press.

Khoury, Dina Rizk. 1997. *State and Provincial Society in the Ottoman Empire.* Cambridge: Cambridge University Press.

Kim, Djun Kil. 2005. *The History of Korea.* Westport, CT: Greenwood Press.

King, Valarie. 2006. "The Antecedents and Consequences of Adolescents' Relationships With Stepfathers and Nonresident Fathers." *Journal of Marriage and Family* 68(4):910–928.

Kingdon, John W. 1989. *Congressmen's Voting Decisions.* Ann Arbor: University of Michigan Press.

Kiser, Edgar. 1999. "Comparing Varieties of Agency Theory in Economics, Political Science, and Sociology: An Illustration from State Policy Implementation." *Sociological Theory* 17(July):146–170.

Kiser, Edgar, and Joachim Schneider. 1994. "Bureaucracy and Efficiency: An Analysis of Taxation in Early Modern Prussia." *American Sociological Review* 59(2):187–204.

Kitsantonis, Niki, and Rachel Donadio. 2012. "Greek Parliament Passes Austerity Plan After Riots Rage." *The New York Times*, February 12.

Kocher, Matthew. 2004. "Human Ecology and Civil War." PhD dissertation, Department of Political Science University of Chicago.

Kohli, Atul. 1997. "Can Democracies Accommodate Ethnic Nationalism? Rise and Decline of Self-Determination Movements in India." *Journal of Asian Studies* 56:325–344.

2002. "State, Society and Development." In *Political Science: State of the Discipline*, edited by Ira Katznelson and Helen V. Milner, 87–117. New York: W.W. Norton; Washington, DC: American Political Science Association.

Koppell, Jonathan G. S. 2010. *World Rule: Accountability, Legitimacy, and the Design of Global Governance.* Chicago: University of Chicago Press.

Krasner, Stephen D. 1999. *Sovereignty: Organized Hypocrisy.* Princeton, NJ: Princeton University Press.

2001. "Rethinking the Sovereign State Model." *Review of International Studies* 27:17–42.

Ku, Dae-yeol. 1985. *Korea under Colonialism*. Seoul: Seoul Computer Press.

Kuran, Timur. 1995. *Private Truths, Public Lies: The Social Consequences of Preference Falsification*. Cambridge, MA: Harvard University Press.

2004. "The Economic Ascent of the Middle East's Religious Minorities: The Role of Islamic Legal Pluralism." *Journal of Legal Studies* 33:475–515.

La Porta, Rafael, Florencio Lopez-de-Silanes, Andrei Shleifer, and Robert Vishny. 1999. "The Quality of Government." *Journal of Law, Economics & Organization* 15(1):222–279.

Laitin, David D. 1992. *Language Repertoires and State Construction in Africa*. New York: Cambridge University Press.

Lake, David A. 2007. "Escape from the State of Nature: Authority and Hierarchy in World Politics." *International Security* 32:47–79.

Lal, Deepak. 2004. *In Praise of Empires: Globalization and Order*. New York and Houndmills: Palgrave Macmillan.

Lamley, Harry J. 1970. "The 1895 Taiwan War of Resistance: Local Chinese Efforts Against a Foreign Power." In *Taiwan: Studies in Chinese Local History*, edited by Leonard H. D. Gordon, 23–77. New York and London: Columbia University Press.

2007. "Taiwan Under Japanese Rule, 1895–1945: The Vicissitudes of Colonialism." In *Taiwan: A New History*, ed. Murray A. Rubenstein, 201–260. Armonk, NY: M.E. Sharpe.

Lammers, Cornelis J. 1988. "The Interorganizational Control of an Occupied Country." *Administrative Science Quarterly* 33:438–457.

2003. "Occupation Regimes Alike and Unlike: British, Dutch and French Patterns of Inter-organizational Control of Foreign Territories." *Organization Studies* 24:1379–1403.

Lange, Matthew, and Andrew Dawson. 2009. "Dividing and Ruling the World? A Statistical Test of the Effects of Colonialism on Postcolonial Civil Violence." *Social Forces* 88(2):785–817.

Lapidus, Ira M. 1990. "Tribes and State Formation in Islamic History." In *Tribes and State Formation in the Middle East*, edited by P.S. Khoury and J. Kostiner, 25–47. Berkeley: University of California Press.

Lasswell, Harold. 1927. "The Theory of Political Propaganda." *American Political Science Review* 21:627–631.

Lawrence, Adria. 2013. *Imperial Rule and the Politics of Nationalism: Anti-Colonialism in the French Empire*. New York: Cambridge University Press.

Lee, Ann. 2012. *What We can Learn From China: An Open-Minded Guide to Treating Our Greatest Competitor as Our Greatest Teacher*. San Francisco: Berrett-Koehler Publishers

Lee, Chong-Sik. 1963. *The Politics of Korean Nationalism*. Berkeley and Los Angeles: University of California Press.

Lee, Chulwoo. 1999. "Modernity, Legality, and Power in Korea Under Japanese Rule." In *Colonial Modernity in Korea*, eds. Gi-Wook Shin and Michael Robinson, 21–51. Cambridge, MA and London: Harvard University Press.

Levi, Margaret. 1988. *Of Rule and Revenue*. Berkeley: University of California Press.

1997. *Consent, Dissent, and Patriotism*. Cambridge: Cambridge University Press.

Lévi-Strauss, Claude. 1969. *The Elementary Structures of Kinship*. Boston: Beacon Press.

Liberman, Peter. 1996. *Does Conquest Pay?: The Exploitation of Occupied Industrial Societies*. Princeton, NJ: Princeton University Press.

Linz, Juan J. 1978. *Crisis, Breakdown and Reequilibration*. Baltimore: Johns Hopkins University Press.

Lipset, Seymour Martin. 1960. *Political Man; The Social Bases of Politics*. Garden City, NY: Doubleday.

1993. "Pacific Divide – American Exceptionalism Japanese Uniqueness." *International Journal of Public Opinion Research* 5(2):121–166.

Lo, Andrew. Forthcoming. "Reading About the Financial Crisis: A 21-Book Review." *Journal of Economic Literature*.

Locke, John. [1690] 1988. *Two Treatises of Government*, edited by Peter Laslett. London and New York: Cambridge University Press.

Lone, Stewart and Gavan McCormack. 1993. *Korea: Since 1850*. New York: Longman Cheshire.

Lukes, Steven. 1974. *Power: A Radical View*. London and New York: Macmillan.

Luttwak, Edward N. 2005. "Iraq: The Logic of Disengagement." *Foreign Affairs* 84(1):26–36.

Lyall, Sarah. 2002. "Lost in Sweden: A Kurdish Daughter is Sacrificed." *New York Times*, July 23.

Lyons, Thomas P. 2003. *China Maritime Customs and China's Trade Statistics, 1859–1948*. Trumansburg, NY: Willow Creek of Trumansburg.

MacKenzie, S. P. 1997. *Revolutionary Armies in the Modern Era. A Revisionist Approach*. London: Routledge.

Macpherson, C. B. 1962. *The Political Theory of Possessive Individualism: Hobbes to Locke*. Oxford: Clarendon Press.

Madsen, Grant. 2012. "Becoming a State-in-the-World: Lessons Learned from the American Occupation of Germany." *Studies in American Political Development* 26(October):163–179.

Maine, Henry Sumner. [1861] 1986. *Ancient Law: Its Connection with the Early History of Society, and Its Relation to Modern Ideas*. Tucson: University of Arizona Press.

Makiya, Kanan. 1998. *Republic of Fear*. Berkeley: University of California Press.

Manin, Bernard. 1987. "On Legitimacy and Political Deliberation," translated by Elly Stein and Jane Mansbridge. *Political Theory* 15(3):338–368.

1997. *The Principles of Representative Government*. Cambridge and New York: Cambridge University Press.

Mansbridge, Jane. 1983. *Beyond Adversary Democracy*. New York: Basic Books.

1999. "Should Blacks Represent Blacks and Women Represent Women? A Contingent 'Yes'." *Journal of Politics* 61(3):628–657.

2009. "A 'Selection Model' of Political Representation." *Journal of Political Philosophy* 17(4):369–398.

Marr, Phebe. 2003. *A History of Modern Iraq*. Boulder, CO: Westview Press.

March, James G., Herbert A. Simon, and Harold Steere Guetzkow. 1993. *Organizations*. Cambridge, MA: Blackwell.

Marquis, Mel, and Etsuko Kameoka. 2012. "The Sun Also Sets: Trending Away from Japanese Exceptionalism in Merger Control and Closer to Global Standards." *Competition Policy International Asia Antitrust*1/8 (February).

Marten, Kimberly Zisk. 2004. *Enforcing the Peace: Learning from the Imperial Past.* New York: Columbia University Press.

Martin, Janet. 2007. *Medieval Russia, 980–1584.* Cambridge and New York: Cambridge University Press.

Marx, Karl, Friedrich Engels, and E. J. Hobsbawm. [1850] 1998. *The Communist Manifesto: A Modern Edition.* London and New York: Verso.

Mathewson, Eric. 2003. "Rebuilding Iraq: Assessing the British Military Occupation." In *U.S. Policy in Post-Saddam Iraq,* edited by Michael Eisenstadt and Eric Mathewson, 52–66. Washington DC: Washington Institute for Near East Policy.

Mathias-Riegel, Barbara. 2004. "A Chair in Your Future." *ASEE Prism* 2004(Summer).http://www.prism-magazine.org/may04/teachingtoolbox.cfm (accessed May 9, 2013).

Mazower, Mark. 2008. *Hitler's Empire: Nazi Rule in Occupied Europe.* London and New York: Allen Lane.

Mazzini, Giuseppe. [1860] 1892. *An Essay on the Duties of Man: Addressed to Workingmen.* New York: Funk & Wagnalls.

McDowall, David. 1992. "The Kurdish Question: A Historical Review." In *The Kurds: A Contemporary Overview,* edited by Philip G. Kreyenbroek and Stefan Sperl, 10–32. New York: Routledge.

McNamara, Dennis L. 1986. "Comparative Colonial Response: Korea and Taiwan." *Korean Studies* 10:54–68.

   1989. "The Keisho and the Korean Business Elite." *The Journal of Asian Studies* 48(2): 310–323.

McNeill, William H. 1986. *Polyethnicity and National Unity in World History.* Toronto: Toronto University Press.

McPherson, M., L. Smith-Lovin, and J. M. Cook. 2001. "Birds of A Feather: Homophily in Social Networks." *Annual Review of Sociology* 27:415–444.

Mendel, Douglas. 1970. *The Politics of Formosan Nationalism.* Berkeley and Los Angeles: University of California Press.

Menees, Stacy B., John M. Inadomi, Sheryl Korsnes, and Grace H. Elta. 2005. "Women Patients' Preference for Women Physicians is a Barrier to Colon Cancer Screening." *Gastrointestinal Endoscopy* 62:219–224.

Meyer, John W. 2010. "World Society, Institutional Theories, and the Actor." *Annual Review of Sociology* 36:1–20.

Meyer, John W., and Brian Rowan. 1977. "Institutionalized Organizations: Formal-Structure as Myth and Ceremony." *American Journal of Sociology* 83(2):340–363.

Meyer, John W., and W. Richard Scott. 1983. *Organizational Environments: Ritual and Rationality.* Beverly Hills, CA: Sage.

Michel, Henri. 1972. *The Shadow War: Resistance in Europe, 1939–1945.* London: Deutsch.

Michels, Robert. 1999. *Political Parties: A Sociological Study of the Oligarchical Tendencies of Modern Democracy.* New Brunswick, NJ: Transaction Publishers.

Mill, John Stuart. [1859] 1956. *On Liberty.* Indianapolis: Bobbs-Merrill.

   [1861] 1963. "Considerations on Representative Government." In *Collected Works,* Vol. 19, edited by J. M. Robson, 371–562. Toronto: University of Toronto Press.

Miller, Warren E., and Donald E. Stokes. 1963. "Constituency Influence in Congress." *American Political Science Review* **57**(1):45–56.

Mitchener, K. J., and M. Weidenmier. 2005. "Empire, Public Goods, and the Roosevelt Corollary." *Journal of Economic History* **65**:658–692.

Moore, Margaret. 1998. *National Self-determination and Secession.* Oxford and New York: Oxford University Press.

Morris Wu, Eleanor B. 2004. *From China to Taiwan: Historical, Anthropological, and Religious Perspectives.* Sankt Augustin: Monumenta Serica Institute.

Morse, Hosea Ballou. 1961. *The International Relations of the Chinese Empire.* New York: Paragon Book Gallery.

Murray, Bridget. 1999. "Department Chairs Call for Leadership Training: Universities Should Bolster Their Guidance of Chairs, Faculty Say." *APA Monitor* **30**(8).

Murray, Douglas J. 2000. "Leading University-Wide Change: Defining New Roles for the Department Chair." *Department Chair*(Summer).http://www.ccubc.ca/murray.pdf (accessed May 9, 2013).

Muthu, Sankar. 2003. *Enlightenment against Empire.* Princeton, NJ and Oxford: Princeton University Press.

Myers, Ramon H. and Yamada, Saburo. 1984. "Agricultural Development in the Empire." In *The Japanese Colonial Empire, 1895–1945,* edited by Ramon H. Myers and Mark R. Peattie, 420–454. Princeton, NJ: Princeton University Press.

Naimark, Norman M. 1995. *The Russians in Germany: A History of the Soviet Zone of Occupation, 1945–1949.* Cambridge, MA: Belknap Press of Harvard University Press.

Nakash, Yitzhak. 1994. *The Shi'is of Iraq.* Princeton, NJ: Princeton University Press.

Nalbandian, John. 1991. *Professionalism in Local Government: Transformations in the Roles, Responsibilities, and Values of City Managers.* San Francisco: Jossey-Bass.

Natali, Denise. 2001. "Manufacturing Identity and Managing Kurds in Iraq." In *Rightsizing the State,* edited by Brendan O'Leary, Ian S. Lustick, and Thomas Callaghy, 253–288. Oxford: Oxford University Press.

Nettl, J.P. 1968. "The State as a Conceptual Variable." *World Politics* **20**(July):559–592.

New York *Times.* 2007. "World Briefing – Asia: South Korea Crackdown on Collaborators" (originally reported by Agence France Presse), May 3.

Neuberg, S. L., D. M. Smith, and T. Asher. 2000. "Why People Stigmatize: Toward a Biocultural Framework."In *The Social Psychology of Stigma,* edited by T. Heatherton, R. Kleck, J. G. Hull, and M. Hebl, 31–61. New York: Guilford.

Neuberg, Steven L., and Catherine Cottrell. 2006. "Evolutionary Basis of Prejudices." In *Evolution and Social Psychology,* edited by M. Schaller, J. A. Simpson, and D. T. Kenrick, 163–187. New York: Psychology Press.

Nieuwenhuis, Tom. 1981. *Politics and Society in Early Modern Iraq.* Boston: Martinus Nijhoff.

Nisbett, Richard E., and Dov Cohen. 1996. *Culture of Honor: The Psychology of Violence in the South.* Boulder, CO: Westview Press.

North, Douglass C. 1990. *Institutions, Institutional Change and Economic Performance.* Cambridge: Cambridge University Press.

  2006. "What Is Missing from Political Economy." In *The Oxford Handbook of Political Economy,* edited by Barry R. Weingast and Donald Wittman, 1003–1009. Oxford: Oxford University Press.

North, Douglass C., and Barry R. Weingast. 1989. "Constitutions and Commitment: The Evolution of Institutions Governing Public Choice in 17th-Century England." *Journal of Economic History* **49**(4):803–832.

North, Douglass C., and Robert Paul Thomas. 1973. *The Rise of the Western World. A New Economic History*. Cambridge: Cambridge University Press.

Nozick, Robert. 1974. *Anarchy, State, and Utopia*. New York: Basic Books.

Oates, Wallace E. 1972. *Fiscal Federalism*. New York: Harcourt Brace Jovanovich.

Oh, Bonnie B.C. 2001. "The Japanese Imperial System and Korean 'Comfort Women' of World War II." In *Legacies of the Comfort Women of World War II*, edited by Margaret Stetz and Bonnie B.C. Oh. Armonk, NY: M.E. Sharpe.

Olie, René. 1990. "Cultural Issues in Transnational Business Ventures." *Studies in Third World Societies* 42 (Special issue on Cross-Cultural Management and Organizational Culture): 145–172.

Olson, Mancur. 1965. *The Logic of Collective Action*. Cambridge, MA: Harvard University Press.

Olsson, Andreas, Jeffrey P. Ebert, Mahzarin R. Banaji, and Elizabeth A. Phelps. 2005. "The Role of Social Groups in the Persistence of Learned Fear." *Science* 309:785–787.

Omissi, David. 1990. *Air Power and Colonial Control: The Royal Air Force 1919–1939*. Manchester: Manchester University Press.

Orwell, George. [1949] 1984. *Nineteen Eighty-four*. Oxford (Oxfordshire), London, and New York: Clarendon Press, Oxford University Press.

Ostrom, Elinor. 1990. *Governing the Commons*. Cambridge: Cambridge University Press.

Ottaway, Marina, and Danial Kaysi. 2012. "The State of Iraq." *The Carnegie Papers: The Carnegie Endowment for International Peace, Washington D.C. Middle East*(February):1–19.

Ouchi, William G. 1981. *Theory Z: How American Business Can Meet the Japanese Challenge*. Reading, MA: Addison-Wesley.

Owen, Roger. 2000. *State, Power and Politics in the Making of the Modern Middle East*. New York: Routledge.

Packer, George. 2005. *The Assassin's Gate: America in Iraq*. New York: Farrar, Straus, and Giroux.

Pape, Robert. 2005. *Dying to Win*. New York: Random House.

Park, Soon-Won. 1999. "Colonial Industrial Growth and the Emergence of a Korean Working Class."In Gi-Wook Shin and Michael Robinson, *Colonial Modernity in Korea*, edited by Gi-Wook Shin and Michael Robinson, 18–160. Cambridge, MA and London: Harvard University Press.

Parker, Ian. 2006. "Letter from Polynesia: Birth of a Nation?" *The New Yorker*, May 1, 66–75..

Parsons, Talcott. 1960. "Authority, Legitimacy, and Political Action."In *Structure and Process in Modern Societies*, edited by Talcott Parsons, 170–198. Glencoe, IL: Free Press.

Paxton, Robert O. 1972. *Vichy France: Old Guard and New Order 1940–1944*. New York: Columbia University Press.

Peic, Goran, and Dan Reiter. 2011. "Foreign-Imposed Regime Change, State Power and Civil War Onset, 1920–2004." *British Journal of Political Science* **41**(3):453–475.

Perdue, Peter C. 2005. *China Marches West: The Qing Conquest of Central Eurasia.* Cambridge: Belknap Press of Harvard University Press.

Perez, Evan, and Eric Bellman. 2009. "Officials Say Investor's Donations Wound Up with Sri Lanka Rebels." *The Wall Street Journal,* October 19, A4.

Peskin, Victor. 2008. *International Justice in Rwanda and the Balkans: Virtual Trials and the Struggle for State Cooperation.* New York: Cambridge University Press.

Petersen, Roger Dale. 2002. *Understanding Ethnic Violence: Fear, Hatred, and Resentment in Twentieth-century Eastern Europe.* Cambridge and New York: Cambridge University Press.

Phillips, Roderick. 1997. "Stepfamilies from a Historical Perspective." *Marriage & Family Review* 26(1–2):5–18.

Phillips, Steven E. 2003. *Between Assimilation and Independence: The Taiwanese Encounter Nationalist China, 1945–1950.* Stanford, CA: Stanford University Press.

Pipes, Daniel. 1989. "The Alawi Capture of Power in Syria." *Middle Eastern Studies* 25(4):429–450.

Pitkin, Hanna Fenichel. 1967. *The Concept of Representation.* Berkeley: University of California Press.

Popkin, Samuel L. 1979. *The Rational Peasant. The Political Economy of Rural Society in Vietnam.* Berkeley: University of California Press.

Powell, Walter W. 1991. "Expanding the Scope of Institutional Analysis." In *The New Institutionalism in Organizational Analysis,* edited by Walter W. Powell and Paul J. DiMaggio, 183–203. Chicago: University of Chicago Press.

Powell, Walter W., and Jeannette A. Colyvas. 2008. "Microfoundations of Institutional Theory." In *The SAGE Handbook of Organizational Institutionalism,* edited by Royston Greenwood, Christine Oliver, Kerstin Sahlin, and Roy Suddaby, 276–298. Los Angeles and London: SAGE.

Powell, Walter W., and Paul DiMaggio. 1991. *The New Institutionalism in Organizational Analysis.* Chicago: University of Chicago Press.

Proudhon, Pierre-Joseph. [1851] 1923. *General Idea of the Revolution in the Nineteenth Century.* London: Freedom Press.

Przeworski, Adam. 1991. *Democracy and the Market: Political and Economic Reforms in Eastern Europe and Latin America.* Cambridge: Cambridge University Press.

Przeworski, Adam, Susan Carol Stokes, and Bernard Manin. 1999. *Democracy, Accountability, and Representation.* Cambridge, and New York: Cambridge University Press.

Putnam, Robert D. 2000. *Bowling Alone: The Collapse and Revival of American Community.* New York: Simon & Schuster.

Rand, Ayn. 1957. *Atlas Shrugged.* New York: Random House.

Rawls, John. 2005. *Political Liberalism.* New York: Columbia University Press.

Rehfeld, Andrew. 2005. *The Concept of Constituency: Political Representation, Democratic Legitimacy, and Institutional Design.* New York: Cambridge University Press.

    2006. "Towards a General Theory of Political Representation." *Journal of Politics* 68(1):1–21.

Rhee, M.J. 1997. *The Doomed Empire: Japan in Colonial Korea.* Aldershot: Ashgate Publishing Company.

Rhee, Syngman. 2001. *The Spirit of Independence: A Primer of Korean Modernization and Reform.* Honolulu: University of Hawai'i Press.

Rhoads, Edward J. M. 2000. *Manchus & Han: Ethnic Relations and Political Power in Late Qing and Early Republican China, 1861–1928*. Seattle and London: University of Washington Press.

Ricks, Thomas E. 2006. *Fiasco: The American Military Adventure in Iraq*. New York: Penguin Press.

2009. *The Gamble: General David Petraeus and the American Military Adventure in Iraq, 2006–2008*. New York: Penguin Press.

Riker, William H. 1964. *Federalism: Origin, Operation, Significance*. Boston: Little, Brown.

Ristović, Milan. 2008. "Rural 'Anti-Utopia' in the Ideology of Serbian Collaborationists in the Second World War." *European Review of History* 15:179–192.

Roberts, Paul William. 2000. "Saddam's Inferno." In *Inside Iraq*, edited by John Miller and Aaron Kenedi, 101–124. New York: Marlowe & Company.

Roberts, Peter W. 2008. "Charting Progress at the Nexus of Institutional Theory and Economics." In *The SAGE Handbook of Organizational Institutionalism*, edited by Royston Greenwood, Christine Oliver, Kerstin Sahlin, and Roy Suddaby, 560–572. Los Angeles; London: SAGE.

Robinson, Michael E. 1988. *Cultural Nationalism in Colonial Korea, 1920–1925*. Seattle and London: University of Washington Press.

2007. *Korea's Twentieth-Century Odyssey*. Honolulu: University of Hawai'i Press.

Robinson, Michael. 1999. "Broadcasting, Cultural Hegemony, and Colonial Modernity in Korea, 1924–1945." In *Colonial Modernity in Korea*, edited by Gi-Wook Shin and Michael Robinson, 52–69. Cambridge, MA and London: Harvard University Press.

Robinson, Ronald. 1972. "Non-European Foundations of European Imperialism: A Sketch for a Theory of Collaboration." In *Studies in the Theory of Imperialism*, edited by Roger Owen and Bob Sutcliffe, 117–142. London: Longman.

Roeder, Philip G. 1991. "Soviet Federalism and Ethnic Mobilization." *World Politics* 43(January):196–232.

Roehner, Bertand M. 2009a. "Relations Between Allied Forces and the Population of Iceland, 1940–2006." Version of April 14, 2009, http://www.lpthe.jussieu.fr/~roehner/occupation.html, accessed September 1, 2009.

2009b. "Relations Between Allied Forces and the Populations of Germany and Austria, 1 May 1945 – 31 December 1958." Version of April 14 2009, http://www.lpthe.jussieu.fr/~roehner/occupation.html, accessed September 1, 2009.

Rogowski, Ronald. 1974. *Rational Legitimacy: A Theory of Political Support*. Princeton, NJ: Princeton University Press.

Romer, Paul. 2010. "Technologies, Rules, and Progress: The Case for Charter Cities." *Center for Global Development*. http://www.cgdev.org/content/publications/detail/1423916:1–11 (accessed May 9, 2013).

Rothstein, Bo. 2009. "Creating Political Legitimacy: Electoral Democracy Versus Quality of Government." *American Behavioral Scientist* 53:311–330.

2011. *The Quality of Government: Corruption, Social Trust, and Inequality in International Perspective*. Chicago: University of Chicago Press.

Rousseau, Jean-Jacques, and Victor Gourevitch. 1997. *The Social Contract and Other Later Political Writings*. Cambridge and New York: Cambridge University Press.

Rowe, Michael. 2003a. "Introduction." In *Collaboration and Resistance in Napoleonic Europe: State Formation in an Age of Upheaval, c. 1800–1815*, edited by Michael Rowe, 1–18 New York: Palgrave Macmillan.

2003b. *From Reich to State: The Rhineland in the Revolutionary Age, 1780–1830.* Cambridge and New York: Cambridge University Press.

Roy, Denny. 2003. *Taiwan: A Political History.* Ithaca, NY and New York: Cornell University Press.

Sales, Amy L., and Philip H. Mirvis. 1984. "When Cultures Collide: Issues in Acquisition" in *Managing Organizational Transitions,* edited by John R. Kimberly and Robert E. Quinn. Homewood, IL: Richard D. Irwin.

Sambanis, Nicholas. 2006. "A Supply and Demand Model of Sovereignty." Department of Political Science, Yale University, New Haven, CT.

Sariola, H., and A. Uutela. 1996. "The Prevalence and Context of Incest Abuse in Finland." *Child Abuse & Neglect* 20(9):843–850.

Sartorius, Rolf E. (Ed.). 1983. *Paternalism.* Minneapolis: University of Minnesota Press.

Schmid, Andre. 2002. *Korea Between Empires, 1895–1919.* New York: Columbia University Press.

Schmitt, Eric, and Thom Shanker. 2008. "U.S. Adapts Cold-War Idea to Fight Terrorists." *The New York Times,* March 18, A1.

Schwartz, Joel. 1984. *The Sexual Politics of Jean-Jacques Rousseau.* Chicago: University of Chicago Press.

Scott, Ian. 1989. *Political Change and the Crisis of Legitimacy in Hong Kong.* London: Hurst.

Scott, James C. 1985. *Weapons of the Weak: Everyday Forms of Peasant Resistance.* New Haven: Yale University Press.

1990. *Domination and the Arts of Resistance: Hidden Transcripts.* New Haven, CT and London: Yale University Press.

1998. *Seeing Like a State: How Certain Schemes to Improve the Human Condition Have Failed.* New Haven, CT and London: Yale University Press.

Selden, S. C., G. A. Brewer, and J. L. Brudney. 1999. "The Role of City Managers: Are They Principals, Agents, or Both?" *American Review of Public Administration* 29(2):124–148.

Seton-Watson, Hugh. 1984. "Military Occupations: Some Reflections from Recent and More Distant History." In *Armies of Occupation,* edited by Roy A. Prete and A. Hamish Ion, 1–15. Waterloo, ON: Wilfred Laurier University Press.

Sharkey, Heather J. 2003. *Living with Colonialism: Nationalism and Culture in the Anglo-Egyptian Sudan.* Berkeley: University of California Press.

Sheehan, James J. 2006. "The Problem of Sovereignty in European History." *American Historical Review* 111(1):1–15.

Shelef, Nadav G. 2010. *Evolving Nationalism: Homeland, Identity, and Religion in Israel, 1925–2005.* Ithaca, NY: Cornell University Press.

Shepard, Todd. 2006. *The Invention of Decolonization: the Algerian War and the Remaking of France.* Ithaca, NY: Cornell University Press.

Shin, Gi-Wook. 2006. *Ethnic Nationalism in Korea: Genealogy, Politics, and Legacy.* Stanford, CA: Stanford University Press.

Shopper, Moisy. 2001. "Stepfathers: Varieties and Job Descriptions." In *Stepparenting: Creating and Recreating Families in America Today,* edited by Stanley H. Cath and Moisy Shopper, 3–18. Hillsdale, NJ: The Analytic Press.

Shweder, Richard. 2004. "George W. Bush & the Missionary Position." *Daedalus* 133:26–36.

Simmel, Georg. [1908] 1950. "Exkurs über den Fremden." In *The Sociology of Georg Simmel*, translated from the German by Kurt H. Wolff, 402–408. Glencoe, IL: Free Press.

[1922] 1955. "The Web of Group Affiliations." In *Conflict and the Web of Group Affiliations*. New York: Free Press.

Simons, Geoff. 1995. *Korea: The Search for Sovereignty*. Houndsmill, Basingstoke, Hampshire and London: MacMillan Press Ltd.

Siroky, David, Valery Dzutsev and Michael Hechter. "The Differential Demand for Indirect Rule: Evidence from the North Caucasus," *Post-Soviet Affairs*. 29 268–286.

Slocum, John W. 1998. "Who, and When, Were the *Inorodtsy*? The Evolution of the Category of 'Aliens' in Imperial Russia." *The Russian Review* 57:173–190.

Sluglett, Marion Farouk, and Peter Sluglett. 1990. *Iraq Since 1958: From Revolution to Dictatorship*. New York: I. B. Taurus.

Sluglett, Peter. 2003. "The British Legacy." In *US Policy in Post-Saddam Iraq: Lessons from the British Experience*, edited by Michael Eisenstadt and Eric Mathewson, 3–14. Washington, DC: Washington Institute for Near East Policy.

Smith, Adam. [1776] 1961. *The Wealth of Nations* London: Methuen.

Smith, William Carlson. 1953. *The Stepchild*. Chicago: University of Chicago Press.

Smooha, Sammy. 2005. *Index of Arab-Jewish Relations in Israel, 2004*. Haifa: The Jewish-Arab Center, University of Haifa.

Staples, Brent. 2005. "Why the United States Should Look to Japan for Better Schools." *New York Times*, November 21.

Stasavage, David. 2011. *States of Credit: Size, Power, and the Development of European Polities*. Princeton: Princeton University Press.

Stinchcombe, Arthur L. 1968. *Constructing Social Theories*. New York: Harcourt Brace & World.

1990. *Information and Organizations*. Berkeley: University of California Press.

1997. "On the Virtues of the Old Institutionalism." In *Annual Review of Sociology*, 1–18.

Stone, Marla. 1998. *The Patron State: Culture & Politics in Fascist Italy*. Princeton, NJ: Princeton University Press.

Stone, Tammy. 2009. "Departments in Academic Receivership: Possible Causes and Solutions." *Innovative Higher Education* 33:229–238.

Strang, David. 1990. "From Dependency to Sovereignty – An Event History Analysis of Decolonization 1870–1987." *American Sociological Review* 55(6):846–860.

Strassmann, Joan E., Owen M. Gilbert, and David C. Queller. 2011. "Kin Discrimination and Cooperation in Microbes." *Annual Review of Microbiology* 65:349–367.

Strauss, Julia C. 2008. "Rethinking Institutional Capacity and Tax Regimes: The Case of the Sino-Foreign Salt Inspectorate in Republican China." In *Taxation and State-Building in Developing Countries: Capacity and Consent*, edited by Deborah Brautigam, Odd-Helge Fjelstad, and Mick Moore, 212–234. Cambridge and New York: Cambridge University Press.

Suchman, Mark C. 1995. "Managing Legitimacy – Strategic and Institutional Approaches." *Academy of Management Review* 20(3):571–610.

Suri, Jeremy. 2011. *Liberty's Surest Guardian: American Nation-Building from the Founders to Obama*. New York: Free Press.

Svara, J. H. 1999. "The Shifting Boundary between Elected Officials and City Managers in Large Council-Manager Cities." *Public Administration Review* 59:44–53.

Swain, Carol M. 1995. *Black Faces, Black Interests: The Representation of African Americans in Congress*. Cambridge, MA: Harvard University Press.

Sweeney, Megan M. 2010. "Remarriage and Stepfamilies: Strategic Sites for Family Scholarship in the 21st Century." *Journal of Marriage and Family* 72(3):667–684.

Taeuber, Irene B. 1961. "Population Growth in a Chinese Microcosm: Taiwan." *Population Index*, 27(2).

Tajfel, Henri (Ed.). 1982. *Social Identity and Intergroup Relations*. Cambridge: Cambridge University Press.

Takekoshi, Yosaburo. 1907. *Japanese Rule in Formosa*. New York, Bombay, Calcutta: Longmans, Green and Co.

Teng, Ssu-yü, and John King Fairbank. 1954. *China's Response to the West: A Documentary Survey, 1839–1923*. Cambridge, MA: Harvard University Press.

Thorpe, I. J. N. 2003. "Anthropology, Archaeology, and the Origin of Warfare." *World Archaeology* 35(1):145–165.

Thucydides. 1954. *History of the Peloponnesian War*. Melbourne and Baltimore: Penguin Books.

Tikhvinski'i, Sergei Leonidovich. 1983. *Modern History of China*. Moscow: Progress Publishers.

Tilly, Charles. 1990. *Coercion, Capital, and European States, AD 990–1990*. Cambridge, Massachusetts: B. Blackwell.

1975. "Food Supply and Public Order in Modern Europe." In *The Formation of National States in Western Europe*, edited by Charles Tilly, 480–555. Princeton, NJ: Princeton University Press.

2004. "Social Boundary Mechanisms." *Philosophy of the Social Sciences* 34:211–236.

Tocqueville, Alexis de. [1848] 1969. *Democracy in America*. New York: Anchor Books.

Toft, Monica Duffy, and Yuri Zhukov. 2012. "Violence in the Caucasus: Global Jihad or Local Grievance." Paper presented at the *Workshop on Ethnicity and Conflict*. University of Uppsala.

Tönnies, Ferdinand. 1988. *Community & Society: (Gemeinschaft und Gesellschaft)*. New Brunswick, NJ: Transaction Books.

Traub, James. 2004. "Making Sense of the Mission." *New York Times*, April 11,32.

Trewartha, Glenn T., Wilbur Zelinsky. 1995. "Population Distribution and Change in Korea: 1925–1949." *Geographical Review*, 45(1).

Tripp, Charles. 2000. *A History of Iraq*. Cambridge: Cambridge University Press.

Trivers, Robert. 2002. *Natural Selection and Social Theory: Selected Papers of Robert Trivers*. New York: Oxford University Press.

Trow, Martin. 1999. "Biology at Berkeley: A Case Study of Reorganization and Its Costs and Benefits." Working paper in the University of California, Berkeley's Center for Studies in Higher Education's Research and Occasional Paper Series: CSHE.1.99. http://cshe.berkeley.edu/publications/docs/PP.Trow.Biology.1.99.pdf (accessed May 9, 2013).

Tse, Kwock-Ping. 2000. "Language and a Rising New Identity in Taiwan." *International Journal of the Sociology of Language* 143: 151–164.

Tse-Han, Lai, Ramon H. Myers, and Wei Wou. 1991. *A Tragic Beginning: The Taiwan Uprising of February 28, 1947*. Stanford, CA: Stanford University Press.

Tsebelis, George. 1990. *Nested Games: Rational Choice in Comparative Politics*. Berkeley: University of California Press.

Tsurumi, E. Patricia. 1979. "Education and Assimilation in Taiwan Under Japanese Rule, 1895–1945." *Modern Asian Studies* 13(4): 617–641.

　1984. "Colonial Education in Korea and Taiwan." In *The Japanese Colonial Empire*, edited by Myers and Peattie. Princeton, NJ: Princeton University Press.

Tung, William L. 1970. *China and the Foreign Powers: The Impact of and Reaction to Unequal Treaties*. Dobbs Ferry, NY: Oceana Publications.

Tyler, Tom R. 2001. "A Psychological Perspective on the Legitimacy of Institutions and Authorities." In *The Psychology of Legitimacy: Emerging Perspectives on Ideology, Justice, and Intergroup Relations*, edited by John T. Jost and Brenda Major, 416–436. Cambridge: Cambridge University Press.

　2006. "Psychological Perspectives on Legitimacy and Legitimation." *Annual Review of Psychology* 57:375–400.

Vail, Leroy. 1989. *The Creation of Tribalism in Southern Africa*. Berkeley: University of California Press.

Varshney, Ashutosh. 2002. *Ethnic Conflict and Civic Life: Hindus and Muslims in India*. New Haven, CT: Yale University Press.

Verkuil, Paul R. 2007. *Outsourcing Sovereignty: Why Privatization of Government Functions Threatens Democracy and What We Can Do About It*. New York: Cambridge University Press.

Virgili, Fabrice. 2002. *Shorn Women: Gender and Punishment in Liberation France*. Oxford and New York: Berg.

Vreeland, James Raymond. 2003. *The IMF and Economic Development*. Cambridge and New York: Cambridge University Press.

Wakeman, Frederic E. 1966. *Strangers at the Gate: Social Disorder in South China, 1839–1861*. Berkeley: University of California Press.

Waley, Daniel. 1988. *The Italian City-Republics*. New York: Longman.

Wallerstein, Immanuel. 1961. *Africa: The Politics of Independence*. New York: Vintage Books.

Waltzer, Herbert. 1975. "The Job of the Academic Department Chairman: Experience and Recommendations from Miami University." An American Council on Education Occasional Paper available through the ACE's Department Chair Online Resource Center. http://www2.acenet.edu/resources/chairs/docs/waltzer.pdf (accessed May 9, 2013).

Warner, Carolyn M. 2007. *The Best System Money Can Buy: Corruption in the European Union*. Ithaca, NY: Cornell University Press.

Warren, Mark. 1999. "Introduction." In *Democracy and Trust*, edited by Mark Warren, 1–21. Cambridge, UK, and New York: Cambridge University Press.

Weatherford, M. Stephen. 1992. "Measuring Political Legitimacy." *American Political Science Review* 86(1):149–166.

Weaver, Shannon E., and Marilyn Coleman. 2010. "Caught in the Middle: Mothers in Stepfamilies." *Journal of Social and Personal Relationships* 27(3):305–326.

Weber, Eugen Joseph. 1976. *Peasants into Frenchmen: The Modernization of Rural France, 1870–1914*. Stanford, CA: Stanford University Press.

Weber, Max. [1919–1920] 1958. "The Protestant Sects and the Spirit of Capitalism." In *From Max Weber: Essays in Sociology*, edited by Hans Gerth and C. Wright Mills, 302–322. New York: Oxford University Press.

    [1922] 1978. *Economy and Society*, edited by G. Roth and C. Wittich. Berkeley: University of California Press.

    1994. "The Basis of Bureaucratic Continuity" In *Max Weber: Sociological Writings*, edited by Wolf Heydebrand, 92–94. New York: Continuum.

Weiss, Penny, and Anne Harper. 2002. "Rousseau's Political Defense of the Sex-Roled Family." In *Feminist Interpretations of Jean-Jacques Rousseau*, edited by Lynda Lange, 42–64. University Park, PA: Pennsylvania State University Press.

Weissberg, Robert. 2010. "A Stranger in Our Midst." *American Thinker* (April 29).http://www.americanthinker.com/2010/04/a_stranger_in_our_midst.html

Welch, Claude Emerson. 1980. *Anatomy of Rebellion*. Albany: State University Press of New York.

Westney, D. Eleanor. 1982. "The Emulation of Western Organizations in Meiji Japan: The Case of The Paris Prefecture of Police and the Keishi-Cho." *Journal of Japanese Studies* 8(2):307–342.

Wilder, Gary. 2005. *The French Imperial Nation-State: Negritude and Colonial Humanism between the Two World Wars*. Chicago: University of Chicago Press.

Williams, Melissa S. 1998. *Voice, Trust, and Memory: Marginalized Groups and the Failings of Liberal Representation*. Princeton, NJ: Princeton University Press.

Williamson, Oliver E. 1975. *Markets and Hierarchies, Analysis and Antitrust Implications: A Study in the Economics of Internal Organization*. New York: Free Press.

Wilson, A. T. 1931. *Loyalties, Mesopotamia, Vol. II: 1917–1920: A Personal and Historical Record*. Oxford: Oxford University Press.

Wilson, Edward O. 1978. *On Human Nature*. Cambridge, MA: Harvard University Press.

Wilson, James Q. 1989. *Bureaucracy : What Government Agencies Do and Why They Do It*. New York: Basic Books.

Wingrove, Elizabeth Rose. 2000. *Rousseau's Republican Romance*. Princeton: Princeton University Press.

Wojahn, Ellen. 1988. *Playing By Different Rules*. New York, NY: AMACOM.

Wood, Frances. 1998. *No Dogs and Not Many Chinese: Treaty Port Life in China 1843–1943*. London: J. Murray.

Wright, Stanley Fowler. 1950. *Hart and the Chinese Customs*. Belfast: Published for the Queen's University by W. Mullan.

Wu, Rwei-Ren. 2003. "The Formosan Ideology: Oriental Colonialism and The Rise of Taiwanese Nationalism, 1895–1945." PhD Dissertation, University of Illinois, Urbana-Champaign.

Yaphe, Judith. 2003. "The Challenge of Nation Building in Iraq." In *US Policy in Post-Saddam Iraq*, edited by Michael Eisenstadt and Eric Mathewson, 38–51. Washington DC: Washington Institute for Near East Policy.

Yoon, Jeongku, and Shane Thye. 2011. "A Theoretical Model and New Test of Managerial Legitimacy in Work Teams." *Social Forces* 90(2):639–659.

Young, Crawford. 1994. *The African Colonial State in Comparative Perspective*. New Haven, CT: Yale University Press.

Yousif, A. S. 1991. "The Struggle for Cultural Hegemony During the Iraqi Revolution." In *The Iraqi Revolution of 1958*, edited by Robert Fernea and Roger Louis, 172–196. New York: I.B. Tauris.

Zelditch Jr., Morris. 2001. "Theories of Legitimacy." In *The Psychology of Legitimacy*, edited by John T. Jost and Brenda Major, 33–53. Cambridge: Cambridge University Press.

Zhao, Dingxin. 2009. "The Mandate of Heaven and Performance Legitimation in Historical and Contemporary China." *American Behavioral Scientist* 53(3):416–433.

Zonderman, Jon. 1995. "Rethinking Philosophy: After a Painful Period of Internal Struggle, a Flagship Department is Still Struggling to Rebuild." *Yale Alumni Magazine* November. http://archives.yalealumnimagazine.com/issues/95_11/philosophy.html (accessed May 9, 2013).

Zucker, Lynne G. 1977. "The Role of Institutionalization in Cultural Persistence." *American Sociological Review* 42(5):726–743.

Index

materialist theory, alien rule and, 9
Mazzini, Giuseppe, 30n. 12
McCaffree, Barry, 47n. 2
membership, alienness and, 2, 2n. 2
microanalysis
  of collaboration, 116–118
  of military occupation regimes, 103–106
Middle Ages
  alien rule in, 32–35
  resistance to alien rule in, 4
  social organization in, 28
military occupation
  adverse factors in failure of, 101n. 10
  as alien rule, 25, 138–139
  cost-effectiveness of, 101–103, 103n. 13
  definitions of, 96n. 1, 96–97
  disruptive effects of, 101n. 10
  exogenous factors in resistance to, 114–116
  historical overview of, 96–97, 97n. 3
  in Korea, 91–93
  legitimation of, 101–103
  macroanalysis of, 97–103
  microanalysis of, 103–106
  Palestinian collaboration in Occupied
    Territories with, 106–110
  regime characteristics of, 97–101
  resistance to, 96n. 2
  societal characteristics of, 111–114
  theories of resistance and, 76–77
  wartime prospects and success of, 114–116
  in World War II, 97n. 3
military structure, national rule in Iraq and
    role of, 67n. 34
Mill, John Stuart, 11n. 20, 22, 30–32
Ming dynasty (China), 2, 35–36n. 27
Miskin, Val D., 128–129
modernity, freedom and, 13
Mukhabarat (Iraqi Party Intelligence), 68
multinational corporate mergers, alien
    rule and, 154
Murray, Douglas, J., 132
Mussolini, Benito, 98–99
MySpace, 13–14n. 27

Napoleonic occupation regimes
  direct rule during, 104n. 14
  elective alien rule and, 32–33n. 21
  indirect rule during, 111n. 26
  resistance to occupation regimes of, 1, 6n.
    13, 97n. 3, 98n. 5
National Democratic Alliance (India), 3–4

national identity, Korean resistance to
    Japanese occupation and, 81–82
nationalism
  barriers to equal treatment and, 140
  British occupation of Iraq and growth of,
    62–63, 64–65
  colonialism and, 1–2n. 1
  decolonization and, 138n. 1, 138–139
  imposed alien rule in China and rise
    of, 37–40
  Italian civic nationalism, 32–35
  in Korea, 78–82, 89–90
  resistance to alien rule and, 4–6, 25,
    29, 30n. 12
National Liberation Front (EAM)
    (Greece), 114
nation-building
  academic receivership compared
    with, 136–137
  alien rule as tool of, 139–140
  centralization of power and, 28
  collective goods provision and,
    102–103, 103n. 12
  colonialism and, 49n. 4
  Japanese colonial cultural policy and, 88n.
    11, 88–91
native intermediaries
  Japanese occupation regimes and,
    83–86, 94–95
  in military occupation regimes, 103–106
  Palestinian collaboration in Occupied
    Territories and, 106–110, 108n. 24
native rule
  in academic receivership, 128–129
  academic receivership and preference
    for, 131–132
  alienness and, 28
  colonial meaning of, 28
  devaluation of, 30n. 12, 30n. 13, 31n. 17
  direct rule and denigration of, 49–51, 50n. 6
  incompetence or breakdown of, 140
  military regime characteristics and, 97–101
  social divisions in, 111–114
natural selection, xenophobia and, 7–9
Nazi Germany. *See also* Germany
  Belorussian collaboration with,
    113, 115n. 18
  Channel Islands occupation by, 99, 99n. 6
  cultural repression in, 98–99
  French (Vichy) collaboration with,
    99–100, 102n. 11, 104, 112, 112–113n.
    29, 115n. 32